SHADOW SOUL

Book One – Narun Duology

M.J. Bavis

Chapter 1

I'm not dead.

A familiar haze wrapped around me, acting as a restraint. I focused on connecting my mind with my body to find a path out of the cloud bank—and regretted it. How long had I dwelt in the bliss of unconsciousness? Could I go back to it? I cracked open an eye, and then the other.

Yup, too late. I was awake. Awake in my thoughts and aware of the reality I didn't want to belong to. Of course, dreams couldn't last forever.

"You're awake!"

My eyes darted around for the source of the startled voice and found the ample figure of a woman, standing by the window. Masses of wild, burgundy curls surrounded her face, the colour striking against her pale green uniform.

"I'll get the doctor. Don't worry, you're going to be okay. You're safe," she assured me, hurrying out of the room.

Safe? I rocked my head from side to side against the pillow, loosening my neck. I wondered which eye-catcher of a story they had cooked up this time: *'Mystery girl in a coma,' 'When Beauty met Beast,' 'Girl found battered—who is she?'* The headlines rarely changed.

Too soon, the redhead was back, trailed by a bearded man in a white coat.

I prepared for the standard questions as the doctor rushed to my side and placed his hand on top of mine.

"Can you hear me, miss? I'm Dr Wood and you're at the Bridleton Royal Infirmary." The doctor glanced at the monitors, his fingertips seeking confirmation of my steady pulse. "And this is Shona." He pointed a light into one eye, and then the other. "She's one of our Healthcare Assistants. You've been in a coma for two months."

1

Blimey, *that* was a record. I'd have to play this carefully. They'd be expecting some brain damage.

I followed the doctor's finger from left to right, and back again. Shona stood at the end of the bed, analysing each blink.

"Do you think she can hear us?" she whispered a tad too loud, in her thick, northern accent. "She might not speak English. *Je-maa-appel Sho-naa.*"

My mouth twitched. *Don't quit your day job, Shona.*

What was a Healthcare Assistant, anyway? You'd think I'd have my head wrapped around all these hospital titles by now.

"Or, um—" Shona carried on. "How does it go again... *Ick been Shooonaaa.*"

Even the good doctor had to find that amusing.

"Okay, Shona, give her a moment." The doctor chuckled and sent her off on a task. *Clever man.* He waited for the door to close before turning to me. "There we go, peace and quiet. You must feel very confused—this is normal. Miss," he narrowed his eyes, "do you understand me? Blink twice if you do."

Right, decision time. I wasn't going to venture down the "blinking" road—last time the lash-fluttering only attracted a migraine. Let them class this as a medical miracle if need be.

I cleared my throat and mumbled a *"Yes"* in a dry, cracked voice. I rubbed my temple for effect. Neither my hand nor my forehead felt like my own.

The doctor's jaw dropped. With the length of the coma, he would've diagnosed me as a lost cause. Which was fair enough: how was he to know my body didn't quite function like everyone else's?

"Well, hello. Nice to finally talk to you, uh...?"

I waited several seconds on purpose, eyes wide open. "Ca...milla. Camilla."

"*Camilla.* That's a beautiful name. And how are you feeling, Camilla?" Dr Wood stared intently, his faded brown eyes catching new life.

"I feel...fine. I don't—I don't remember. How did I get here?"

"We hoped you could tell us that." The doctor lowered his brow. "One of our nurses found you outside the hospital. You were unconscious with swelling in your brain. We had to induce a medical coma. Unfortunately, your brain decided to stay under longer than we would've liked."

Now that was interesting. Who took me to the hospital?

The doctor read the confusion on my face and continued, "Do you remember anything about what happened to you?"

I angled my head to the side, staring at the light blue walls. The room's décor screamed hospital—clinical and unimaginative. The air was thick with the smell of plastic and detergent.

"I'm not sure," I started. "I remember a park and then...I don't know." It always helped to add a bit of hesitation.

"All right, dear. Not to worry. That's perfectly normal. Mild amnesia and disorientation come with this stage. You suffered quite a blow to your head. It's a miracle you're alive, let alone coherent! Let's take it a day at a time."

The door flew open. The Return of the Redhead.

Shona handed a piece of paper to the doctor and he inhaled deeply, his chest puffing. He nodded to Shona who retreated a few steps.

"Camilla," the doctor frowned, "is there—"

"*Camilla?*" Shona repeated loudly. "Your name is Camilla? I knew it'd be something exotic!"

That's exotic?

My attention shifted back to the doctor as he enquired of family members to contact. I hadn't matched any of the police's missing person files, and they presumed the perpetrator had stolen all forms of identification. I simply shook my head, confusion stamped on my forehead. Inwardly, I sighed in relief that I had thoroughly covered my tracks.

Disappointment spread on Shona's face like a knocked-over tub of paint as my supposed amnesia dawned on her. People always wanted the gossip. Regardless, she held her tongue while the doctor scribbled notes in his folder. He clicked his pen on and off between each glance at the monitors.

3

"We'll leave you to rest for now. You must feel overwhelmed. I'll be back to do a full check-up. Unless, of course, there's anything I can do for you?" Like most doctors, Dr Wood wasn't one to loiter.

I cleared my throat, feeling like my mouth was full of cotton balls. "Did I have any other injuries?" As if I couldn't feel the two fractured ribs healing, the torn tendons and ligaments of my ankle, and the tender shoulder after it'd been set back into place. Of course, there was the blow to the head that drove me down to coma alley. The bruises would've faded by now. And the swelling was long gone.

As expected, the doctor recounted the same. "...but you've made a remarkable recovery. You're very lucky to be alive."

If it was down to luck I would've been dead a long time ago.

"And no one has been to see me?" I had to be sure.

"No one, love, not a soul," Shona blurted, and the doctor threw her a stern look. "Other than the police, of course," she added hastily.

"All right, then." The doctor clicked his pen one last time and placed it in the breast pocket of his coat. "Camilla, do use your call button if you need anything. I'll be back to run some tests, and the police are eager to talk to you. Our in-house psychiatrist will also be popping down to introduce herself, in case you feel like talking to someone."

And to assess if I'm a nut job. Then again, maybe I am.

I offered a thankful smile as the doctor literally pushed Shona out of the room.

I inhaled deeply, finally able to lower my defences. The vivid images, the memories—all of it—came crashing down on me. The intolerable anguish swelled inside, devouring everything in its path. I exhaled, taking control.

No more.

I focused meticulously on the paintbrush strokes on the ceiling until my thoughts were back in line.

So. Two months in the hospital, unconscious, no unexpected injuries. Nothing unusual there, except for the long hospitalisation; must have been a statistical error. The only question was, how was I found *outside* the hospital? Someone found me at Cumber Park, drove me over and...left me outside?

A crease formed between my eyebrows as my fingers pressed gentle circles on my temples; the first touches always felt a little like stroking a doll.

Either the standard for helping a fellow human out was seriously slipping, or my Good Samaritan was acting bashful for a reason.

Neither option filled me with confidence.

Chapter 2

"Good morning, beautiful!" A nurse dressed in a royal-blue uniform burst into my room.

Guess the knock was only out of courtesy.

"Morning." The plastic cover on the mattress rustled as I wriggled to straighten up on the bed.

"Ah, that's more like it." The nurse smiled. "I was growing rather tired of one-way conversations."

"Yes, well, I got tired of listening," I muttered with the beginnings of a smile.

The nurse laughed heartily. Her face was heart-shaped, eyes a rich shade of brown, contrasting her blonde hair well.

"I'm Anita, by the way." She stepped to the window, pulling the heavy, cream-coloured curtain to one side, and opened the blinds. The grey sky hardly brightened the room. I was beginning to realise seasons in England only worked in theory.

"Camilla." I pointed a finger to my chest. "But I'm assuming you already know that."

"Indeed, you're quite the celebrity around here."

I grimaced inside. The last thing I wanted was attention.

Anita walked to my side. "How are you feeling today?" She busied herself, tucking a loose corner of the sheet under the mattress.

"It's nice to see the light of day again," I said, bending the truth.

Her lips curved to a genuine smile as she checked the drip stand at the head of the bed.

"You were the one who found me, weren't you?" I took a wild guess.

She halted, her hands dropping to fidget near the hem of her tunic. "Um, yes, that's right." Her slight blush intrigued me. Why was she embarrassed about it?

Without thinking about it, I shifted my legs to hang off the edge of the bed. I needed a stretch. A two-month lie-in sure could make a person stiff.

7

Suddenly, a firm grip came to circle my arm. "Don't be getting any ideas, now. The physio needs to assess your ankle before you—"

"Don't worry." I lifted a hand, changing my mind. "I'll just sit for a bit." The ankle was strong enough, but I guessed I'd better wait until Anita wasn't present.

Anita nodded in approval, her jaw endearingly firm. "Good." She patted my arm as she let go, grabbed the jug on my bedside table, and walked to the door. "I'll get you some more water."

"Wait, Anita… I want to ask you something." Anita paused at the doorway, hand resting on the door handle. "When you found me outside the hospital…did you see anyone?"

She sighed, a shadow of disappointment crossing her face. "No, there was no one around and the police said the surveillance cameras were disabled."

The security cameras being out was admittedly convenient—a little too convenient.

"Okay. Thank you."

Anita hesitated, her thumb rubbing along her wedding ring. "For what it's worth, I'm really sorry about what happened to you."

I was glad she didn't wait for a reply. Guilt covered me like a sheet of lead. Her face—radiating the kind of empathy a mother would have for her own—said enough. I imagined she checked up on me daily. I bet she had brushed my long, sable hair, bathed me and spent hours scrolling through the missing people's website. She probably went the extra mile because she thought I was alone, a victim of a heinous crime.

If only she knew the truth.

*

It took the doctors a week to accept I really was something of a medical miracle with my quick recovery. During my time at the hospital, Anita became the only person who made the days bearable. She went from caregiver to friend in record time. To me, she was a distraction, and I reminded her of someone she wished she'd had a second chance in helping.

But I let things go too far.

We pulled into the drive of a stone-built, semi-detached house that looked the part of a family home: an outdoor trampoline with a safety net, a kid's bike resting against the garage door, a slightly deflated ball weathered by the outdoors.

How had I let this happen? Accepting Anita's invitation to stay at her house while I "adjusted back to society" and regained my memory was not only idiotic but verged on unethical. Yet her kindness had melted something inside me.

Evidently, my common sense.

"Your house looks lovely." I forced a smile as I dragged my feet down the path to the door.

"Come on," she beckoned. "David will bring in your luggage."

David, Anita's husband, had picked us up from the hospital. He'd barely spoken two words to me during the drive, clearly wary of letting a stranger bunk at their home. It seemed we had both fallen victim to Anita's persuasion.

I threw David a quick glance as he rubbed his bald head and picked up my "luggage"—a plastic bag— and followed Anita inside.

The hallway was deceptively spacious, with a lounge on the left and kitchen on the right, and a staircase leading to the second floor. The wooden floorboards were brightened by a colourful rug. A large family photo hung on the wall.

Anita gave me the tour, drawing attention to framed photos of their five-year-old son, Aaron, who was visiting his grandmother during the school summer holiday.

My room, the attic guest room—wallpapered with natural colours, kept sparsely furnished and free of clutter—was small, but had its own bathroom. A pile of spring-scented towels lay on the bed.

Anita left me to get acquainted with my new living quarters. I dug into the carrier bag and placed my basic hospital toiletries by the sink. My change of clothes looked lonesome hanging in the wardrobe. And that was me unpacked. Sighing, I finally turned to the large box with a red ribbon laying on the bed. My name was written on a white tag in bold, black capitals.

The gift was another one of Anita's acts of kindness: pyjamas, makeup, underwear, moisturiser, T-shirts, a hooded jumper and a box of chocolates.

She is too generous.

My pounding conscience was getting harder to tame. Anita had showered me with support to get me back on my feet and to deal with my supposed amnesia, yet I repaid her by lying to her and her family.

I shifted the box to the floor.

Was this really the kind of person I had become? Would it matter that the goal was the same? Yes, I did have it all in my head—the memories, the people, the terrible things I had done—but I wanted nothing to do with the past.

Anita would never have to know that everything about me was a lie.

Chapter 3

"Yo, Camilla! Wait up!"

"Walk faster, Tony," I called back and kept my pace. The indistinct grumble behind me made me smirk. Tony, the only friend I'd made since moving in with Anita nearly three months ago, changed his long stride into a jog.

"What's the rush, Milla?" Tony caught up with me as I marched across the stone-paved grounds of Bridleton University. His short bronze hair was flat on one side, the result of leaning on his palm for an entire lecture.

"I've somewhere to be," I said, zipping up my jumper.

"Oh. I was gonna ask if you wanted to get a bite to eat. I'm starving."

I laughed lightly. "Lunch was less than two hours ago, Tony."

"I'm a growing man."

"Width-wise yes…" Truth was, Tony could eat a cow a day and it wouldn't make a difference to his physique thanks to the sheer amount of sports he played.

He adjusted his hold on his bag strap, now at ease with my brisk step. "Where are you going, anyway?"

"I told you. *Somewhere.*" I picked up speed. I was running late for the appointment as it was.

"Can't it wait?" Tony grumbled. "I need company. I'm bored!"

"I thought you were hungry?"

"I am. Hungry, bored—"

"Whingy."

Tony took a hold of my rucksack and yanked me back a step. "If I'm whingy, it's only because you make me. Now can't you do your thing later? You know Jill's out of town and I'm miserable."

Tony reminded me of a dog begging for a stroll—minus the tail wagging. He was a little lost without his girlfriend.

"So, I'm second best?"

11

"Maybe third, but yeah." He grinned as I bit my lower lip pensively. I did enjoy his company; we operated much on the same wavelength. Plus, like most guys, he rarely asked unnecessary questions, which suited my complex living situation with Anita's family.

"Fine," I sighed, "where'd you wanna go?"

Tony did his usual victory dance, seized me by the shoulders and spun me around. "I don't know, but I'm driving."

"You know I don't drive."

"And the world is safer for it." He shot me a teasing smile.

I climbed into Tony's silver Ford Fiesta, with all honesty, feeling relieved. The meeting with the hypnotherapist could wait.

Indefinitely.

The smell of chips and bacon lingered thickly in the air as we walked inside a cosy-looking pub called the Woollen Wonka. Tony headed to the men's room and I watched his broad back disappear behind a swinging door. I ordered drinks and picked a corner table by the window.

Tony was my first friend in years if Anita didn't count. Although I'd only known him for a few weeks, it felt like a lifetime. Since I hadn't landed a job, Anita had hired me. I walked Aaron to and from school, cleaned the house, and ran errands. After a while, she'd urged me to take up a few modules at the local university to associate with people of my age. On my third day of lectures, Tony and I had been paired for group work and failed equally on knowing anything about the topic. Since then, we'd bumped into each other almost daily. When he introduced me to his girlfriend, Jill, we officially became mates.

I was pulled from my thoughts as Tony joined me at the table.

"I got you a beer," I said, and Tony reached for the pint. I twirled a straw in my drink as Tony speed-read the menu and went to order.

I jolted as the phone in my pocket vibrated—I wasn't quite used to the thing yet—and dug it out to read the message.

Anita: Hope everything goes well at the therapist. Thinking of you! x

12

I pinched the bridge of my nose, stifling the tremors of guilt in my gut. She was still trying to help me "figure out my past" even though there hadn't been any progress. And there wouldn't be.

I replied with a reason why I couldn't attend the session she'd arranged for me—again. Even as the text sent, I knew Anita would be suspicious. My excuses were in the same boat as the dog that ate the homework.

I sucked in a quick breath of the greasy air, itching to throw something that smashed. Preferably a chair through a window. Or my head.

"Bad news?" Tony snuck up on me.

I put the phone away and smoothed out the frown. "No, no. Just business with Anita."

"Your landlady?" he asked, and I nodded.

The less Tony knew about Anita, the better. Amnesia had proven a tricky lie, and when starting university, I'd decided not to venture down that path. In the end, I had no intention of letting either party meet.

*

My abs were getting a free workout from all the laughing. Tony and I were now accompanied by a few of his friends who happened to stop at the pub.

Matthew, a bona fide survival expert, was the most laid-back person I'd ever met. He worked as a park warden and his job description entailed enjoying the fresh air and collecting kids' wind-swept balls from the duck pond. Tony's other friends, Jake and Stan, were Business students. Both sported the typical student look: chinos, shirts with rolled up sleeves and man-bags boasting Hollister and Calvin Klein logos, respectively. *Student loans going to good use, no doubt.*

"You want another drink, Milla? I'm heading over." Jake was half up, pointing a thumb towards the bar. Although impressed that we were already on a nickname basis, I declined the offer.

"So, Milla, you're not actually a full-time student, then?" Matthew asked, and I shook my head. "But you share lectures with

Tony?" He leaned towards me, pushing aside an empty glass on the table.

"Yup, two classes."

"Right." Matthew rubbed his chin. "And where are you from again? I can't place your accent."

Tony scoffed and shot me a pointed look. "Good luck getting anything out of her... She's a vault of secrets."

"Whaaat...I'm an open book!"

"Yeah, with a lot of blank pages." Tony took a long swig of his beer and returned the pint down empty.

I shot a glare Tony's way and turned to Matthew. "I'm from out of town." *To say the least.* "You won't know the place, it's small. Plus, we moved around a lot."

"Try me. I got Google Maps."

"It won't show on Google." *Or on any map.* I brushed off the images of my real home knocking on the door of my mind.

"That small, eh? No wonder you joined us city folk."

"Precisely, Matt."

"*Matthew*," he corrected. "I go by 'Matthew.'"

"Whatever, *Mattie.*" I rolled my eyes, knowing it would kill the questions.

Jake returned with another round of drinks and passed them around. Perhaps I should've had one after all. I wasn't quite caught up on the social norms yet.

Matthew jolted up in his chair, drawing in our attention. "Man, I can't believe I forgot to tell you guys! This is sick." He drummed the table with his fingers in excitement. "Remember ages ago I saw that beat-up girl in the park, and she was in a coma for months, yeah?"

My breaths stilled.

"The battered lass on the local news?" Stan frowned as if trying to bring up details of an old story back to his memory. "What about her?"

My heart racing, I concentrated on keeping a calm front. Only my foot refused to stop jiggling under the table.

"She. Woke. Up." Matthew drew out the words and I feigned surprise with the others.

14

Did he know it was me?

One of the guys must've asked for more details as Matthew answered, "It wasn't in the news. I overheard two nurses talking about it last week whilst visiting my nan in the hospital. Apparently, she woke up months ago."

"I thought the papers wrote her off." Jake touched up his gelled hair. "Where's she now?"

I swallowed, a little painfully. Was there a chance it wasn't me? *Pretty thread-thin of a chance.*

"Don't know, mate. She's in some kind of a witness protection scheme; that's what the police officer implied on the night." Matthew took a sip of beer.

Eh? What police officer?

"I must've missed the story in the news." I eased my locked spine. "Where'd you find this girl? What happened?"

Matthew's face lit up. "Right, so I was going home through the park one night and I see this *heap* of a girl on the ground all messed up, with this young guy kneeling next to her. I stop, and he notices me, and jumps up, clearly upset." Matthew wafted a hand in the air. "Anyhow, the guy says he's an undercover cop, hands me a number to call for my statement, and basically gets rid of me. So, I go. And the next day it's all over the news."

I bit my inner cheek to allow my alarmed body some release. *Did Matthew not recognise me? What cop?*

I leaned my hand on my head to make sure it was still attached to my body.

This could ruin my already questionable new life.

I wanted to ask questions, but I was afraid they'd see through me. Instead, I picked at the Bombay mix on the table. Finger food made you look less guilty. *Right?*

"So, did you actually see her face?" Stan asked, and I knew the answer had to be a no.

"Nope," Matthew said. "The cop made sure of that. He didn't want her identity leaking to the media, I guess."

"Mate, look at you! Cops, villains, and a hot bird." Jake elongated his last words, snapping his fingers in the air.

"*Dude.*" Matthew pulled a face, unimpressed. "She was unconscious and caked in blood."

"Still, that's sick man, sick."

I was about to excuse myself and leave the boys to their chatter, when I realised Tony had been silent the whole time, gazing out the window, deep in thought.

I should kick myself in the neck. I'd been so wrapped up in stopping my heart from pounding out of my chest that I'd forgotten him. *Was he not interested?*

"So, what's your theory, Tony?" I pitched my voice just loud enough to draw his attention. His eyes remained glazed until I snapped my fingers by his ear. "What's your take?" I repeated as he glanced at me. "As in, what happened to the girl Matthew found? Hey, you still with us?"

Tony looked everywhere but directly at me. "I don't know," he grunted and straightened up. "Can I use your phone? My battery's dead and I forgot I needed to call someone."

Taken back by his abrupt manner, I handed him my phone and watched him disappear outside.

Something was off.

*

The engine was particularly loud, old as the car was. I was frustrated Tony had rushed off, but the opportunity to quiz Matthew for more details, as he drove me to Anita's, was welcome.

"Oh, you know that police officer you met at the park? Was his name Dave, by any chance? He's a friend of mine on the force," I queried innocently.

"He didn't give me his name." Matthew flicked the button on the radio to find a better station. I would never have guessed he'd settle on jazz.

"Right. I don't suppose he was kind of short and round with blonde hair?"

"No, the exact opposite actually." The car struggled on the cobblestone road. "Tall, dark-haired. He looked young, like twenty, twenty-one? I wouldn't have believed him, but he did flash a badge."

I'd fancy having a look at that badge myself.

16

"Do you still have the number he gave you?"

"Nah, I threw it away after I'd given my statement," Matthew said. "Why do you ask, anyway?"

"Just curious."

Matthew drummed his thumbs on the steering wheel. "Yeah, I wish I knew what happened to her."

I scoffed, recalling the sound my shoulder had made that night as it popped out of place. "She was probably a druggie, beat up by debt collectors or a punter."

"No. Not her. I didn't see much but I didn't get that vibe. Plus, the cop's reaction wasn't one a druggie would get. Before he saw me, he was sort of *stroking* her hair." Matthew placed both hands on the wheel, sliding them to the top.

I pressed my tongue to the roof of my mouth to keep myself from retorting with a torrent of questions.

"Odd, I guess." I threw in a yawn to feign disinterest and left the topic.

A few minutes later, Matthew pulled up by Anita's and I slipped into the house and up to my room unseen. The bed protested as I crashed on it. A headache was imminent. The ground under my house-of-cards-of-a-life trembled. Why was I even still in this city? And taking classes at university...?

The truth was, being on the run had lost its appeal, and its purpose. I'd grown attached to Anita and Tony, and the thought of settling down. It was a distraction, a pain relief that worked better than any hospital bed. The loss and the guilt were numbed under the illusion of a normal life.

But what if the truth came out and Anita found out I lied? What if she found out about all the other times I'd put myself in hospital?

I'd end up on the WANTED poster in both worlds.

I flipped onto my back on the bed. It was unlikely. I always covered my tracks and Matthew clearly had no idea who I was, but the other guy...troubled me. A cop wouldn't have dropped me outside the hospital; clearly, he was lying. Had someone from home found me? Had I crossed paths with a Scout or a Hunter? *Then why had they let me live?*

I balled my fists against my forehead.
I wasn't going to like what I'd have to do next.

Chapter 4

A night of fitful sleep did the trick—I wasn't going to let some mystery man drive me to rash decisions. I was going to stay. If he'd wanted to cause trouble, he'd had plenty of chances to cause it.

I stayed in my room all morning until Anita came to get me down for lunch. Her stilted body language confirmed to me she wasn't pleased I'd, yet again, cancelled the appointment with the therapist.

I grabbed her arm on the stairs. "I'm sorry," I blurted. Anita's fingers wrapped around the railing. "About yesterday. For missing the...thing."

Anita sucked in a sharp breath. "Are you really? Don't get me wrong but it seems every time I try to help, you find some way to cancel or have some..." she trailed off, fixing up a strand of hair to her usual bun. "Camilla, you *must* have family or someone looking for you and—" Anita swallowed the rest as a soft groan escaped my lips.

I'd told her time and time again I had a strong feeling I had no family, but she wouldn't believe me. Of course, she was right not to, but that was beside the point.

"Never mind, I'm sorry," she said, much softer this time. "You don't need this. I can only imagine how difficult this must be."

Typical Anita. She always put others first.

"No, you're right," I admitted. "I have been putting off...well, everything." A picture of Anita's son stared at me from the wall, driving the guilt home further. "The truth is, I'm settling into this life and I'm afraid getting my memory back will ruin it."

Anita's eyes searched mine until the usual warmth radiated through from them. "Of course. I understand. Take your time." She beckoned with her head, grinning. "Come on, lunch is ready—my boys don't wait."

After lunch, I left for the city centre. I wanted to give Anita's family some alone time and I was down for meeting Tony at the cinema later in the afternoon.

The bus was still slightly in motion as I hopped on to the pavement. The police station stood in its majestic, familiar frame across the road. Anita had dragged me over there several times demanding a progress report, only to hear the same: without my memory, the case was at a dead end.

Hands in my jeans' pockets, I eyed the old Victorian building, crossed the road, and walked in the opposite direction.

I wish I'd never lied about having amnesia. Anita would've understood if I didn't want to talk about my past, but would she forgive me if she found out I lied? After all, she'd trusted me to look after her son.

The rolling clouds swallowed the warmth of the sun as I strolled onto the grounds of an old townhouse that had been converted into a museum. A path, lined by trees, directed my steps. The smell of lemon trees injected a tidal-wave of memories: faces, tree-topped mountains, rays of sun bouncing off the long, marble corridors... All images of what I once called home.

There were things I missed, people my heart ached to see. But for as long as home was tainted with the memory of *him*...

I headed down the road of self-destruction and allowed the images to saturate my mind.

His face alone carried marks of our history: the neat scar on his hairline that was barely visible, the impending laughter lines around his mouth, the cheekbones that caught freckles after a day of training in the sun. He was patient when I struggled, comforting when I missed my family, gentle when I messed up—

A hole punched through my chest. The heartfelt memories iced over, spreading their unforgiving frost inside of me, as his last words resounded in my ear.

"*...Kali, no!*" he'd screamed, face twisting in pain. "*Don't!*"

I staggered back. The words sounded physical as if spoken next to me. Grief wrapped its fingers around my throat; the guilt suffocated.

20

Enough.

I clutched the back of my neck and focused on the oxygen flowing through my nose. Slowly, I regained control, fighting to take captive the straying thoughts.

The metaphorical ice retreated inside me, leaving a damp trail, and then even that vaporised. I regained composure.

My exhale was loud in the otherwise quiet surroundings.

Over a year of running hadn't healed the wounds. But here, surrounded by ordinary people's lives, it was easier to forget, easier to be someone else.

Going back home had never been an option, even if I was allowed to return.

Being *Camilla* was my only chance of having somewhat of a life.

*

"Awesome film!" Tony zipped up his jacket. "I wish I could kick butt like that."

We stepped out of the cinema and walked along the quietening streets. The pub I had suggested wasn't far.

"It was okay. Typical action film." I was a little brain-dead from the mindless violence.

"Mate, didn't you see those moves? Hijaaaaannng!" Tony's impromptu side-kick nearly knocked out both me and a bin. I ducked, but the bin wasn't so lucky.

"Careful, Van Damme. I'd rather get home in one piece." I placed my hands on the bin to stop the metallic rattle.

"Sorry." Tony checked for eyewitnesses. "Don't you think it'd be so cool to know how to do all that stuff?"

I grinned, tickled inside. There was a part of me, a rather large part, that missed the fighting and the training. I had always been one for the adrenaline rush.

"You'd make a good fighter, Tony. You're balanced." I bit my lip. *Why had I said that?*

"*Balanced?* What's that supposed to mean?"

"Um, you seem to have a good...balance." I dug my hands into my pockets.

21

From the corner of my eye, I saw Tony glance at me. "Okay, weirdo."

"Takes one to know one." Why did I have the urge to tell him? I shouldn't be thinking on those lines. It was in the past and I was no longer who I used to be.

"Hey, do you know that guy?" Tony's elbow in my ribs summoned my attention as he pointed to a guy down the street, presumably waiting for the bus. There was something familiar about him—his stance? —but I couldn't place him.

"Don't think so. Why?"

"I keep seeing him around campus."

I cocked my head to the side. "Have you considered he might be a student?"

"Maybe." Tony ignored the sarcasm. "It's just that I normally see him hanging around. You know, not really doing anything. Seems out of place sometimes."

My eyes narrowed. The guy's face was shadowed by his cap, hiding his features. Surely, I would've noticed if someone was following Tony around. I did spend most of my time with him.

"So, do you think he's after you for your one-line lecture notes or your winsome personality?"

Tony gave me a dirty look. I bumped my shoulder into him but made a mental note to pay more attention the next time I was on campus. Or anywhere else. There could be people looking for me.

"Or…maybe *you* have a secret admirer?"

"*Me?* I thought he was following *you?*"

"First of all," —Tony swung his arm around my shoulders and leaned in— "he's not *following*. He's just there, mainly when I'm with you. Come to think of it, he only has eyes for you…"

I shoved his arm off me. "Knock it off. You're reaching." *Although, he probably isn't.* After all, I did have some mysterious cop-wannabe after me.

"Come on, you're a pretty girl," Tony teased. "In that unusual kind of way."

"Okay, I know we're just friends, but you need to work on your compliments. For Jill's sake."

Tony laughed. "I didn't mean it like that. You look a bit...foreign, that's all. You got that exotic look. Don't worry. Guys dig that."

"And you call *me* a weirdo."

Tony tackled me into a hug, pinning my arms against my ribcage. I shook him off and turned the conversation back to the film, swapping lazy ideas for a sequel.

As we neared Cumber Park, I pointed at the metal gates. "Let's take a shortcut through the park. The pub's on the other side." I grabbed a handful of Tony's jacket and pulled him towards the entry.

"What? No way." He yanked free the slippery material of his jacket from my grasp. His chin lowered down a second too late; I'd already registered the flinch on his face.

"What's up with you?" I narrowed in on the subtle changes in his facial expression. "Scared of the dark?"

"Nothing's up." Tony snorted. I bit my teeth together repeatedly as if sending a message in Morse code while Tony dug his fingers in his hair. "Sorry," he muttered into the air. "I overreacted."

I'll say. Tony inched further from the park as if afraid the shadows might come alive. "Come on, it's getting late—"

"*No.*" I set my jaw. "Not until you tell me what's going on. You were acting strange yesterday as well."

"What you on about?" Tony's darting eyes failed him.

"Yesterday at the pub, something seriously bugged you. And now this!" I flicked my thumb towards the park.

"Milla, you're imagining things."

I stepped back from him, looking deeper into his eyes, which now faced the park.

Tony squinted, focusing on something, his chin slightly raised. "It's...him. That's him again, the guy I was on about!" Tony's face scrunched in disbelief.

My head whipped around and met the object of his stare. Within a stone's throw from the park's entrance, under the branches of a willow tree, stood a form, slender and tall. A cap hid his face, but his features were now familiar in their unfamiliarity.

My legs sprang into action and I raced towards him. I leapt over a flowerbed, eyes glued on his dark form. The guy stayed still, his chin slightly lowered, even as I swallowed the distance between us. And then, in a blink, he vanished, leaving behind nothing but the whooshing branches. I came to an instant halt, scanning the surroundings frantically.

He was gone.

Tony's panting voice rang nearer and soon he caught up with me. *"What are you doing?"*

Accepting there wasn't a trace left of the guy, I faced Tony's puffing cheeks. His expression was one to record: a blend of confusion and astonishment.

"Are you out of your mind? He'll think you're a psycho, running after him like that!" Tony steadied his breath with three long inhales, and I released my tensed shoulders.

"It was him, the guy from earlier. He was *right* there!" I couldn't be bothered to point.

"I know." Tony turned his voice down a notch. "I'm the one who saw him, *remember*? What were you thinking charging at him like that?"

Granted, I felt a little dumb. "He's been stalking you—"

Tony's grunt interrupted me. "What do I know? A blind mouse is more perceptive than I am!"

"You said he's been following you!" I insisted, chin jutting out and my cheeks catching a tint of red.

"I know what I said. I didn't think you'd chase after him like a maniac! And by the way, I'm signing you up for the track team."

I sighed out the frustration and rubbed my thudding temples. Stalker or not, I knew what I'd seen. It was not down to chance we'd seen the guy twice within such a short period. Cap or no cap, I could have sworn his eyes were drilled on me. Besides, why would he disappear into thin air if he had nothing to hide?

Tony waved a hand at face level. "Oy, are you even listening?"

No. I was not.

"I said: did you see the guy's face?" Tony repeated.

I sniffed. "No, his hat was too low." I had another scan of the area. Nothing but abandoned park trails, trees, and flowers that'd lost their colour to the night sky.

"I think we've watched too many spy films. Next time pick a rom-com. Like a normal girl." He headed back towards the gates, muttering to himself.

I rubbed my hand along the length of my face and allowed myself a quick glance back. He was probably right, yet the uneasiness wouldn't shake off. The guy knew what he was doing. There were only few who could vanish seemingly into thin air, and none of them had business anywhere near here.

Tony and I walked in silence the rest of the way. The incident in the park played on repeat in my head. Plus, with Tony acting weird earlier on—*Hold on.*

Tony bumped into me as I stopped on the doorstep of the pub.

"Whoa, little warning would be nice," he remarked.

I apologised and walked to the nearest empty table. Tony unzipped his jacket but left it on.

Once the waiter had taken our food order, I set my elbows on the table. It was time for some answers. "Now, tell me, why you been acting so strange?"

Tony shrugged; I gave him a warning look.

"Fine." He rubbed his chin with his thumb. "It has nothing to do with you. But this is going to sound strange."

"I'm strange. It'll be right up my street." I smiled close to flirty.

Tony offered a slight chuckle, but he didn't sound humorous. *Come on, Tony,* slugs would finish slithering a marathon at this pace.

"I've been stumbling across some interesting articles lately." He leaned in and I relaxed a little. "Seems wherever I look I read things about police asking for information regarding a Jane Doe, or a girl getting beat up and ending up in hospital. I mean, some of the stuff looks like police reports so I have no idea how they ended up in my path but...they did."

The blood drained from my face and I took a gulp of my drink. "Okay," I cleared my throat, "what does that have to do with anything?"

"Well, nothing." Tony fidgeted. "But when Matthew brought up the girl last night, something clicked. Even though they're all

25

seemingly separate events, I think the articles are all about the *same* girl."

My pulse resembled a game of professional ping pong. "I'd no idea you were such a detective."

"I'm fascinated, what can I say. *If* it is the same girl...I may be onto something newsworthy!" Tony reached for his drink.

I smoothed the top of my hair a few times, fighting for a clear head. I needed to know exactly what he knew. "What makes you think it's the same girl?"

Tony inhaled between his teeth. "Similarities. She's always described as a young girl, late teens. Skinny. Straight, black hair, kinda like yours, I guess." Tony stopped to point at my hair. *Note to self: buy hair dye.* "She never has any ID, no one visits at the hospital, and then she seems to just disappear."

I crinkled my nose, needing to kill Tony's curiosity. "All probably coincidental. If she was the same girl, the police would know. They'd have pictures and she'd be a person-of-interest." As far as I was aware, I'd burned all the photos the crime scene investigators had taken.

"Maybe. I don't know. Some of these articles or reports, or whatever they are, are from abroad, though, so...*maybe* no one's connected the dots."

I felt like someone punched me in the jaw, the blow making me dig my fingernails into my palms. The food arrived just in time to give me a saving few seconds. Tony dug in like he hadn't eaten for days.

"How" —I tapped my teeth together a few times— "*exactly* did you come across all this stuff?"

Tony wiped a smear of ketchup from his face. "Totally" —he stopped to swallow— "by chance. Like I sit at a café and there's a newspaper folded open, or at lectures, a previous student has left an analysis of a police report." He ignored my questioning glare and carried on eating.

For a moment, the past year fast-forwarded in my mind: the different countries I didn't care to recall, the cities blending into one, the people whose faces were a blur, and I—fallen out of grace—in the middle of it all. All Tony could see was me twirling a strand of hair, occasionally dipping a chicken strip into sauce, when under the surface my thoughts kickboxed each other.

It all sounded too coincidental, too ridiculous, too unbelievable. If I was the one who Tony was unknowingly building up a case against—and the evidence was piling up against me— how did such a trace still exist? And how did it end up in Tony's path?

I'd have to see these stories Tony was referring to. And destroy them.

"It all sounds pretty far-fetched, Tony," I finally said. "Without a photo—"

"I bet I could find one."

"What? Why? How?"

Tony gave me a peculiar look. "It *is* the digital age. There's bound to be a police report or a social media account somewhere with a picture."

Panic circulated in my veins. I couldn't have this come out; I didn't want to face it. If Tony did follow the breadcrumbs, somehow Anita might find out the truth.

It was too big a risk.

"As for why," Tony continued, but I barely heard him. "I'm officially interested. When I was a kid, I wanted to become a detective. Guess that part of me never grew up." Tony winked and dug out his ringing phone from his pocket. He signalled he was taking the call outside and hurried out, pressing the phone to his ear.

I lingered on the memory of him for a few seconds. *It'd been nice knowing him.*

Fighting the gnawing emptiness inside of me, I threw down a few notes on the table and snuck out through a side entrance.

This is it then.

I had to get back on the road. Forget Anita and Tony. Forget the idea of a home. Forget about having friends ever again. I couldn't have my lies hurting anyone ever again.

I'd hurt enough people in my life.

Chapter 5

I surveyed the still silhouette of Anita's house from across the road.

She deserved a goodbye.

As I stepped through the front door, I sensed something was amiss. Anita sat in the lounge, staring blankly at the phone in her hand. She remained motionless even when I walked in the room.

"Hi," I greeted softly.

Anita sucked in a sharp breath as if waking from a dream. Tendons on her neck bulged as she faced me.

I prepared for the worst.

"Your friend Tony rang." The iciness of her voice gave me chills.

Worst was an understatement.

"How'd—" I stuttered, panic promoting my every nerve on high alert.

"You're not the only one who can keep secrets." Anita placed the phone down, her thumb moving to slide along her wedding ring. "Tony got my number off your phone yesterday." *Why would he do that?* "Ironically, he just wanted my insight as a nurse in the hospital that treated, well, *you.*"

Me? What had Tony said?

"Oh." I sat down opposite her. *I should've sacked goodbyes and hopped on the bus instead.*

"*Oh?* That's all? That's *all* you have to say?"

"I'm so sorry." I stared at her blankly, mind racing to figure out how much Tony knew and to what extent he'd connected the dots.

"For what?" she spat out.

"I thought Tony—"

"Oh, he did. He told me *everything.* The comas, disappearing acts, cover stories, amnesia...you name it."

I blanched at her words. I didn't understand how but she knew. He knew. I was officially a fraud.

"There's no point in acting clueless," Anita finally said. "We know what you do."

29

Panic again rang in my ears. This was bad—really, *really* bad. What was worse, all I could do was gape.

"Aren't you going to say anything?" Her tone became more demanding.

"I..." I said voiceless and had to start again. "I don't know what there is to say. Except that I'm sorry. I never meant to—"

"Meant to what?" Anita stood up. "Get beat up so you'd end up in a coma? Lie your way into people's lives and then disappear? And for what? Money? Drugs? Free hospital bed?"

I tried to stop my fidgeting hands by pressing a thumb into the middle of my palm. "It's not what you think."

"Then tell me," Anita retorted as if returning a slap.

I'd walked into that one. But how could I explain? How could I make her believe I never meant to hurt anyone but myself? That the physical pain relieved the anguish inside? That all I had wanted was for time to pass while I lay there unconscious, not having the constant torment of my thoughts assaulting me?

"I'm not who you think I am," was all I could muster to say.

Anita laughed wryly. "Well, that's obvious."

The lump in my throat made swallowing difficult. "You're right. There's nothing I can say to make things right. I'm not a good person. I never *meant* any harm. Though, I guess I can't help but...cause it." My palms slid along my jeans. "I really did care for your family and it killed me to lie to you—"

"You don't lie to and hurt the people you care about." Her voice carried sufficient disappointment to nearly strangle me. Her eyes reflected how I'd let her down. "You should go."

I stood immediately, unable to bear her condemning scrutiny any longer.

"You have one night," she added. "David will ring the police in the morning."

I nodded, emotionally battered. "Thank you. For everything."

I turned to walk to the door as Aaron stepped down the stairs. Suddenly, my body came alive in a way it hadn't done in a long time, every sense heightened, every muscle begging to listen to my instincts. I recognised the voice of my internal radar, telling me exactly what was wrong with Aaron.

My eyes flashed to him and I knew. Inside, unseen to the eye, he was bleeding to death. He didn't have long.

"Mummy, I want some water," the little boy mumbled sleepily.

"What happened to him?" I demanded.

"Just a minute, honey," Anita reassured her son. "Camilla, I need you to go *now*."

"What *happened* to him? How did he hurt himself?"

Aaron portrayed a blue plaster on his forearm. "I fell out of a tree. Mummy said I was really brave."

Blood drained from my cheeks. "Anita, you need to take him to A&E. *Now*." There was no time for explanations. She would never believe me. She would never believe I was born with an intuition that was more accurate than an MRI scan.

Anita pinched the bridge of her nose with her thumb and forefinger. "Aaron, go upstairs, please. Mummy will bring you some water in a minute." Obediently, Aaron lifted a leg up a stair.

"No, you need to listen: if you don't take him to the hospital *right now*, your son's going to die." I tried to lower my voice for Aaron's benefit, but I had to get through to her.

Anita threw daggers at me while Aaron's frame twisted, and he fixed his upset, hazel eyes at his mum.

"Camilla, please, I've had enough. *Enough* of the lies! Go before I call the police."

In seconds, I assessed the situation. She wasn't going to listen; why would she? And Aaron didn't have the time for me to explain my unconventional gifting. I had to get him out of the house within the next few minutes for him to live.

I reached and pressed my thumb and fingers on the carotid arteries pressure points in the front of Anita's neck, causing her blood pressure to plummet. Suddenly lightheaded, her knees wobbled. I took her weight as she fell to the floor unconscious. Aaron whimpered as he watched his mother crumble. Without a second to waste, I picked him up and dashed outside. Thankfully, Anita had a tendency of leaving her car keys in the ignition.

31

Ignoring Aaron's growing resistance, I fastened him in his car seat and jumped in the front. Driving lesson number one would have to be a crash course.

The engine roared as I reversed out of the driveway, barely missing a lamp post.

"Aaron, I need you to listen to me carefully." I glanced at the sobbing boy from the rear-view mirror. He was in shock. "Everything's gonna be fine. Mummy's fine, she's only sleeping. She'll meet us at the hospital." Grinding the gears, I passed a learner driver and almost made them veer into a ditch. "Aaron, I need you to trust me and be really brave, like you said you were before? I'm taking you to the hospital, so the doctors can make you better, okay?"

Aaron begged for his mummy, kicking against the seat in front. The traffic camera's flash caused little dark spots in my vision.

My reassurances falling on deaf ears, I dialled for Tony. It only took two rings for him to pick up.

"Tony, it's me. I know I'm the last person you wanna talk to, but you need to listen: it's about Anita."

Tony hesitated but I didn't have time to wait for him to decide. "Look, I've got Aaron, Anita's son, and I'm taking him to the hospital. Anita's at home and she'll be waking up any minute. I need you to call her and tell her to meet us at the hospital ASAP."

"Wait, what? What's going on?"

I repeated myself, and still didn't get through to him. Frustrated, I yelled at the phone, "Tony, *call Anita*. Hospital. *Now.*"

Aaron's cries were rattling my eardrums.

With little time to spare I pulled in front of A&E. I grabbed the struggling Aaron and ran inside without locking the car. Heads whipped in our direction due to the dramatic entrance. I cut in the queue and interrupted a woman talking with the receptionist.

"This boy needs to be seen immediately. He has severe abdominal bleeding and—" Aaron's pupils drew back as his body went limp on my arms. The nurses at the desk stared at me dumbfounded. "He needs surgery now!"

"Are you a doctor?" The older of the nurses asked, doubtful of my young age, but her hand moved towards the phone.

"Yes—no, pre-med. I know his medical history. He's had a fall and he needs help now!" Would they take me seriously? I wouldn't.

The fresh-faced nurse jumped from her seat, calling for a doctor. From there, I was impressed by the swiftness of everyone's actions. A doctor came running in, taking Aaron into his arms. I quickly explained what had happened and where the bleeding was. The doctor shouted instructions for the nurses and disappeared into the restricted areas. Staring at the swinging door in front of me, I sighed in relief before informing the front desk of Anita's imminent arrival. Then, I fled into the night.

Choosing a longer detour, I drove back to Anita's. The house was empty as anticipated. I gathered my few belongings, wrote a note of apology, and—with a heavy heart—shut the front door.

It wasn't until I was checked into a motel and behind locked doors that I allowed the raging emotions to pour in, only to shove them aside to another corner of my mind—I was in no mood to process them.

I gave the small but clean room a scan. Had Anita not been a super-generous employer, I'd be sleeping on the streets.

I sat on the neatly-made bed and flopped backwards. Instantly, the vibration against my thigh pushed me up. *Tony.* Pacing along the floor, phone in hand, I talked myself into taking the call.

Tony's greeting was official yet somewhat relieved. I waited, holding my breath.

"I thought you'd wanna know Aaron made it to surgery on time and he's gonna be fine," he said. "Anita and David are here with him."

He was at the hospital. Anita would've filled him in on the details.

Oh boy.

"Thanks, it's good to hear," I said quietly. The silence felt strange.

"Soooo… Anita says thanks."

I scoffed humourlessly. "There's no need. I did steal her car and technically kidnap her son."

"But you saved his life," Tony said each word slowly. "The doctors said if he'd been a couple of minutes later he would've died."

On purpose, I mumbled something barely audible.

"How did you know?" Tony asked.

"I had a hunch." I rubbed my neck with my free hand, knowing the answer would do nothing to satisfy Tony. I was buying time. For what—who knew.

"Seriously, I'm not an idiot, and I'm not in the mood. The doctor told me word for word what you said and even he doesn't understand how you could've known."

I pressed my lips together and sucked them in. I could just hang up the phone.

"It doesn't matter how as long as Aaron's fine, right?"

"That's what Anita said." Tony scoffed. "She's letting go of all the other stuff because you saved her son. But it's not good enough: I want to know how you did it."

I weighed the options. I could tell him. I could hang up. Could I trust him with the truth? Was there any point if I was never going to see him again?

Tony cleared his throat, probably sensing I was about to end the call. "Where are you? I wanna see you."

"Why?" Out of instinct, I took a step closer to the door and gave the room a once-over as if Tony was going to float through the walls.

"Because you have *a lot* of explaining to do, missy. And not just about tonight."

"I don't have anything to say. Besides, I'm leaving first thing tomorrow." The line was quiet for a while and, again, I toyed with the idea of hanging up.

"I don't want you to leave."

"Maybe you should've thought of that before telling Anita," I retorted, and then thought better than to risk riling him up with my tone. "How did you put it all together, anyway?"

"With a lot of luck and sheer intelligence," Tony dead-panned. "Anita had the right to know. Plus, you went missing from the pub. I didn't want you to do anything stupid." He sighed heavily. "Look, I'm not angry. I just want to see you. It'll be easier to talk in person."

My tongue slid along my bottom lip, left and right. Tony must have some ulterior motive. Anyone with any sense would stay away from me. I only caused pain. *I was in pain.*

I clicked my tongue. "I'm at the Bay Horse Motel. Room 34."

Chapter 6

Time dragged like a slug. I debated the possible outcomes of Tony's visit, heart pumping on overdrive. *Why had I agreed to see him?* Surely there was no way to salvage the beginnings of my new life in Bridleton. It would be better for everyone if I left.

Yet I couldn't make myself run away. Not this time.

Sharing the truth was a gamble, and I was about to take it.

My sighs multiplied until I wanted to pull my hair at the sound of one. Tonight would be a milestone: I was letting someone in. Or I'd be spending the night in a prison cell. I might prefer the cell.

A knock demanded my attention. I tiptoed to the door. *Here goes nothing.*

Tony stood in the corridor, hands in his jeans' pockets. I struggled to read his expression. With a slight nod, he walked past me.

I popped my head into the corridor. "No cops. Or are they outside?"

"I see your sense of humour wasn't a lie. It's still atrocious," Tony answered flatly. "Why would I bring cops?"

"Kidnapping, carjacking, fraud… Need I continue? And Anita said—"

"No one's throwing you in jail. You'll just have to find other ways of paying me back. And society at large." The tiniest smile flickered on Tony's face; I drew confidence from it. "Besides, like I said, saving Aaron was your redeeming act—no cops."

I pursed my lips and folded my arms in front of me. "Then why did you wanna see me?"

"I want the truth. I wanna know what drove you to do what you did. You know, whether you really are nuts." Tony's smirk came without the twinkle in his eye.

I perched on the bed, keeping a keen eye on him. He kept his hands firmly tucked away in his pockets, still scanning the surroundings. He reminded me of a TV-movie detective.

"And once you get your answers, then what?"

"Then," Tony shrugged, "we can move on. Or get you some help—accordingly." I glared at him and he continued, "*Come on.* The suicidal tendencies... Obviously, you have issues."

"I'm not suicidal." *Although, I could see why he'd arrive at the conclusion.*

"Then what are you?" Tony sat on the leather armchair. He leaned on his elbows, facing me inquisitively.

I took a raspy breath, more for time than lack of oxygen. My gut told me I could trust him, but where would I even start?

"Start from the beginning," Tony said, reading my mind. "Tell me who you really are and where you're from?"

"It's...not that simple."

"Right. Well, are you human?"

I couldn't help but grin. "Yes."

"Good. That's a start." Tony surprised me; he was verging on comical. "How many times have you pretended to be in a coma?"

"I never *pretended* to be comatose. That would've been counterproductive. But, twice I've 'caused' my body to shut down like that."

Tony scrunched his face. "*Caused?*"

Here we go. "Let's just say I know my body *very* well. I know what kills it and what shuts it down for a nice little nap."

Tony brushed his hand through his bronzed hair, his blank expression signalling his need for clarification.

"I don't know how to explain it." I pressed a thumb to the dimple on my chin as I studied the beige carpet. "It's something I was born with. A special *ability*, I guess, that allows me to know what's medically, or emotionally, wrong with myself and others. Like I can *read* their weaknesses. I don't know the 'logistics' of it; the information comes to me like knowing if I'm hungry or thirsty. Like a hyper-perceptiveness." I cleared my throat. "It seems to also accelerate the healing process in my body."

Tony stared at me blank. I waited.

"Okay," he found his voice, "then why'd you use this ability to harm yourself?"

38

I squirmed within my skin. How could I make him understand? "To escape from myself, my thoughts. Haven't you ever wanted to just...sleep?"

"Haven't you ever heard of sleeping pills?"

I cast my gaze to the white ceiling fan, and back to meet Tony's scrutinising look. There was no way I could explain it. "Sometimes I can't cope with everything going on in my head. One night I was at a train station, struggling to sleep because I was wrestling with bad memories and I just thought *'if only I could punch myself to sleep'*. So, I did. And it worked." *Kind of.*

Tony cleared his throat, clearly not impressed. "Um, bit extreme. But I'll go with that for now." His furrowed forehead was evidence of his struggling thoughts. "Then what's so bad you can't bear to live with it?"

My feet itched to run. I could disappear. I could forget this day. Only...my body didn't take the hint.

My toes tapped the ground; I pressed one foot on top of the other. "That's not an easy question to answer—" Before Tony could object I added hastily, "But I'll try my best." *Sink or swim.* I shifted my weight on the bed, rubbing my knuckles with my fingers. "I need to start from the beginning for this to make any sense."

Bracing himself, Tony straightened his posture and inhaled audibly. He leaned backwards and intertwined his fingers.

"Remember when I told you I'm from out of town? Well, it was a bit of an understatement. I come from a very different *world*—"

"You're an alien?" Tony's eyes ballooned.

"Not *that* different of a world." I rolled my eyes. "I'm from the Kingdom of Narun. It's sort of an island, or a whole new continent, if you will." It was strange talking about home in such a way—out loud.

"But it's on this planet?"

"Yes, on this planet! I told you, I'm not an alien and I don't want to take over the world or suck your blood for that matter."

Tony held his arms up. "Can't blame me for asking."

"Ha-ha," I retorted dryly. I had to admit Tony was handling this well so far.

39

"Why haven't I heard of this place?"

"Because, technically, it doesn't exist. It's not on any map; you need to know where it is to find it. We're kind of our own hidden race." *How do you explain to an embryo there's a whole world beyond the womb?* "Anyway," I continued, in a serious tone. "I left nearly two years ago and have been travelling in your world ever since."

"Why'd you leave? And how did you know about us if we don't know about you?"

"It's not important right now. I came because I needed to get away. It all reminded me of—" Goosebumps surfaced on my skin at the thought of *him*. The pain felt raw.

I swallowed air. "—someone I lost." A stain on the carpet drew my focus. I remembered why I hadn't chosen the truthful route before—it was uncomfortable, unbearable.

"Is that the reason for the comas? You're trying to forget someone?"

"Yes." I stood up, my back to Tony. "So, now you know."

"Whoa, you're not getting away that easy! Get back here, and don't you dare give me that bulletproof exterior. I want the *whole* story, the whole shebang."

Reluctantly, I sat back down. "I told you. That's why I'm running: I want to forget everything."

"Right. Well, no offence, but that sounds a bit weak."

I wanted to growl at him. In fact, I could have thumped him. What does he know about loss?

"Now you're angry," Tony observed.

"Well spotted."

"But why? You've not really explained anything. So, you're from some secret place and you're beating yourself up because someone died. You're holding back." Tony was his usual straight self. And he was right. I wasn't giving him the whole story.

I raised the corners of my mouth as a sign of peace. "It's just not easy. I haven't told anyone about any of this. Ever."

Tony reached out his hand and clipped me gently on my arm. "Sorry, kid."

"Ask me something. It's easier to answer questions."

"Explain Aaron. How'd you know about him?"

Keep up, Tony. "Like I said, I know people's weaknesses. It's mainly physical things as it helps in combat. For example, your left arm is weaker than your right." I paused to scoff as Tony compared the bulk on his arms. "And if I'm familiar with the person I can better read their emotional weaknesses and specific medical issues. I'm not sure how it works exactly. It's a gift." *Or a curse.*

"Right." Tony sucked in a breath. "First of all, I'm going to ignore the 'weak arm' comment...but I still don't get it. Are you a superhuman or something?"

"Don't be daft. It's just a gift, a talent."

"Can everyone from, err, Nauru, do that?"

"*Narun,*" I corrected. "No. But some others have different sorts of gifts and skills. Things to help them in battle, like enhanced speed, or being able to track or... I don't know, skills." I sucked my lips in; other people's talents weren't for me to reveal.

"You keep mentioning battles." Tony frowned. "Are you in constant war in this place?"

"Not in so many words," I stalled. "The atmosphere is unsteady, explosive. Life used to be more peaceful, but when I was a toddler, the Queen was murdered by an enemy tribe and things changed. Attacks became frequent and the Crown Prince had to be placed into hiding as they feared for his life—to this day he remains the Lost Prince." I took inventory—the depth of the crease between Tony's eyes, his rigid posture, the straight line of his mouth. "Things have calmed, but the threat of open war is always there."

Tony drew a circle in the air with his finger, encouraging me to continue.

I took a deep breath. "We're an old tribe of people defending our kingdom and its values. Most of our people are 'normal' in your sense of the word—families, traders, farmers, teachers—but some of us have been born with a special skill. Those of us become part of the Royal Guard, defending our King and Land. We're set apart as children and trained to defend the Kingdom either as a Defender, an Attacker, a Tracker or an Advisor, depending on our natural gifting."

41

I paused to see if Tony was following or freaking out. It seemed safe to carry on.

"When we reach level three training, most of us are paired with a partner of the opposite gender, someone destined to complement our gift."

Tony's face twisted like someone had placed a bucket of fish guts in front of him. "You get married?"

"No. You train together and become partners for life; it makes you stronger to fight. The pair normally serves for a period of time and then they step down, start a family, and train the younger ones." The textbook approach worked: I could distance myself emotionally.

I leaned back to get a bottle of water from the bedside table.

"Sounds like something from a movie. You better not be playing me, Milla." Tony's disbelieving look spoke volumes; I assured him I was telling the truth. He scratched his beardless chin, digesting my words, and I allowed him the time, my pulse steady.

"Let's say I believe you," Tony said slowly, eyes shut but his forehead smoothed. "What was your role?"

"I was a Defender." I ignored the pang in my chest.

"Really?" He perked up. "Does that mean you can do all that Kung Fu stuff?"

A corner of my mouth rose involuntarily. "I can handle myself."

Tony shuffled forward, begging me to show him what I could do. I shot him down. Metaphorically.

"I won't believe you unless you show me." He was clearly disappointed—and annoyed at my indifferent shrug. "Wait, what about your partner?"

It took the time of me lowering the bottle onto the floor for Tony to cotton on.

"Right. He was the one who died. Sorry." He cringed.

I studied the stain on the floor again. Hearing someone say it out loud twisted the knife sticking in my chest.

Tony came next to me, wrapping his arm around my shoulders. I shoved the pain down back into its pit.

"It's okay," I lied and straightened against the weight of his arm. "Now you know my little secret. Any more questions?"

"Tons." Tony laughed. "But I'll leave them for another time." He tightened his grip on my shoulder before releasing me.

"What happens now?"

Tony opened his mouth, and shut it, taking a moment. "Nothing has to change. I can keep your secret, if you want, and we can pick up where we left off."

That simple? *Really?* "What about Anita and her family? And Jill? And—" The list would be too long.

Tony examined the room again, peeking into the bathroom. "You best stay away from Anita's family. They live at the outskirts, anyway, so you're unlikely to bump into them. As for Jill, I can't really keep this from her, not without it causing problems."

A shiver crept up my spine. I nodded, although I was anything but convinced. I had only met Jill maybe four times in passing. I'd have to be at the mercy of Tony's good judgement.

"Don't worry." Tony touched my arm. "She'll understand, and she won't tell anyone. Let me explain it to her, though. Your narration kinda sucks."

"Yeah, whatever." If anyone, I'd rather he told her than me anyway. "Hey, Tony, thanks for being so cool about this."

"Yeah, and what do I get in return" —Tony pinched his left bicep— "weak arm, my eye."

I knew he wouldn't let it go.

Tony left after making plans to meet the next day, leaving me alone with an anxious knot in my stomach. The unknown unsettled me.

That night, the sword, tainted with blood, haunted me more than it had in a long time.

Chapter 7

I wiped the steam from the bathroom mirror. The face staring back at me was that of an acquaintance, at best—one I hadn't properly given a second look in years.

I'd lost weight: the sunken cheeks cried out for better care. The contours of my face had sharpened and the dent on my chin resembled the Grand Canyon. My green eyes were faded, my tanned complexion more ashen. The ends of my hair brushed the small of my back—the longest I'd ever let it grow.

I scoffed at the reflection and combed the dripping hair into the usual sleek ponytail.

The knock on the door startled me as I fastened my jeans. *It had to be Tony or room service.*

The knock repeated itself and I checked the peephole to find my first guess correct.

"It's about time," Tony huffed as I let him in and waved something brown in front of me. "I brought you a filled bagel—chicken mayo. Even Wonder Woman has to eat." He pushed past me, shoving a paper bag against my chest.

"I thought we were meeting at uni." I closed the door. "At lunch."

"It's two o'clock, Mil."

My eyes darted around, searching. *What sort of a motel room doesn't have a clock?*

"Oops. I'd no idea. Sorry." I dug into the bag. The smell of fresh bagel provoked my stomach to produce a demanding rumble. Although we were rarely offered bread to eat on the Guard, I'd grown more than accustomed to eating it here.

"Why didn't you answer my call?" Tony walked to the bedside table, picked up my phone, and tossed it on the unmade bed. "Your phone's dead."

"Again—sorry. I slept in." I bit into the bagel. "Thanks for breakfast."

"Don't mention it. It was 'buy one, get one'."

I wiped a smear of mayonnaise from my chin. "You look tired."

Tony rubbed his jaw, dismissing the concern in my voice with a quick shrug. "Didn't sleep well. Had a lot to think about."

I had kind of shoved a load on Tony.

I took the rest of the bagel in one hand and threw the empty bag in the bin.

"Oh, by the way, Jill's back," Tony said. "I met up with her this morning. So, she knows now."

Uncertainty rushed through me. "How'd… she take it?" The last time I saw her, she'd barely spoken to me. Not that I had been much better at small talk.

"She took it well, considering." Tony pulled out his car keys from his pocket and buried them in his palm. "It's a lot to digest."

It's a good thing I only scratched the surface then. Had I told the whole story, I doubt they would've been so understanding.

"If it helps, think of me as a foreigner. That's all I am."

"Yeah, a foreigner with some freakish gift that can detect internal bleeding, and kick butt." Tony shot me a glare and moved to the doorway. "Although, the jury's still out on the last point."

Rolling my eyes, I slid some cash into my pocket, gave the room a scan and followed Tony outside.

Jill sat by a corner table at our usual study lounge, her handbag and jumper reserving two empty seats—not that there was a shortage of seats. Her wavy, sand-coloured, jaw-length hair hung on the sides of her face as her head was bowed, fixed marginally at the wrong angle for her to be reading the book in front of her.

"Hey, babe. Sorry we're late. Milla overslept." Tony kissed Jill's cheek and took the jumper on his lap as he sat down. I slid onto the free chair and apologised for making her wait. She smiled back coyly and folded a corner of a page before shutting the book.

Hmm, awkward silence.

Tony stroked the back of Jill's hand, staring at nothing, while she looked down, blushing. What had Tony made me out to be like?

"So..." *Someone needs to break the ice.* "Should we address the elephant in the room?" I quipped, a knot forming in my stomach.

"Sorry, Camilla. I didn't mean to—" Jill spoke softly. "I didn't want to make you feel uncomfortable."

I hurried to shake my head. "I should be the one apologising. I'm sorry I lied to you both."

"It's okay." Jill straightened her posture to near perfect. "You weren't in a good place. Tony told me what you did for Aaron: you saved his life." She smiled warmly; I'd never realised how pretty she was.

"It doesn't make up for anything. What I did—"

"What's done is done." Tony lifted his hand to cover a yawn. "Let's forget it and start off on a clean slate."

I eyed the pair of them. I didn't deserve this. I didn't deserve *them.*

My conscience pounded my insides. Surely, there'd be internal bleeding soon. "It's not right what I did."

Jill and Tony exchanged glances. Tony cleared his throat. "Mil, really, it's not like we've never lied. Honestly, we sort of get it. Well, maybe not the fascination with death" —Tony shook his finger at me— "but the only person you *really* hurt was yourself."

"We want to help." Jill reached forward.

I felt like I'd been brought to therapy.

"Guys, I'm *not* suicidal," I clarified. Another exchanged glance. Would they stop with that lovers' telepathy?

"Tony said you're trying to forget someone," Jill said. "Maybe we could help you, so you could go back home."

I shifted on my seat, uneasy. I had run away from home and betrayed our people by fleeing from my duty. And still, treason was the least of my crimes.

There was no going back.

The shreds of my life were now here and the two people in front of me were the only ones holding it together.

I forced a polite smile. "Thanks, but going back isn't an option."

"Then we'll help you move on." Jill's chocolate-button eyes were the dictionary definition for 'empathy'.

47

I mumbled my gratitude.

"Right, so," Tony spoke up, scratching his chin. "In that case, we need to find you a place to stay. Unless you were a millionaire back in... *wherever* you can't stay at a motel. You can crash on my couch until we find something permanent."

"You sure?" I aimed the query more at Jill than Tony, and she reassured me rather enthusiastically. She certainly wasn't one for jealousy, or she trusted Tony when he said we were just friends.

Tony winked and made a comment about me doing his housework in return for the favour.

Could it be that easy? Could settling down be the answer to finding peace within myself? Or was I only postponing the day I'd have to pay for what really happened the day I left Narun?

One thing became clear. If I was to live in peace, without always glancing over my shoulder for people looking for me, there was one thing I had to do before anything else.

When I was six years old, I'd taken an oath in blood to serve the King as Guard. To settle the Blood Debt, I'd have to spill blood once again. Perhaps then I could find peace.

*

"All right, line it up, kids," Bar'Aelia said for the second time in his serious voice.

We shuffled into two lines, elbows knocking into each other. The boys behind us were the first to quieten down; a few girls beside me let out a nervous snicker. Bar'Aelia stood poised to the right of me, his playful smile reminding me of my father.

It had been three weeks since I'd last seen home—my old home. The King's palace was my home now. The kids around me, the Guard, were my family.

And yet I barely knew their names.

The girl next to me, the one with the quick heart rate making her dizzy with nerves, shifted her feet so our arms no longer grazed each other.

She knew. They all knew. Nobody wanted to get too close to the girl who could write a shopping list of their shortcomings.

I imprisoned my bottom lip under my teeth and focused on the powdery dirt of the training ground. I willed Bar'Aelia to get started with the lesson.

A stone, skimming to knock against my heel, made me take a quick glance back.

The stocky boy with crewcut hair smiled at me again.

Chapter 8

"You almost done, love?" The janitor jingled a bunch of keys as a subtle hint.

I tied the bin bag, hooked it on a finger, and placed the broom back in the cleaning cupboard. The janitor whistled a tune as he strode towards the exit, and soon I followed, walking through the door he held open for me.

"See you in a few days, Arthur." I took the rubbish to the bin and quickened my pace in the chill air. The few hours of work dusting and sweeping floors at the dance studio were just what I needed: adequate money, low profile and had nothing to do with the past me.

Too bad not everything could be swept under the rug so easily.

Letting Tony and Jill in the loop was a relief in some ways but starting over was only simple on paper—the decision had done little to help me forget *him* and what I'd done. Tony insisted I'd find a way to move on, but *he* wasn't someone to move on from. *He* had been the very core of me. What was worse, now that the previous pain relief method was no longer an option, I had to learn to live with it: day, night and in between.

Yet, having a job and my own place had at least offered a distraction. *A bit too much of a distraction.*

Resolving the Blood Debt had taken persistent residence on my to-do list.

I sped into a jog as a faint thunder rumbled above. I should make my one-bedroom flat before the heavens opened.

"Hello, stranger."

My jog halted mid-air, if it was possible. The voice came from a young man leaning against a light post. He hadn't been there a second ago.

I assessed his features, which I somewhat recognised. *It's been a while.* He looked slightly older than me—early twenties, I guessed—and had brooding eyes that could turn faces. His dark hair previously covered by a cap was now tousled by the breeze. He stood a head taller to me, but his slender build was deceiving. He knew how to handle himself.

"Looks like rain, don't you think?" he said with a crooked smile. *What a cliché.*

"I know you." For a fraction of a second doubt flickered in his eyes. "You're that guy. From the park."

He arched an eyebrow. "From the park."

Was that a question or a statement? "Who are you and what do you want?" I took a step back as he straightened his posture.

"A friend." His voice toyed with me.

Which question did he answer? "I have enough friends." I checked to see if the road was clear for crossing.

"It's not wise to talk to strangers, you know," he said as I stepped off the curb.

I glanced over my shoulder, baffled. "You ought to heed your own advice then." I hurried across the road, not giving him a chance to respond. As I turned the corner, I heard one set of footsteps—my own.

I slowed to a walk. A stone presented itself along the path at the opportune moment. The tip of my shoe launched it in the air, curving the rock off the pavement. It skipped, resting next to a car wheel.

Late nights really do bring out the weirdos. Why did the guy have to resurface now? Why hadn't I demanded answers out of him?

A few drops of rain tied the distance from sky to ground.

I was semi-succeeding at having a life as *Camilla.* I couldn't take a complication. I didn't want to know who he was.

*

Head leaning on one hand, I enforced the figure eight shape I'd doodled on my notebook. The guest lecturer droned on about the charity he'd founded. He'd lost me during the first quarter. The girl next to me sported equal enthusiasm: her notepad was full of flowers, signature rehearsing, squares and stick men. Neither of us excelled in art.

A nudge to my ribs made me jolt.

"You have an admirer," my fellow doodler whispered in a Scottish burr. Her strong perfume lingered in the air around me.

"Say what?" I replied too loud. The lecturer paused and searched for the source of the voice. The girl next to me waited until he carried on with his slides.

"Fourth row, to the right of me." She barely moved her lips as she spoke. "The guy keeps staring at ye."

I angled my head, darting my eyes back the second they met his. *What is he doing here?*

"He fancies you," my neighbour persisted in a sing-song voice. "He's hot."

Yeah, he was a real kettle of boiling water.

I slammed my notebook shut. Student or not, it wasn't a coincidence he was here, not after last night. Annoyance swelled up in me. *What does he want?*

"Do you know him?" the girl asked, but my firm 'No' was drowned in the mandatory applause as the lecturer finished. I was out of the lecture theatre, notebook in hand before the clapping faded.

I marched along the corridor, took an abrupt left and sneaked outside through a side exit. The swinging door narrowly missed a guy squatting by the side of the building. I left a mumbled "Sorry" to hover in the air. When the cigarette smoke no longer found me, I dropped the notebook to the ground in a statement, flung a leg over a bench and sat on it. Sooner or later I'd have to confront this guy.

Today was not the day.

"Hey."

The voice behind me caught me off guard and my neck spasmed at the abrupt turn of my head.

"You left this." The guy placed my bag beside me. I drilled my eyes into him, annoyed I hadn't even noticed my bag missing, and because he'd once again surprised me.

He sure is light on his feet.

"What do you want?"

"I think it's time we talk, Camilla." He sat on the bench, opposite me, ignoring my scowl.

I shuffled back, annoyed at the intrusion to my personal space, and stuffed the notepad in the bag. "You can start by telling me your name since you already know mine."

"You can call me Leo."

"Okay, *Le-o*." I mocked for no particular reason. "Why are you following me?"

He flashed his pearly whites with an assuming grin. "Maybe I like what I see, rosebud."

Rosebud? Did he have a death wish?

"So, you admit you've been following me?" I took in his relaxed composure, close to rehearsed in its perfection. Last night I hadn't noticed the colour of his eyes: piercing blue, like the deep of the Caribbean Sea.

"Would that flatter you?" He cocked his eyebrow to match mine.

If I weren't so annoyed, I'd laugh. "Stay away from me." I stood up, but his sudden grip on my arm pulled me back. "You have three seconds to—"

"And what are you going to do after three seconds?" Leo challenged.

"You have no idea what I can do *in* three seconds."

"Likewise." The playfulness melted from his face. A blink later the glimmer was back in his eye.

My muscles tensed under his grip as a shot of adrenaline deluged through me. I recognised the surge of fire bubbling inside. I'd missed it. Raising my free arm, I bent my fingers halfway, ready to—

"Yo, Mil, you finished for the day?"

My arm went limp at the sound of Tony's call. I threw Leo a warning look. With a wink, he let go of my arm, tilting his head to smile at the approaching Tony.

"What's going on here?" Tony asked, catching the tense vibe and no doubt the exasperation written all over me. I walked up to him and let my expression ease. Bringing Tony in on this would make it an issue.

"Nothing." I smiled. "Come on, let's go."

Tony ignored my tugging hand. "You're that guy who keeps turning up everywhere." Leo got up and introduced himself. Tony pounded his extended fist and measured up Leo from head to toe with quick, repeated scans. "Do you know each other?"

"We don't."

"Well, that's not entirely true, Milla," Leo added, once again passing me my bag.

"Yeah? How so?" Tony turned to me, searching for an explanation for my apparent hostility.

"Apparently, we share a lecture," I said under my breath, and Tony eased his poise, theories of stalker behaviour wiped from his mind.

I shot a glance at Leo as he cleared his throat. "To be completely truthful" —he smirked in my direction— "I've actually been plucking up the courage to ask her out."

I wanted to pluck *him* bit by bit. He was either one for a gamble or he could read Tony well. I gathered the latter as Tony burst out in hearty laughter. He placed his arm around Leo's shoulders and started to tutor him on how to win me over. So much for loyalty.

I spun on my heels, intentionally flinging my bag so it smacked Tony's chest.

This is not over, Leo.

Trampling the ground flat, I pushed the dining hall doors open and tossed my bag on the nearest free table. The chair screeched along the floor as I pulled it out.

What did the guy want with me? He came across awfully confident, and he was fast on his feet. That time in the park he was gone within a blink. He was agile, lean. *Egotistic, annoying, pretentious...*

Personal feelings aside... Obviously, he wasn't from Gorah, or I wouldn't be standing tall anymore, but could he be from Narun? There was something familiar in his features, but if he was Guard, I should've recognised him, not to mention, he would've just said so. It was unlikely another fugitive was searching me out.

I shook my head to rid myself of the idea and hoped the only thing off about him was his stinking personality.

*

After my final lecture of the day, Jill picked me up with her red Mini and drove us to a shopping centre. We'd become closer since she found out about where I came from; her down-to-earthiness was like a safety blanket to me.

I trailed her from shop to shop as she searched for a dress for a family occasion.

This was new to me. I'd had girl-friends in Narun, but our days were spent training or riding or playing Tackle with the others. I had never felt comfortable having heart-to-hearts with other girls. *He* had been the only one who knew me inside out.

Jill appeared from the dressing room in a golden, tunic-like dress. Her petite, ex-ballerina figure complimented the attire and I gave her the thumbs up. As she disappeared behind the curtain again I glanced at my watch—we were going to be late. Tony had rung to invite us over for bowling with his friends.

I'd never bowled, but I'd seen people do it on TV. But how hard could it be to hit a few pins with a ball?

After a few wrong turns, Jill found the low ceiling building with large, neon letters lightning up its side: Hollywood Bowl.

I followed Jill inside through the glass doors. The entrance hall was spacious, opening wider into rows of bowling lanes. Vending machines and games, ranging from shooting to dance mats, filled a room to the left of the entrance. A cashier's desk welcomed us on the right.

I scanned the people: a few families, some students, all and all rather quiet. By the furthest lane, Tony cheered an apparent strike.

"What shoe size, Mil?" Jill held a pair of black and red bowling shoes in her hand. I stated my size; a young guy handed me a pair and returned to his book. My thanks barely received an acknowledgement.

We made our way to Tony.

"Hey, there you are... What took you so long?" Tony brushed a kiss on Jill's cheek and let his gaze linger on her face. *They're good together*, I thought, as Jill explained our tardy arrival. I checked the scoreboard hanging from the low roof. Two initials stood side by side on the screen.

"Who are you playing against? Who's 'L'?"

Tony waved his thumb at something on the side of us. I turned—and froze.

"Surely you haven't forgotten me yet, Rosebud?" Leo grinned, turning a black ball between his hands.

My head snapped towards the amused Tony. "What's he doing here?"

"Easy, he's right there…"

"*I know*, Tony." I placed myself between him and Leo, my back to Leo. "But what is he *doing* here?"

"He's your blind date." Tony winked. "It's about time you found other people to hang with." Tony man-handled me aside.

I wasn't sure who to be angrier with, Leo or Tony, but I swallowed the bitter pill of defeat, nonetheless.

Jill gave Leo a coy wave of a hand and introduced herself.

"Come on then, let's play. Girls against boys? Too unfair?" Tony nudged my arm. He'd obviously missed a calling somewhere if matchmaking brought him so much joy.

"Girls against boys is fine." I twirled around, my ponytail swishing inches from Leo's chest. "Come on, Jill, let's show them how it's done."

"Actually, Milla," Jill smiled wryly, "I'm not that good at bowling."

"Well, I am," I snapped back, and hoped bowling was like target practice: breathe, focus, aim, release.

Twenty minutes later Tony was dancing his victory dance, punching his fists in the air. Leo's score, much like mine, was near to perfection. I got the feeling he missed some bowls on purpose.

Annoyance brewed inside me. I had to get some cooling off time. Alone.

I excused myself to the toilet, but snuck outside through a staff door, leading to a narrow alley aligned with the building. Littered with bins, it was an obstacle course. The smell of decomposing food mixed with soiled tins and cardboard hung in the air. For the sake of a moment of peace, I sucked it up.

I walked to the end of the alley and kicked a bin, a little too hard. It thudded against a wall, rattling until the last of its contents had settled. *What is it about this guy that gets to me so much?* So he was good at bowling. So he befriended Tony. So he followed me around.

I inhaled deeply, holding the air inside my lungs until I literally tasted the rubbish, and then released it. Of course, there was something more to him. He wasn't after a date, that was a given.

I froze as someone called my name. *Figures.*

"What do you want?" I faced Leo, vexed.

"To talk."

"Then talk."

Leo took four steps forward, leaving a calculated space between us. He hid his hands in his pockets. Light was scarce but there was enough to reveal the shreds of self-reproach shining through his eyes.

"You played well," he said, his tone soft, verging on complimentary. I raised a shoulder and Leo continued, "Your aim is precise. Rehearsed?"

"I got lucky." I rubbed my fingertips together, increasing in pressure, as we stared at each other, undisturbed by the surroundings.

"You're not from around here, are you?"

"I wasn't born in Bridleton, no," I said, aloof.

Leo sighed. "Let's speed this up a notch. I know where you're from."

I maintained my composure to a tee. *Of course, he knew.* I just hadn't wanted to admit it. Or let him call off my cards so easily.

"Oh yeah?" I kept up my stance of feigned boredom. "And where's that then?"

"Narun," he answered simply.

"*Narun?* Is that a brand of cleaning detergent?" I considered marching back inside but to reach the door I'd have to go past Leo. I suspected that wasn't going to happen.

"Why don't we cut the denial and get to the chase? I know you're from Narun, and I know you used to be a Defender." Leo levelled his gaze on me. "They sent me from Narun to find you."

58

Chapter 9

It felt like fire ants ran up and down my back. Leo stepped forward, halting as my arm rose to warn him.

"Camilla," Leo's voice wavered. "I know I should've told you straight away, but I wanted to make sure it was you."

"Who are you?" I held him tight in my vision, alarm bells ringing.

"I'm a Messenger. I travel to find fugitives, like yourself." Leo bowed his head slightly towards me. "I'm basically the human version of pigeon post."

I gave myself a moment, focusing on being angry to have a better hold of my raging emotions.

"How did you find me?"

"Trade secrets, my friend." He tapped the side of his nose. "It wasn't easy but after observing, or stalking as you so aptly put it, for some time I knew it had to be you."

"What, you never saw a picture?"

"I did. You look different."

He had me there. I had changed. "Right. And what message do you have for me?" I bit my lip as the memories of my last days at Narun raced through my mind.

What did they want? How much did they know?

"They asked me to escort you back home. They want you to re-join the Guard."

My lips parted; it wasn't what I had expected. Had I been pardoned? Did they not know? Was it a trap? *What does it mean?*

I focused on the one thing I did know.

"If you think you can throw me over your shoulder and drag me back, you're mistaken."

"As delightful as that sounds, I'll give you some time to think about it." His playful wink grated my nerves like they were a chunk of cheese.

But I couldn't think about it, not with the memories pounding on the door of my thought-life. Not with anxiousness choking me. And definitely not with his smirking face distracting me while Tony and Jill waited inside.

I needed an exit.

"Whoa, not so fast." Leo stepped in front of me as I started for the door. "That's it? You don't have any questions? You don't want to talk?"

"Not here, not now," I bit out and added a glower for good measure. "Get out of my way before I physically remove you."

Leo laughed but moved. "Alright, hotshot. We'll take a rain check." He reached for the handle, bowing theatrically as he opened the door. "Please, be my guest."

I marched inside and stopped short as the noise in the bowling alley stunned me. It had gotten busy. I brushed a hand across my forehead, melting the creases under my palm. I did *not* want to get into this with Tony and Jill.

Speaking of whom…

"There you are! We've been looking for you." Tony sauntered over with his arm anchored on Jill's shoulders. I smiled as if nothing had happened. "Ah, I see what's going on. You two are hitting it off, eh?" The wink of approval he threw Leo nearly made me tilt him.

"No, that's not—" I had to stop mid-sentence. A hand rested on my shoulder, sliding to the front of me until it lay horizontal across my shoulders. Before I had time to react, the firm grip pulled me towards itself, making me stumble. My back thumped against Leo's chest.

"You called it, Tony." Leo's voice was fluid. "It's like we've always known each other."

Tony chuckled, utterly misreading the situation.

"Get. Off." I shoved against Leo's arm, without much luck. Jill mumbled something in my defence but was cut off by Tony's suggestion to move to the games' room.

Leo told them to go ahead as I squirmed against his hold, digging my fingernails in the skin of his arm. As I was about to kick him in the shin, his grip pulled me even closer. He lowered his head next to mine, his lips mere inches from my ear. "Go on, I dare you."

Flames burned my vision. He was *trying* to make me use my skills!

I met Jill's eyes as she glanced back over her shoulder before hurrying after Tony. *Not here.* I swallowed hard, and let my arms fall to my sides limply.

"Can you please let go of me?" *You arrogant goat.*

Leo dropped his arm, copying my polite tone. "Of course, my apologies. Thanks for asking nicely."

I dusted myself off and sped after Jill without glancing at Leo.

"What was that all about?" Jill asked me wide-eyed as I caught up with her. "Are you...you know, is it true you're hitting it off?" Her voice hardly amounted to a whisper. My glare said it all. "But Leo—"

"Leo is trying to wind me up." *And doing a good job with it.*

Tony deposited a coin into a machine called *Need for Speed.* Leo took the seat next to him, and Jill and I watched as the boys started the game. Jill kept giving me a look; I kept my focus on the screens. Now wasn't the time to get into it.

"Are you going to explain what's going on with you two?"

She had to ask. "There's nothing going on." I licked my dry lips. Jill didn't deserve the abrupt tone. "Sorry," I added hastily. "He winds me up."

"He seems like a nice guy," Jill tried softly.

Traitor. "I can't believe Tony brainwashed you too. You only *just* met the guy."

Jill shushed me and glanced to see if the boys heard us. "I mean in general, he's nice. Tony spent the afternoon with him and he can't stop singing his praises."

I scoffed, blood pooling under the skin of my cheeks, and turned my focus back to the boys' race. *Why does he irritate me so much?* And why did I get the feeling he was bending the truth?

Tony slammed his hands on the wheel as his screen flashed 'Game Over'. Leo's car passed the finish line five seconds later.

"Can I have a go?" The others stared at me, perhaps because my tone indicated otherwise. "I wanna play against Leo..." everyone followed my extended finger towards a virtual boxing ring on the other side of the room, "on that."

Leo cocked his head at me. Tony showed his approval, and with a hesitant Jill in tow, he walked towards the ring.

"You sure that's a good idea?" Leo's voice was hushed as he caught my arm.

"I think it's a great idea," I hissed and marched to the boxing ring.

"You gotta play nice now, Milla," Tony said, and turned to Leo. "Last time we played on the Xbox she got so riled up she broke the controls." Tony chuckled at the memory until Jill jabbed him in the ribs. He had to keep reminding me of the one time I was having a bad day. Other than today.

"Duly noted—sore loser, tendency for violence." Leo cringed playfully.

"Right, kids, no real hitting. It's called *virtual* for a reason." Tony handed us helmets and two sticks to hold in each hand. A large screen lit up on the side of us.

"You ready?" Tony held a finger on the green button, excited about the prospect of a fight, even a virtual one. I nodded, and so did Leo.

For a game, the surroundings felt surprisingly real. I was transported into a boxing ring, faced with a character of Leo crouching in front of me, his fists held up to block his face. A smile flickered on my lips. I motioned towards Leo, raised my hands, and took a stance.

Leo threw a punch, one easy to block; I went for his chin with a jab. With reflexes like a hawk, he dodged it, hitting both my arms down. Within a split second my knee was in his gut, and then he was behind me, holding me in a strangling grip. I freed myself by smacking his side and Leo's virtual character doubled; it was weaker than the real him. A moment later, we faced each other with a matching warrior pose, the characters making it look off. If anyone other than Jill and Tony were watching they'd think we were being theatrical. Or nuts.

Virtual Leo attacked, mixing hooks with jabs against my blocks. We exchanged blows, ducking and diving, and taking the occasional hit onto our virtual bodies. The few second delay was frustrating, and the scrabble didn't produce anywhere near the effect I was after.

Yet it wasn't the poor technology that made me fume. A thought in the back of my head was becoming clearer. When the match ended and announced a draw, I knew my hypothesis valid.

I yanked the helmet off and launched it at the unsuspecting Leo. "You lied to me!" My words flew like darts and hit the bullseye.

"What—" Leo started, but was finished by Tony, "—*was that?* How did you get them to do that?" Tony's eyes resembled beach balls.

"Did you think I wouldn't find out? That I wouldn't figure it out?" I shoved at Leo, who still looked at me baffled.

"Calm down, Milla. It was just a game," Tony attempted from the sidelines. I blatantly ignored him.

"Drop the act, Leo, you know exactly what I mean! A *Messenger?* Really?"

Leo straightened his posture, glancing at Tony and Jill as they took in every accusation. "Why don't we go talk—"

"Did you think I wouldn't put two and two together? *Messengers* aren't trained as we are. Your reflexes, your composure, your aim, and your moves... I don't care if it was virtual; I could tell *those* moves from anywhere!" I shoved Leo's chest.

"I'm not sure I follow." Leo clasped my wrists, holding them inches away from his chest.

"Don't give me that. You're an *Attacker*, aren't you? The story about being a Messenger was a *lie.*"

In an instant, Leo grew serious, his jaw tight. "Calm down or you're going to say something you regret," he said between his teeth, trying to appeal to my good senses.

"Like expose you in front of everyone? They already know who I am; it's only fair they know the truth about you." I wavered even as it came out. Truthfully, I didn't want to drag Tony and Jill into this. But I had already said too much.

"The truth, Leo. What are you really doing here and how come I've never met you before?"

"I don't think this is the place." With a stern look, he pressed towards me so that my hands were now resting on my chest, my back slightly arched due to him towering over me. "I'll tell you the truth, but not here. If you'll clear your head from psycho mode, you'll see we've pulled quite the audience." He leaned in even closer, making sure I was the only one hearing him. "Fugitive or not, you still don't want any harm on our Land, do you?"

I flinched, and something switched in my brain. Curious observers stood by the doorway. I slowed down my pulse and gave Leo a sharp nod.

"Can we borrow your car, Tony?" Leo addressed our immediate audience.

"Only if we can come with you." Jill's voice surprised me as it cut Tony's out.

Leo took inventory, before agreeing.

Jill was the first to move. As she turned, half a dozen observers disappeared from the entrance of the game room. Tony followed her, glancing back to make sure *we* followed.

Leo escorted me outside, gripping my arm the whole way, and shoved me on the back-seat of Tony's car, sliding in next to me. Jill and Tony mounted the front. Heavy on the gas pedal, Tony reversed out of the car park.

We drove in silence, the others perhaps afraid to say anything that might spark another torrent of accusations from my part. I waited, stock-still, until Tony had parked in a quieter neighbourhood. As soon as the engine flicked off, I jabbed Leo's bicep. Jill gasped, taken back.

"Never touch me again!"

Leo didn't grant me the pleasure of rubbing his arm.

"Okay, *what* is going on?" Tony stared us down, leaning on the wheel.

"Yes, Leo, why don't you tell us what's going on and who you *really* are? And what you're doing here?" The questions flooded out.

"Okay, hothead." Leo pulled some slack on his seatbelt. "Take it easy or you'll pop a vein."

I scowled, and a grin flashed on Leo's face. A blink later it was gone.

"Why didn't you admit you're an Attacker?" I ignored Tony and Jill staring at us the best I could.

"I didn't think it was relevant."

"So, you admit you lied?"

"I might've misled you a little." Leo remained frustratingly calm. "But the rest is true."

Tony's eyes popped as the penny finally dropped. "Wait, you're from Nauru too?"

"*Narun,*" Leo and I corrected in unison. Leo continued, "That's right. I'm pleased you know our true origin."

"Did your spying eyes not figure that one out?" I folded my arms in a statement; everyone ignored me. My emotions were definitely attempting a coup.

"We haven't known for long," Tony said. "Camilla only told us because we kind of found out."

Leo let his gaze rest on me a moment too long. "Good for you, Rosebud, letting your friends close."

I gripped onto self-control like it was the pin holding the grenade. "You still haven't told me what you're doing here and why you lied to me."

"I did tell you," Leo replied. "I was sent here to give you a message."

"What message?" Jill blurted, curiosity widening her eyes. She pulled away as I shot her a glare. My foot tapped the air furiously while Leo reiterated what he'd told me in the alley.

"You expect me to believe they sent an Attacker all the way here to ask me to come back? That's insane."

Leo lifted a shoulder. "Their purpose is not for me to know."

I started but snapped my mouth shut. There was some truth in what he'd said. We were often assigned missions with little explanations; our job wasn't to question.

"It still doesn't explain why you lied to me. Where is your partner, anyway?"

"Alright," Leo said. "I admit lying wasn't the best move. I guess I didn't want to come across as a threat. As for a partner, I'm a Solo. You know not all Attackers are paired up."

"Then how come I don't know you?" I drew my words out with purpose. *Thick-skulled as he was.* "You can't be much older than me. I should've seen you around; we would've trained together, lived under the same roof. I *should've* seen you."

"We must've missed each other. Easily done with different missions. I'm a couple of years above you."

I rubbed my lips together, staring at my feet. I hated that my case crumbled. Maybe we had missed each other; he was an Attacker after all. Maybe I had forgotten a face. *Maybe.*

I pinched the bridge of my nose, frustrated that Leo could see my defences were silk-thin.

Tony cleared his throat. "Well, this has been intriguing," he said. "Does that mean you'll be leaving us, Milla?"

I shook my head. "No. I don't know. I—look, can you just take me home, please? I want to be alone." I turned to the window to shake Leo's gaze off me. After a moment, the engine hummed to life.

"Leo, you'll have to teach me some of that Kung Fu," Tony said as he joined the road. "Milla refuses to."

"Sorry, Tony," I cut in. "He won't be staying."

I caught Leo's amused reflection in the window I was facing.

"I don't think I'll be leaving quite yet."

"Oh, you *are*."

"Don't listen to her." Tony flickered his headlights to make the temporary traffic lights turn to green faster. "You should definitely stay for a while. Right, Jill?"

Jill lowered her chin as if feeling the burn of my glare on the back of her skull.

"Fine, take his side," I huffed to myself. "You have known him all of *one* day..."

Tuning out the others' conversation, I focused on the dark streets lit up by lamp posts and house lights.

I was lightyears away from Narun when suddenly Narun came to me.

My life as Camilla was nearing its end.

Chapter 10

Stupid alarm clock. I turned to my side under the duvet, in no mood to get up. The night had been a long episode of REM sleep: muddled dreams I didn't care to remember. I wanted to forget about Leo and the message he brought. I wanted to ignore it and shut the world out of—

I lifted an arm over my ear. The shrill alarm was a stubborn sort. *Fine.*

I slapped the clock on its head. Whoever invented alarm clocks must've hated sleep. Or regretted decapitating their rooster.

I kicked the duvet off, shivering as the chill air grazed my skin. If I finished at work quickly, I'd have time for a run in the park before my date with Tony and Jill. After all, I needed to get in shape.

A hospital bed was a killer for fitness.

*

I paused at the coffee shop entrance and spotted Tony and Jill sitting by a square table, next to a large potted plant. Their heads were down, both focused on reading the newspaper sprawled across the table. A few menus lay on a vacant chair by Tony, along with his jacket—a new one, I noted.

"What's so interesting?" I pulled out a chair, eyeing the paper.

"Hey, you—" Jill gasped. "Oh my word, your hair!"

"I thought you were at work this morning, not the hairdresser's," Tony said, accusatory.

"I cut it myself." I flicked my newly-shortened hair and grinned. "Half an hour ago, to be precise." Free-running in the park had reminded me how I'd always found long hair a nuisance.

"It's so much shorter! It looks great; no way you did that yourself!"

I brushed my now barely shoulder-length locks. "Thanks for the confidence, Jill." I laughed.

"No, no, I meant that—"

"That there's no way she could cut a straight line? Or is that why you went for the choppy layers?" Tony shoved into Jill's defences.

"Funny. Can we eat? I'm starving."

"Me too." Jill snapped herself out of staring at my hair. "But seriously, your hair's great. It makes you look more—"

"Like a hot ninja?" Tony quipped.

"Stop finishing my sentences, Tony!" Jill elbowed him in the arm.

I scoffed, amused, as they continued their couple's bicker that was bound to end in a kiss, and grabbed a menu. A low rumble shivered the pit of my stomach as I decided what to have.

"You guys ready to order?" I got up. "I'll get this."

Tony and Jill broke off their smooch to state their orders. Jill lifted a hand towards her purse. "Are you sure you don't mind...?"

"Not at all, you guys pay for me all the time."

"I don't think I've paid for you once, Mil," Tony retorted.

"Your friendship is all the gold I need, Tony." I winked and Tony pretended to gag. Hair whooshed to the side of my face as I turned. I'd have to get used to that again.

"Can I have a tray, please?"

Two cups of coffee and a tall glass of water sat on the counter, next to a small vase with a wooden spoon with the number twenty-three on it.

"I'll give you a hand." The voice next to my ear made me tense up, and then crashed me back to earth.

"Oh jolly. There I was hoping meeting you had just been a bad dream."

"Happy to see you, too." A cheery Leo leaned against the counter.

I slapped his hand as he reached for the cups. "I got this."

"You can grow a third arm later, Rosebud, but Tony's caffeine addiction won't wait." Leo took the cups. "By the way, we need to talk," he remarked under his breath before walking to the table. Begrudged, I followed.

"Leo, my man! That was a long phone call." Tony moved the menus from the chair next to him. Tony's jacket—I guess it was Leo's jacket. They were trying to get us to get along. Or send me back home. Who knew if they even knew.

I considered leaving but Jill caught my train of thought and pulled on my sleeve. Her eyes pleaded for me to stay. Surely, I could act civilised for the time it took to inhale an omelette. It should make up for acting like a spoiled brat at bowling yesterday.

"Nice." Leo pointed at my locks, his chin dipped. Something about his gaze threw me. "Close to how you used to have it, nearly as short."

I felt a flush of heat under the skin of my cheeks. "How'd you know I used to have it shorter?"

"I've seen a photo, remember."

"Whatever." *Like that didn't emphasise my maturity.* From the corner of my eye, I noted Leo holding back a chuckle.

"You used to have it even shorter?" Jill asked.

"Oh yeah, she used to have it about *yay*-high." Leo moved his hand back and forth in a line across his jaw before turning to me. "It suited you. Though I'm not complaining about this look…Fetching." Leo grinned so wide I could almost count his teeth. *A lot of pearly whites to knock out.*

Tony chuckled. "Mate, you're poking at a bee's nest…"

I pulled a face at Tony and craned my neck to see what was taking the waiter so long. Of course, even toast wouldn't have popped in the time lapsed.

"Mate," Tony leaned forward, folding his arms on the table, "you gotta give us some dirt on her. She never tells us ANYTHING."

"You utter one word—"

"Yeah, and it'll be my last." Leo cut off my warning with a hurried tone, turning to Tony and Jill. "What do you wanna know?"

"Leo, seriously—"

"*Relax*, Rosebud." Leo laughed. "To be honest, there's nothing I can say. What I *can* tell you, is that she looks different these days. Skinnier for one."

Was that reproach I detected in his voice? How could he even tell that based on a picture? I didn't recall my face being that chubby.

71

"You *have* lost weight in the last few weeks," Tony agreed. "Maybe I do need to start paying for your food."

I cast my eyes heavenwards and glanced over my shoulder again. "Where is the food?"

"Hopefully here soon, or you might waste away, Rosebud." Once again Leo managed to throw me; his tone and expression contradicted. Our eyes locked for a fraction of a second, and then Leo pulled his gaze away. Something about it infuriated me, and I downed several violent gulps of water.

"A question, bro: why do you keep calling her 'rosebud'?" Tony asked. "I get that you're trying to get on her good side but flattery ain't going to tame this one. Trust me."

"Why don't you ask Camilla?"

"Me? What makes you think I know the workings of your degenerate brain?"

Leo looked at me slightly baffled, for once lost for words. He faked a cough and resumed his aloofness. "I think it's the resemblance. Tall, skinny... prickly."

Tony swallowed his laughter; Jill made sure of it by kicking his shin.

I'd had about enough. I got up, about to excuse myself to the bathroom when Leo let out a dry laugh.

"Running away again?" His voice rang harshly for once. I swallowed, about to set him straight when he continued, "We all know that's what you're good at." He examined me openly as Jill gasped and Tony choked on his drink.

My posture rose as my lungs widened with air. "What game are you playing, Leo? I'm sure befriending the locals wasn't part of your mission."

"You know why I'm here. We can do this the easy way or the hard way, but I'm not leaving without you."

Locked in a battle of wills, I took a step towards him, ignoring the other customers openly watching our show-down. "Why do they want me back on the Guard?"

"I told you: I don't know," Leo said. "You'll have to find out for yourself."

"I don't believe you. There's no reason for them to send you to find me."

"Really?" Leo lifted his chin. "Are you sure about that?"

His question was like a kick in the stomach and I recoiled, unable to stop myself. My front broke only for a second but it didn't escape him. He knew he'd gotten under my skin.

"You don't know anything." I made my exit and disappeared into lunchtime traffic.

*

I approached him, my heart racing to a destiny I could not yet see. He was familiar and secure to me. It couldn't have been anyone else.

I was relieved. I was ecstatic. He was my friend and now he was officially my partner.

He was with me for life.

He nudged his head towards the door and I followed him out of the hustle and bustle of the common room and into the weapons' storage.

"You and me, lass," he said, pressing the door shut behind me. "How do you feel?"

"Good." I smiled. "At ease."

He returned my smile. I had always known he'd be there for me, ever since he started taking my side at training when he saw the others were wary of me. Ever since he'd started whispering encouragements in my ear. And ever since he realised my gift was overwhelming me, he'd been there to catch me.

He knew me.

The Elders were right. I needed him.

Chapter 11

The phone vibrated in my pocket. I couldn't muster the will to talk to Tony, much less get into what the episode in the café had been about.

I sat at the edge of the pier, legs swinging back and forth, one at a time, as the waves of the sea mesmerised me. The sun caused the surface to sparkle but failed to warm the air. Thoughts were trying to knock themselves through into conscious sentences. I'd have to give in at some point, and I'd have to talk to Leo, find out if there was more to his message.

Meanwhile, I'd happily cling on to oblivion, stagnation, and ignorance like they were the only lifeboat on a sinking ship.

Another vibration tickled my thigh. I pursed my lips, moving them from side to side. I should let Tony know I was fine. After all, I was fine. Fine, fine, fine. If only Leo had never shown up. Everything had fallen into place, and then he had to ruin it by presenting me with a no-win choice. If I returned and they pardoned me for leaving, and let me re-join the Guard, how could I face my friends and family after what I'd done? How could I serve as Guard when everything reminded me of *him*? Even if they didn't know about what I'd done, how could I be the warrior they presumed me to be when I knew that not only was I not a warrior, but I wasn't even the hero of the story?

I raised my arms to lean on the rail above my head. My forehead soon found rest in my arms.

There was no reason to go back.

Except for the proverbial *but*. If I didn't return, I'd be disobeying an order; this was my last chance for a pardon. I'd officially be cast out, never able to return, never to see my family, my home... I'd have no purpose, no destiny, nothing left to live for. I would've let the King and my people down. I would've let *him* down. I deserved to live under the curse of a Blood Debt, but bringing shame on my family...

No-win.

Oh, for crying out loud. I slapped my palm to my temple. I needed a distraction. *Before I talk to Leo I won't be making any life-altering decisions anyway.* I pulled out my phone, and replied to Tony's text, agreeing to meet him.

"My phone—Someone's taken my phone!"

I glanced behind and to the side of me. A girl close to my age swivelled around, looking at the people around her, her hands digging in and out of her pockets. A group of people—seemingly her friends—motioned with their hands in jerky movements. I scanned the line of curious observers and whipped my head to the few guys walking down the pier. It wasn't hard to pick out the offender— hands in pockets, hasty steps and complete disregard to the commotion behind him.

I leapt up and anticipated the guy's path. I vaulted over a set of benches and stopped to wait behind a parked ice cream van.

"Hand it over, mate." I grabbed the guy's arm as he passed me and slammed him against the van.

The guy, visibly taken back, shook my hand off his arm. "What you on about?"

"The phone you stole. Give it here and I'll let you off with a warning."

The young Rebel-Without-a-Cause swore and flicked a pocket knife at me.

"Cute. Did it come with a fork?" I pointed at the knife, and as he lifted his hand up, I struck my wrist against his, simultaneously smacking my other arm on the base of his neck. I rotated my arm behind him, pulled, driving the hand with a knife further away, and finished him with a knee jab to his groin. As he dropped to his knees with a groan, I picked up the stolen, glitter-covered phone from his pocket.

"Make this the last time. Okay, mate?" I gave him a final look and jogged over to give the phone back to its owner.

"Oh my gosh, where did you find it?" the girl shrieked in relief, worry melting from her face.

"Found it on the ground. Near the van."

"Oh, I must've dropped it earlier" —the girl brought her palms up to her cheeks— "I thought someone stole it!"

I smiled dismissively as she thanked me and left the girl with her friends. As I was two paces away from her, a hand brushed my elbow.

"Hey, you're Camilla, right?" A guy with shaggy, honey-coloured hair faced me, his fingers tapping his thigh. His eyes were light blue like the sky.

"Do I know you?"

"Not really," he laughed softly, "I'm Sebastian. We share a lecture on Thursdays, Professor Richmond's."

I met his extended hand. His face carried a familiarity. "Oh, right, yes. Four hours of Richmond." I winced.

"Tell me about it." He widened his eyes playfully. "Anyway, I just wanted to say hi, and thanks for returning my sister's phone."

I mouthed a 'Hi' and waved mechanically.

"So" —Sebastian took an awkward step back— "I'll see you on Thursday, I guess."

I nodded and walked off. Tony awaited.

The familiar block of apartments towered in front of me. Tony buzzed me in and I jogged up the three flights of stairs to his flat. His door waited for me ajar; the familiar man-flat fragrance hit me as I stepped in. The two weeks I had crashed on Tony's couch had made it feel like a second home. A lot of good memories.

Tony wrapped me into a bear hug upon entry.

I scrambled out of it. "I'm fine. Stop overreacting."

Jill lounged on the couch, resting on her elbow. She put down the magazine she was reading.

"I shouldn't have invited Leo today." Tony scrunched his face. "My bad."

"Got that right. Maybe a lesson for next time?" I slapped his arm, and sat down next to Jill, pulling my legs underneath me.

"I still think you'd make the perfect couple. You'll see." Tony sat on a bean bag opposite us, a grin not far from his lips.

"I knew you weren't that sorry."

Tony stretched his arms behind him, and I declined Jill's offer for a drink, soon regretting the decision as an uncomfortable silence fell in the room.

"What's up with you two?" I narrowed my eyes as Jill and Tony glanced at each other. Tony nudged his chin towards Jill.

"Okay," she said in her usual wary style. "Here's what we think. Although we understand—"

Tony huffed, lifting a hand. "You'll hear it straighter from me: Leo was out of line, but so are you. The 'avoiding everything' act is getting a little old. We like you but this 'buddies' thing works both ways. So, in threat of sounding like a girl, you have to start opening up and trusting us."

Huh. I rubbed my face and left my fingers to trace my mouth.

"Try seeing it from our point of view," Jill suggested. "You're saying the world as we know isn't the world as we know it after all and then—then we're just left with no right to ask any questions."

I rolled my bottom lip out and back again. *Guess I wasn't the only one with a lot on their mind.* "You're right. What do you wanna know?" I looked at Tony under my brows. "Don't wait too long or I'll change my mind," I added, smiling a little.

"Start by telling us what Narun is like," Jill said coyly.

I gripped my legs tighter, a vision of home filling my mind. Whenever my thoughts flew home, I first pictured a bird's eye view of the land, followed by an image of the long corridor leading up to the inner courtyard in the palace.

"It's beautiful." The gulp was louder than anticipated. "Nothing like this concrete jungle. Nature has a freedom to it, a wildness. Green hills, rivers, lakes and plenty of fertile land. Our people value the land, so we take care of it. And it's peaceful—quiet, you know."

"No cars and hence no pollution must help, eh?" Tony dug himself deeper into the bean bag. It took me a moment until the penny dropped.

"*Leo.* He's already told you some things, hasn't he?"

"He is a lot more cooperative than you, little missy," Tony said, unapologetic.

I shook my head in disbelief. "You've known him, what, two days?" *Had it really only been that?* Leo seemed like part of the furniture, like an old heirloom coffee table that had no other purpose than to trip you over.

"Like I said," Tony repeated, "he's *a lot* more open."

"But we don't know anything about you." Jill's statement hardly took me by surprise. Of course, they weren't after a geological overview. Who was?

"Well, as you know" —I hugged my arms, wishing I'd brought a hoodie— "I was part of the Royal Guard. You don't choose to join; you're chosen or destined for it, if you like. When a child is born, the Elders, Wa-Elah, lay hands on the child to see if they have a special calling and whether they will become Guard. If yes, the child stays with their parents until they're six. Then the parents bring the child over to the Inner City where they'll take an oath and are trained."

"Wow. That's harsh," Tony blurted.

"Yeah, being taken away from your family so young." Jill scrunched her nose. "That must be tough on the parents, and the child! What if you don't want to be part of the Guard?"

Not off to a great start here. "No, no, it's not like that. It's an honour. Only a few are chosen. Plus, your family can visit whenever." Neither of them looked convinced. "Look, training and being Guard is great. It's not some army drill camp; it's a family and a lifestyle. Then when you're around eight you're partnered up with a suitable fighting partner and when considered ready, you move on to active duty."

"Child marriage?" The size of Jill's pupils made me laugh.

"No! *No*, you're getting it all wrong! You don't get married; you're *paired* with your fighting partner. You train together, get to know each other. The reason it's so young is so you'll know each other in and out. It makes it safer for both of you. I mean yeah, eventually when you have served your term, whatever length it is, you're given the choice to marry and settle down for a family. But *no*, Tony, there's nothing dodgy going on."

Judging from Tony's expression, and the pillow that hit his face by Jill's hand, I had guessed his train of thought correctly.

"Just checking." He lifted his hands up in defence.

"What if you don't like the person? Who makes the decision, anyway?" It wasn't hard to see Jill struggled with the concept. I didn't expect them to understand. They had grown up with a different set of beliefs.

"The Elders have the final say; many of them have the gift of foresight. Although it often happens naturally. I've not known of anyone who hasn't got on with their partner. If it's meant to be it's meant to be."

"You said each 'couple'" —Tony quoted the air with his fingers— "serve a length of a term before they retire—how long?"

"There's no set time. You move on when it feels right. Some have served only a few years due to injuries, some over thirty. Oh, by 'serving', I mean being on active duty. After, you move onto other roles, usually within the palace."

Tony feigned interest in the ceiling tiles and Jill fiddled with a cushion. I waited for the information to absorb.

"What's the training like then?" Tony asked after a moment.

"Took you long enough to ask." I cracked my neck gently. "And again, I can't, and I *won't* tell you." Tony turned on his puppy eyes. "Sorry," I added, not feeling sorry at all. "Code of Honour, top secret stuff, classified. You get the drill."

"Come on, it's not like you're there anymore," he persisted.

"That's where the 'won't' comes in." Now the pillow flew towards me. I placed it on my lap.

"You're such a bore." Tony crossed his arms on his chest. "Leo doesn't have a problem in complying."

That's because he's probably playing you.

"You've really hit it off with him, haven't you?" I said. "How have you even had the time?"

"Bromance," Jill whispered to me, shaking her head.

"He stayed over last night. He's cool. We clicked," Tony explained.

"You don't even know him. He could be trouble."

"You should give him a chance. He might be your ticket into forgetting this guy you lost."

I was standing before my mind registered it. "He wasn't just 'some guy'! And I could *never* forget him, especially over someone as obnoxious as Leo!" I stomped to the door, opened it, and slammed it shut in front of me. The epiphany hit as I faced the closed door. Jill whispered something behind me.

I touched my forehead on the door. "Leo was dead on the money after all; I do keep running away." I looked down at my palms, rubbing my fingers together. What was going on with my temper these days?

Finally, I lifted my chin. "Tony, can you get a hold of Leo? I need to speak with him."

Chapter 12

The knock hardly came as a surprise. After I'd booted Jill and Tony out—from his own flat—I'd barely blinked my eyes off the window. It had taken Leo less than a minute to reach Tony's front door after entering the building.

Twice, I ran my fingers through my hair before opening the door.

I scanned Leo's frame from the tip of his black trainers, along his dark jeans, passing his navy jacket, and set my focus on his eyes. There wasn't much to be found in them. In fact, his exterior was as mine: it didn't give anything away.

"Are you going to invite me in?" A brief smile broke his sculpted face.

"I'm still debating." I walked away from the door.

There was a delay in Leo's steps before he closed the door. "You alright?"

"Do you care?" *He brought it out of me so easily.*

"If you're looking for another scrap, I think we've filled our quota for the day."

"Sorry." I faced him, folding my arms. "I didn't ask you here to fight."

Leo stood tall near the sofa, easily demanding attention from the simply decorated flat. "Look, Camilla," he rubbed his eyebrow with his thumb, "I'm sorry about this morning. I was out of line."

I blinked twice, indifferent. His posture matched mine and briefly, he looked as off-put as I did. He held my gaze for a couple more seconds, and then there was the grin. The next moment, he threw himself on the sofa and picked up the magazine Jill had been reading earlier.

"Let me know when you're ready to talk." He lifted the magazine so it hid his face.

I stepped towards him, about to snatch the tabloid from him, when he slid to the side, out of my grasp. I pressed my palm against the back of the sofa to correct my balance, and quickly straightened up.

"You're too predictable, and my reflexes are better than yours." He stood up and tilted his head in thought. "It's like you haven't even figured out what I'm *not* so good at."

"How, and why, would I do that?"

"That's your gift, isn't it? Knowing what weaknesses people have? I thought it was more of an autopilot thing than a conscious decision." Leo picked up a squash ball from the bookshelf, tossed it in the air, and placed it back on the shelf. "Or then you're working really hard on tuning it out."

I flushed, much to my annoyance. "How do you know that?"

"Give me some credit."

My lip ached from biting it so hard as I tried to focus on the reason I'd asked him to come. The sooner we'd talk, the sooner he would leave.

"I want the truth, Leo," I said. "That's why I asked you to come. Why did they really send you and what do they want with me?"

Leo straightened his back, stretching his spine, and defaulted to his relaxed stance. Hesitation flickered in his eyes.

"Leo. *Please.* If I'm going to consider coming back, I need to know the facts." I lowered my defences further. Although, I was starting to realise he'd see through me even if I was I made of concrete.

Leo sat down on a wooden chair on the other side of the room—elbows resting on his knees, palms together. He looked at the space between us, and then lifted his eyes to meet mine. He was even more confusing to read when he tried to be genuine.

"As you wish. I'll give you the whole truth if you answer one question. Truthfully."

How bad could one question be?

"Why did you really leave Narun?"

Unless it was that question. I had no doubt he could see the slight twitch on my cheek. I stifled the urge to fidget.

"I don't see why that makes a difference but fine," I spoke breathlessly. "My partner was killed on a mission and there was no reason for me to stay." The steady tone deserved applause, but I failed to draw my eyes off the floor.

Leo clicking his tongue made me finally glance at him. "Now that's not the whole truth, is it?"

"What makes you—"

"Because I know the truth." Leo stood up, matching my risen tone. "And that's not the *whole* truth." He paused. "*Kalika.*"

There was a fine line between letting your legs give in and telling them to do so. Whatever the case, I found my knees folded underneath myself on the wooden floor. It wasn't so much a spin my thoughts were in, more of a scramble. I trusted my ears to have heard correctly. That wasn't the problem. The problem was, it was too late to un-hear it.

"Are you okay?" He was actually concerned. That meant my face reflected the shock sinking in from the mention of my name. It had been too long since I had heard it; it carried too many memories with it.

I lowered my chin into a nod. It never quite made it back up again.

"Did you really think I didn't know your real name? They do tell you the basics when you're tracking someone." Leo was trying to lighten the mood but the emotion behind it translated ingenuine. "Why else do you think I call you 'rosebud'? That's what your real name means, *Kalika.*"

"Stop saying it! That's not me anymore."

"And Camilla is?" he scolded.

"*Yes.*" I forced myself back to my feet to distract him from my shaky words. Leo followed suit; I hadn't even registered when he'd knelt in front of me. Instinctive, I backed a few steps.

"Why are you doing this to yourself?" Leo asked with a softer tone. "You're not running away from Narun; you're running away from *yourself.*" He paused, indecision making him choose his words carefully. "It kills me to see what you've done to yourself."

My chest suddenly felt heavy. *He doesn't know me.* "Why would you care? You don't know me from the next girl! You're a Tracker, Attacker, whatever. Why should you care?"

85

"Because" —Leo rubbed his head as if fighting off a migraine— "you're one of us and we take care of our own. And I don't want to see you hurt."

"If you haven't noticed, I'm fine." If only the tremble in my chin would agree.

"*Argh!* You're so stubborn, Kalika! You're withdrawing yourself as you can't bear to face the facts. Stop running away from every—"

"I am *not* running away," I cut in harshly, pointing a finger to the floor. "I'm starting a new life. Is that so hard to believe?"

Leo looked at me as if I'd just declared I was made of cheese.

"A new life? Which number of a 'new life' is this then? Wasn't cage fighting, jumping off cliffs, and putting yourself into a coma a fascinating enough life? Huh?" I pictured Leo's imaginary hands shaking me. "You want to start again? Jump out the window and tomorrow you can be Casey or Carol or Cassandra. How about it? Anything to avoid being *you*. Isn't that how it works?"

As his stare eased on me for a second, I took a step forward and pretended to stumble. Leo caught me by the arm; I used the distraction to floor him. Air squeezed out of his lungs on impact with the laminate flooring. The same instant, I pounced on top of him, pressing his good arm with my foot, holding the other down on his chest. Livid, I narrowed my eyes on him as he recovered from the blow. A small tugging underneath my foot made me apply more force on his arm. It didn't take long until I felt his muscles relax. A victorious smile spread on his lips.

I restrained the urge to take an easy punch.

"How long have you been following me?" I waited for his smile to vanish; I wasn't going to let him off this time.

"Like I said, you were a tough cookie to track." Leo smacked his lips. "I found you eleven months ago. In your underground cage fighting days," he added with reproach.

"Eleven?" I pressed against his hard chest—harder. "Eleven *months?* Why didn't you approach me then?"

"You weren't ready."

"Ready for what?"

"To come back." Leo rotated his shoulders, and I released his arms and got my head back in gear.

"So, you're saying you've been stalking me for nearly a year?" *How in the world had I not noticed?* I cringed at the thought of someone being there to witness my darkest hours.

Leo placed his freed hands behind his neck. "Not stalking, looking after you. And boy, did you need it! Trust me, there was many a time I wanted to interfere, many a time I tried to stop you from—"

"Wait, it was you, wasn't it? That undercover officer in the park? You took me to the hospital."

Leo glanced to the side, and back to me again. There was something raw about his look, and for a second, I felt...embarrassed.

He pushed himself up with ease, shifting me to the floor.

"Tony's friend, Matthew, saw you that night," I thought out loud. "You came up with the story."

"First thing that popped in my head. I admit, very Hollywood."

I barely heard him as a memory of Matthew's words floated to me. Hadn't he said something about the cop "stroking my hair"?

I bent a knee and leaned my elbow on it. I couldn't muster a reason to get up from the floor. Leo had moved back to lean against a chair, one leg straight, one bent. I tried to organise my thoughts. How many more emotions could I go through in one day?

"You want a joke to lighten the mood?" Leo quipped, and lifted his hands defensively as I shot him an eyeful.

"Leo," I said quietly. "I need answers." I could see fragments of his thought process on his face and for a second it seemed like he wrestled with himself.

"What do you wanna know?" he finally said.

"You're saying you've been trailing me for over a year." I sought for confirmation, and he nodded. "How have I not seen you?"

"You haven't exactly been the most observant person lately. It seems the longer you've been here the more you've tried to block out everything you are."

"*Was*," I corrected. "I'm not that person anymore."

"Precisely. You've filled yourself with that rubbish."

87

I let the comment slide. "Why did you stick around so long without delivering the message? You should've been back home a long time ago. Surely they're wondering where you are?"

"You weren't ready. You would've run a mile if you even suspected I was from Narun. They knew that, so I was allowed the time."

"So, now you think I'm ready?"

Leo grinned. "Getting there…"

"It's an awful lot of time to give from your life to follow me around." Who would follow a stranger around for eleven months? *The guy is definitely on the wrong side of right in the head.*

"A mission's a mission."

"Flattering. Why didn't you go back and say I wasn't ready?"

"And let you literally throw yourself to your death?"

I picked up the condemnation in his voice. Or was it my conscience that condemned me?

Goosebumps covered my forearms, but I hardened myself up to his scrutiny.

"You didn't know me… I was just another mission." I stared him down, but he gave me nothing but a stone-cold wall again.

"Seeing you here wasn't the first time I've seen you, Kalika."

I slowed down my breathing, gritting my teeth. Somehow, I expected that.

"Explain."

"I've seen you around in Narun." *Too vague.*

"That's impossible. I would remember." Then again, my facial recognition system has been experiencing a few glitches.

"I didn't say we've met. In fact, you never met me." I shook my head and Leo continued, "Like I said it was just in the Guard, in passing."

"You're telling me," I enunciated slowly, "that seeing me in some assembly made you care enough to give a year of your life to shadow me? That's the biggest load of rubbish."

Leo shrugged, and I felt like ripping his shoulders off. "Maybe I felt sorry for you. You used to be full of life, and over here… there's nothing left in you."

"Yeah, right." It was obvious my voice lacked conviction. I turned away from him.

"You know full well how much you've changed. Let's leave it at that." Leo's words were thick with emotion. There was still so much he was hiding.

"What do they want from me?" My eyes searched for his darting ones.

"They want you back on the Guard; they have a need for your special kind of gifting," he said after a moment. "They want you to be my partner, Kalika."

It was like being hit with a bazooka.

"*Never*. Never in a million years will I be your partner, you lying dung fly!" I yelled, self-restraint blown to bits. "How could you even think for a second I would go with such a ridiculous idea? Did you really think you could replace...you could never—" I sucked in air through my teeth, feeling my temperature rising a degree.

"Kalika, this wasn't my idea! Things are changing, and they need more fighters, especially ones with gifting like yours. Plus, they don't want you to lose your way. We're a family—one suffers, we all suffer."

That answered one question: they didn't know of the events that led to my departure.

But if going back meant Leo would become my partner, it tipped the scales. I'd rather lose my honour than trample on *his* memory. *He* would always come before me.

"Don't, okay, *don't*. I don't want to hear it. Consider your job done. You can tell them I'm not coming back. Tell them... I'm already lost." I stormed to the door, ready to jerk it open. "Oh, FYI— I'm not running away. I'm leaving because we're *done*."

I yanked at the door handle and left an un-opposing Leo alone in Tony's apartment.

*

It was late, or early morning, when I got back to my place. I'd been all over, from the beach to the woods. I dropped the keys on a table near the door and headed to the kitchen. With a glass in one hand, I let the water run through my numb fingers. The fire may have died but the ember still heated my insides. The events of the afternoon refused to digest.

I washed my face and dried off with a kitchen towel.

A new partner? *Leo?* The very thought offended me, no, appalled me. *He* could not be replaced.

I walked into my tiny bedroom and sat on the bed, knowing my thoughts would allow no rest. Darkness strangled the room. The past had been getting the better of me all night, slicing what felt like physical wounds on my body.

Of course, the thought had been there. It forced itself into my consciousness. It demanded to be thought through.

It wasn't just me Leo would've seen in Narun; he would've seen *him*. He might have even trained with *him*, talked with *him*.

My only saving grace was that at least Leo didn't know I had killed *him*.

Chapter 13

The sky threatened with thunderclouds, the air filling with anticipation of the coming storm. My head rested against his chest, my knees pointing to the sky. There was no place in Narun that made me feel more at ease. The rock was our rock, the view down below our homeland, his lap—mine.

"It'll rain soon." He played with my hair, brushing the short length of it through his fingers. "We should head back."

"We should." Neither of us made an effort to get up.

"I have business in town tomorrow morning, so I won't be at breakfast."

"I can come with you." I swiped away a strand of hair from my face that he'd dropped.

He leaned back on his hands and I adjusted my position. "No," he retorted and chuckled under his breath. "I wouldn't dare take you away from food."

"Good. It is Scrambled eggs-Friday tomorrow." I turned on my side, squashing my cheek against his abs. He smelled like...cocoa.

"Seriously, Kali. It'll rain soon." He made an attempt at shifting me, but I wrapped my arms around his torso. "Come on, clingy."

I squeezed him harder. I never wanted to move. I never wanted to part from him. In so many ways, he was a part of me, and he had made me who I was. Otherwise, I'd still be lost, trying to cope under the pressure of a gift I'd always considered a curse.

A raindrop splashed against my temple. He wiped it dry.

"Oy." He got up laughing, with me still holding onto him. "Come oooon, I don't wanna get wet. Wet frizzes my hair."

I let go of him. "Pftt. Yeah, all two inches of it…"

He gave me a peck and took my hand.

I'd follow him anywhere. Storm or calm.

Chapter 14

A girl giggled a few seats from me.

I glanced at her, guessing her studies had moved to the back-burner while she updated her social media. The library was slowly losing its students, yet my essay was only half-way finished. I'd left it to the last minute out of laziness. I'd had the time. What I lacked was the motivation.

Nearly two weeks had passed since my chat with Leo, and he still hadn't left. Obviously, he had issues with accepting rejection. Or he felt his life purpose was to complicate my life.

I did my best to avoid him, but it was becoming difficult as he worked his way up the social ladder, befriending my only, few friends. Somehow, Leo's explanation, "Never knew I had a look-alike on the police force", had even done the trick in satisfying Matthew when it came to looking exactly like the undercover cop he'd stumbled upon in the park where he'd found me.

Apparently, you could sell anything these days.

Of course, the biggest problem wasn't him wrapping Tony and Jill under his spell: barely a day went by without him attempting to talk to me. I had to give him one thing: he was persistent.

If only I could figure out a way to get him to leave.

"Burning the midnight oil?" a guy asked, catching me off-guard.

"Yeah, deadline." I faced the person now perching on the desk. "Sebastian, right?" I picked a name from memory; he was the brother of the girl who'd lost her phone, and we shared a lecture.

"You remembered." His face lit up. "How much do you have left?"

I leaned back on my chair, grimacing. "Around a thousand words."

"Oh, bags of time." Sebastian glanced at the screen dismissively. His shaggy hair was brushed back as if he'd just had a shower. "What exactly do you study?" Sebastian nodded to the books sprawled around the keyboard.

"Actually, I only take a few modules. Just figuring out what I wanna do." While re-thinking my life's purpose from this point onwards... "But this one," I tapped the books, "is Community Studies. What about you?"

"Psychology," he replied. "It's fascinating. I never knew there were so many ways in which a person could be a bit of a nut."

A guy in the corner of the room woke up to my laughter. "What you doing here at this time, anyway?" I twirled left and right on the chair, one leg bent.

"Borrowing a book. Well, I teach a Taekwondo class here on Wednesday nights. So, killing two birds with one stone."

Should've guessed. He was toned and carried himself with a certain confidence. "You must be pretty good to teach it."

"That, or the students are *really* bad." Sebastian grimaced.

"I doubt it. You're pretty fit."

Sebastian burst into clumsy laughter. "Thanks... It's not every day you hear a pretty girl say that to you."

My cheeks flushed. It wasn't exactly what I'd meant by it. "I meant that," I swallowed, "that you're in good shape. Physically."

Sebastian eyed me, amused.

I slapped his arm. "Ignore me. My brain died an hour ago." I turned back to the screen, willing the blush to cool down.

Sebastian pulled a chair for himself and lifted a finger to tap on the desk. "Do you drive?"

I shook my head and glanced at the time. Hopefully, I'd be finished by midnight.

"I'll give you a lift back, then."

"No, it's okay. I'll still be a good while." I ran a word count; it didn't impress. "I couldn't ask you to do that."

"You're not." Sebastian dug out headphones and a tablet out of his bag. "I'm offering." He grinned and surrendered his attention to the tablet.

Guess the matter was settled.

Minutes past midnight, I followed Sebastian out into the breezy night. His pink car, borrowed from his mother, jolted several times until kicking into a smooth purr. We chatted through the short journey until Sebastian pulled over in front of my house. Even for a local boy, he was great with directions.

Looked like I'd made a new friend.

*

The next morning, I arrived at my lectures early. I took a seat near the back and slumped into the royal blue, fabric chair, casually scanning the students as they trickled in.

"Hey, stranger." Tony shoved my bag to the floor and claimed the seat next to mine. "Seems like the only times I see you anymore are at lectures." He pulled out a notepad and pen from his bag.

"I've been busy."

"Busy avoiding us." Tony set his face.

"You know I'm not avoiding you…"

"Just who we hang with," Tony added knowingly.

My lips pursed, and I swayed a pen between my fingers. I couldn't exactly be angry. Tony and Jill had been more than accommodating, respecting my wish not to hear, see, or speak of Leo. Ultimately, they were the ones left juggling.

"I take it you remembered assignment deadline this morning?" I asked.

Tony took the pen from me and placed it on the table. "Of course, I finished it ages ago."

"Sure you did — geek."

Tony grinned, settling deeper into the chair as he took in the room. "How've you been, anyway?" His head was angled towards me, but he watched a guy a few rows ahead showing off a tattoo on his arm.

"Good. Studies, work. You know, the mundane."

Tony brought his focus back to me. "Jill misses you."

"I saw her last week, and I talked to her a few days ago." Tony raised an eyebrow and I faltered. "Okay, I know, *I know*. I'll arrange something with her. What about you? What you been up to?"

"Same old. Been hanging out with people. You're missing out, lass."

I pulled my shoulders inwards. The last few weeks had been rather lonely.

95

"You and Jill free tonight?"

Tony said they were all going out, and we shared a look. "I see. I have to give it to Leo. He's suddenly everyone's best buddy."

If Leo's tactic was to alienate me from my friends so that I'd return, it wasn't going to work.

"It's not like that." Tony rubbed his beardless chin. "You should cut him some slack—talk to him. Did you even know someone tried to mug him the other night?"

If someone tried to rob Leo—an Attacker in the Royal Guard—I felt for the mugger.

"He can look after himself," I noted.

"True. But he also said he didn't think it was random. He thought it might've been someone from wherever you're from."

"*Narun,* Tony," I muttered. "And that's insane. Why would someone from Narun attack Leo?"

"He said they were probably after you."

I picked up the pen again and tapped it on the desk. If they were after me, why attack Leo? "*Or* he's just trying to get me to talk to him. The guy will stoop to any level."

I didn't catch what Tony mumbled in reply.

After the lecture, I sat with Tony in the cafeteria, nibbling on a cheese sandwich, while Tony filled in an application to volunteer at a youth centre—his long-term dream was to run a sports club for children in need. I couldn't think of anyone more suited for such a role.

I swallowed the last dry bite, scrunched the used cling film into a ball and tossed it in the bin as Tony and I parted ways.

I wasn't looking forward to my four-hour, mega lecture.

A group of students had already gathered by the door of the large lecture theatre. No one seemed particularly eager to go in and I slowed my pace until I registered the casual, one-leg-up-the-wall, pose. As usual, Leo wasn't going to let a day pass without attempting at a conversation.

Hard-faced, I picked up the tempo.

"Still no 'hello'?" Leo's good-humoured voice reached my ears.

"It's not looking promising." I passed him without a glance.

"Come on already, we're going to have to talk one of these days."

I was about to lay down the law for the hundredth time when I spotted my new friend— the only friend I now had who Leo didn't know.

"Hey, Sebastian, wait up!" I rushed over to him, jerking at his arm and feeling the force of Leo's glare on my back. "I wanted to say thank you for last night."

Sebastian greeted me, throwing an arm over my shoulder like we'd know each other for years, and led me to the lecture hall. Leo didn't follow.

*

Half past seven in the evening, I pushed open the two sets of heavy glass doors to the cinema. Groups of teenagers stood scattered in the high-ceiling entrance lounge. Sebastian's mop of hair and green Hollister hoodie caught my eye near the stairs. He held out two tickets between his fingers.

"I was impatient." He fanned the tickets. "I thought there'd be a queue, so I got here early."

I took the ticket from Sebastian's extended arm. *'Not a date, not a date'*, I repeated the mantra in my head. He'd just asked me to the movies. After *that* lecture, we needed a treat. Besides, I could only spend so many nights playing tic-tac-toe by myself.

Then why was I having a boxing match with my conscience?

"Thanks. You were right." I nodded towards the snake-like queue. "Must be a popular night."

"*Or a popular film*," stated a familiar voice behind me.

My heart skipped a much-needed beat.

I turned to face Jill, Tony, Stan, and Leo, sizing us up, intrigued.

Jill's gaze flittered to Sebastian, but Tony was the one to ask the obvious. "Who's your friend?"

My smile was all teeth, no emotion, as I introduced everyone, ignoring Leo's prying eyes.

Sebastian smiled, holding out his ticket like a business card. "So, you're here for '*Sobriety*' as well?"

"You bet. Wouldn't miss it." Tony took in the queue with a frown. "And on that note, we need to get tickets." Stan followed Tony to the end of the swerving snake.

Jill stalled, adding up things between the lines. "You know each other from uni?"

"That's right." I nudged my head to the side knowingly and thankfully, Jill got the message. She hurried away with a quick smile. I suspected she'd be bombarding me with text messages soon enough.

"So, Sebastian" —Leo took a demanding step forward— "have we met?" His tone may have fooled the Queen of England, but the sour twist of his lips spoke louder.

"You haven't," I cut in as Sebastian was about to reply and took his arm. "Let's get a drink." I yanked Sebastian towards the stairs and shot Leo a warning behind Sebastian's back.

He wasn't going to steal this friend, too.

I gulped the last of my drink, shaking the cup to get the drops trapped within the ice cubes. Surrendering, I shoved it back in the holder. My head fell against the head-rest. The action sequence was never-ending. Surely killing innocent people in road crashes didn't justify the hero's quest to save his family.

I jiggled on the seat—and jiggled again. *Great*, I needed the toilet. Engrossed in the film, I doubted Sebastian heard me excuse myself. A few irritated murmurs followed me out of the room as I slipped into the dimly-lit corridor.

The restroom was empty, so I passed a few extra minutes reading the wannabe graffiti artists' writings on the cubicle doors. It would be unheard of in Narun to write profanities on walls.

I sighed—the mirror sympathised. This had all been one dysfunctional idea. The connotations of the night looking like a date didn't sit right with me. And Leo's burning stare on the back of my skull for the entirety of the evening had given me a headache. Someone ought to educate Leo; a cinema trip was a happy occasion.

Speaking of which... I should join the film before Sebastian got suspicious.

"What are you doing?"

The restroom door nearly knocked my back as I was confronted by Leo inches from me.

"Coming from the toilet. Obviously." I pushed past him, only to be pressed back against the doorframe. I resisted the urge to go Krav Maga on him.

Leo stared down my face, hard as marble. "Who is he and what are you doing with him?"

"What's it to you?" My attitude was thick as wool.

"Who is he?" he repeated, leaning in further.

"Seriously, none of your business. Get off me." I pushed his face away, but he returned his stare.

For a few seconds, Leo measured me, then let go, and backed up a step. A tight line formed in place of his usual grin.

"Is that how it is then?" he stated, or asked? Who knew?

I steeled myself further. "And if it is, then it is. We're not partners, Leo. We never will be, so you don't get a say in my life and I definitely don't need to tell you who I go out with."

"He's your date?"

That's what he gets out of what I said? I glanced up at the ceiling in frustration. I'd had enough of this conversation.

"I'm missing the film," I muttered and walked off, surprised he let me pass.

"I guess you didn't find it so hard to move on after all."

My hand seized up on the door handle to the theatre, and I exhaled from the blow. There was remorse in Leo's voice even as he said it, but he didn't try to take it back.

Biting my lip, I yanked at the door and hid into the darkness.

Leo was an idiot, yet I was the one left feeling rotten.

Chapter 15

I hopped into Jill's car, tossing a bottle of water and a punnet of grapes on the back seat. Jill's sand-coloured hair was tied in a ponytail with strands failing to reach the band, framing her face.

"I thought you knew where this place was." I pointed at the satellite navigation as she pulled onto the road.

"I do. I just don't know how to get there."

The navigation estimated that the time to travel to our destination—a reservoir surrounded by moors—would be thirty-eight minutes. When I'd rang Jill last night to give the obligatory explanation for mine and Sebastian's 'date', we'd decided to go out hiking the next day.

Jill reached for the radio and turned it down. "How did Narun come to be? Or has it always...been? You know, what's its history?"

I laughed lightly, taken aback by the nature of the questions. I had a hunch cornering me had been Jill's plan for the trip all along.

"You sure don't waste any time." I placed an elbow on the window and sighed. I'd better oblige.

"It's always been, but it hasn't always been known about," I started. "Our people first settled the lands a little over two thousand years ago. It was discovered by a people led by a man called Aviel, who'd been travelling, searching for a place to build a community based on their, *our*, values." I took a shallow breath.

"So, the people settled down and increased in number, but soon found out there were some amongst them who chose different lifestyles, ones against our beliefs. These people—the Gorahites—attempted to kill Aviel but failed and were forced to leave Narun with their families. They then settled down on the other side of the river dividing the land, and built their own nation called Gorah."

I paused for a quick glance at Jill and continued when she nodded along, "But the leader of the people, who became their King, harboured a grudge against Aviel and since that day the Gorahites' purpose has been to destroy Narun, our King, people, and to claim the land. So, ever since then our nations have been at war, sometimes active, sometimes passive." I played with a strand of hair, a little nostalgic. "Most of my lifetime has been peaceful," I added.

Jill lowered her hands to the bottom of the steering wheel. "Wow. That's...that's...something." She eyed the road ahead of us pensively. "This war though, how come the hatred didn't die with the first King?"

I let the question marinate for a moment. "Each generation shapes the next; what parents imprint on their kids determines how they see the world. The Gorahites are basically brought up to hate us."

"And you're brought up to fight them?"

"To *defend* our home, yes. As you know, some of our people have been given natural tendencies, or gifts, to fight—and to fight well."

Jill was quiet for a minute and I wondered if it was because she was concentrating on joining the motorway, or if it was something I said.

"Does a person have to be born in Narun to live there?"

"Um, in theory, no." I straightened against the seat. "We have to be careful who we take in. Spies and other infiltrators from Gorah have always tried to force their way in. Hence people only join us if brought in by someone—a native who can vouch for them. Although, it's quite rare. We're not really meant to travel to your world." No one had any reason to. Unless they fled. Like me. "Of course, there is that little thing of Narun being a *hidden* nation."

"Yeah, how come no one's ever seen or heard of Narun?"

"It's not that simple. You need to understand Narun isn't like another country; it's almost like another dimension, another way of life. Think of it as—"

"The Matrix?" Jill perked up.

"Uh, little more reality, less film. It's like if the world was a square cardboard box, Narun would be a round, glass ball inside it. *In* it, but not made of it." I crinkled my nose, not sure if I hit the nail or the thumb with the metaphor.

"Hmm." I guessed she wasn't fully sold. "So, why is it kept hidden?"

"To protect our way of life. If our location was known, people would come in and ruin the lands, bring cars, and with it, pollution, and most importantly the world's—as you know it—way of life. Our beliefs would get diluted into other cultures, and those of us with special gifts would probably be examined or stuck in a circus. Or an army. Like I said, people do join us from your world but only once they share our beliefs. Otherwise, well, if you mix ice with water, eventually they'll become the same."

"Aren't you full of metaphors..." Jill grinned. "Which begs the question: what are these beliefs that make you different?"

"In a nutshell," I glanced at the moors, "we believe our lives are there to serve the King, and each other, by using our natural skills and tendencies. As a people, we're one. For example, everything is shared in terms of material possessions; we don't use money but trade in goods. Those who can work do so, and those who can't are taken care of. Food can be collected from the market for free. We're all there to help, support, guide, and to share life with each other." I sucked in a breath, deciding enough was said of the matter.

I glanced at Jill rapping her fingers against the gear stick, mulling over the conversation. I was curious how it all sounded in the ears of a foreigner, but first and foremost, all I could think of was how much I missed home.

*

The sun had set as we returned to my flat. Neither of us had intended on staying so long, but the afternoon had run away with us.

As I peeled my tired legs out of the car, Jill reminded me they'd be gone for the weekend for a concert down in London. I wished I could've joined them. A weekend alone sounded like too much time to myself.

"Camilla!"

I whisked around, my arm still in the air from waving Jill off, and clocked Sebastian running towards me from across the road.

What is he doing here?

It was barely six-o'clock but the sky was grey, straining to shed enough light where street lights failed. Yet, I still saw it.

"What happened to you?" I reached to graze Sebastian's black eye, but he winced away. *Hardly two hours old.*

"Oh, it's nothing." Sebastian rubbed the back of his neck. "Martial arts."

I crinkled my nose and mouthed an 'ouch'. "What are you doing here?"

"My cousin lives around the corner." Sebastian flicked his thumb somewhere behind him and took a sharp breath. "Hey, you wanna take a walk? In the park, maybe?"

We cut through a ditch to get to the bottom of the park which was illuminated by street lights and jogged across a field to a bandstand, eerie in its solitude. The fresh mud hardly made a difference to the state of my shoes from a day of hiking.

Sebastian hopped the few steps up to the bandstand and sat on the built-in bench. His fingers drummed his knees. Something was bothering him.

"You alright?" I sat next to him.

He cleared his throat as if to buy time while deciding what to say—or whether to say anything at all. "I gotta ask... What's the deal with you and that guy?"

I stared back, dumbfounded. "I don't follow."

Sebastian rubbed his neck again. "I taught an extra class today at uni—Taekwondo, that is—and your friend, Leo, from the cinema, was there."

Where would he not be? "Did he give you that?" I pointed at the bruise, my blood heating up in anger.

"Oh no, no—well, technically, *yes*. But it was an accident. I thought he was a rookie, so I didn't have my guard up when we trained."

I'll kick Leo over the border myself.

"Really, it's not a big deal. To be honest, it was all the questions he was asking about you and me, and my background, that didn't sit right with me."

My jaw worked over time as I swallowed a few choice words aimed at Leo. "What did you tell him?"

"About me—not much. It's none of his business. You—I just said we were friends, but he told me to stay away from you, anyway."

Leo sure had some nerve.

"I'm so sorry." I reached over to grasp Sebastian's wrist. "He's...deluded. He's like a friend of a friend." I knew I had to give him more even before Sebastian frowned. "We went out once ages ago and since then he thinks he has the right to butt into my life."

Easier than explaining 'deranged stalker from an unknown land trying to get me to become his partner'.

Sebastian's mouth curved as if tasting something that had passed its sell-by date. "That's not cool—that's majorly possessive. How come your friends still hang out with him?"

"It's complicated. They go way back." I lowered my eyes for a few seconds. "Look, just leave it. I can handle him. I'll get him off your back. I'm really sorry." I released Sebastian's wrist, suddenly conscious of touching him.

"Hey" —Sebastian nudged his shoulder against mine— "if you need a hand in getting rid of him, let me know." He winked, and winced, lifting his palm to hover over the bruise.

"Tempting...but it's okay. I'll teach him a lesson on what's socially acceptable behaviour. He's obviously failing hard."

I had let Leo get away with too much, sitting on the issue because... because I didn't want to deal with it. But he had officially forced my hand. The gloves were now off.

Chapter 16

I walked Sebastian to his bus stop and waved him off, feeling more like I had downed several double espressos instead of hiking all day.

Flicking the hood up on my jumper, I headed back towards the park. Stale indoor air didn't appeal. I kicked loose stones on the path whilst hurling insults aimed at Leo.

He had to go. He had to. Not only had he crossed the line in messing with my friends, but I couldn't keep living here with a constant reminder of home—a constant reminder of who I'd been.

A cloud of frustration trailed me like a puppy. Although I hated to admit it, Leo was only part of the problem. I was the one who had taken a metaphorical sledgehammer and gone to work on my life. I would never find peace within myself if I didn't strive to do some good with my life as Camilla, and right the only wrong that I could: The Blood Debt.

It was taught that in rare circumstances the King could release someone from the oath and so resolve the Blood Debt. However, I had once stumbled on another way in the Scrolls: *What was bound with blood, could be unbound by it, too.*

For every year I had been Guard, I'd have to kill a Gorahite soldier and shed my blood over them.

Fourteen kills. Fourteen scars on my forearm. Then the debt would be paid off.

A plan was birthing itself in my mind. To go against the Gorahites, I had to be strong—lethal. I had to sharpen my skills.

I swivelled around and jogged towards the exit.

I knew exactly where to go.

"I want in." I slapped a palm against the table. The man sitting on a plastic foldable chair inspected me, bemused.

"This isn't sign-in for Zumba, love." He locked his fingers together behind his head, his legs stretched on a trestle table.

His feet fell on the floor as I yanked at the table.

"I'm here to fight."

Stone-faced, the man eyed my slim appearance. "Again, this ain't no place for pretty, little lasses."

"Appearances can be deceiving," I challenged, hearing how ridiculous I sounded.

The man scoffed and cocked his head towards the exit. "Go home, kiddo." He pulled the table back.

"Look, I take full responsibility. Just one fight. You've nothing to lose."

The man's mouth moved as if he was chewing gum. "You're awfully sure about yourself."

"This isn't my first fight."

The man spat and coughed out a shred of laughter. "Suit yourself then, love. Enjoy explaining a busted nose to your daddy." He gestured me towards the hall and I hurried along before he changed his mind.

A stale smell floated in the corridor as I marched to the end of it and pushed open the rusty metal door. A raucous of shouting and cheering hit me as the scene set. Sweat, tangled with testosterone, hung in the air. A mass of men huddled in a tight circle. Scantily dressed women hovered in the outer circle, holding trays of drinks.

A little theatrical for my liking.

Based on the aggressive chanting I gathered a fight was drawing to an end. I unzipped my jumper, tossed it on the floor, and elbowed my way through the mass to the forefront.

"I'm next."

I breathed deep, in and out, jumping on the spot to warm up. The chunk of a man I was up against—with half a face decorated with a tattoo—argued with the man calling the fights. *No one wants to fight a girl.* The crowd growing impatient determined the outcome of the debate: we were to fight.

I rounded my posture, fixing my balance point. *The man has no real training.* Within a second from the start of the fight, I jumped up from the man's leg and climbed on his back. He tried to throw me down but ended up bringing himself down with me. I rolled on impact and wrapped my legs around his neck. It didn't take long for him to tap out.

The next guy was equally easy. Block and duck, jab, jab, kick to the ribs, floor him, and finish with a death grip. For the third guy, I took a few hits for the show before finishing him by nearly ripping his arm out of its socket. A roar of shouts erupted as I released my hold on him and lifted a foot off his back. His ego wounded, he shoved his way out of the circle. I swung my arms back and forth, craving for the next opponent. The bookie took bets from the pumped-up crowd as someone shoved me a glass of water. Grateful, I downed it with big gulps.

Another man took to the circle, hurling insults. He was tall, well-built, and stereotypically a skinhead. His knuckles popped white as he clenched his fists in front of his face. They never learned.

I stepped forward—and stumbled. Black spots hit my vision, forcing me to stagger towards the crowd. Voices turned to murmur. I reached out to grab a hold of anything stable as my head spun violently, but the effort was in vain. I fell, back first, against the wall of people.

At that moment, a pair of arms tucked under my shoulders, and the distance between me and the enraged crowd started growing. Limbs paralysed, I could but surrender.

A blink later, there was more space, less shouting. The surroundings blurred as someone lifted me up and my upper body slammed against someone's back, my arms hanging down. Although the blood dripping into my brain eased the spinning, it did nothing to inject fight into my jellified muscles.

I was losing the battle against unconsciousness when fresh air assaulted my skin and the cold, hard surface of tarmac shocked my body. A murmur of speech echoed near.

"…She's…yours. Who…work for?"

And then darkness claimed me.

Chapter 17

I gasped as I came to. It took me a moment to find focus.

"Shh, it's all right—easy," a man said.

"Who...?" I tried to raise my arm to rub my eyes, but it refused to cooperate, slumping on my nose.

"If you're trying to hit yourself, I'd be happy to assist."

The source of the dry tone materialised.

"Leo...?"

"Yup." He crouched next to the bed I was lying on.

"What—"

"They spiked your drink," Leo explained, his clipped tone giving away the emotions he was trying to hold back.

I concentrated on bringing myself back on track. The man at the door, fighting, water, hard floor. *Yes,* there was something foreign in my body, and it really didn't agree with me.

"Where am I?"

The bed dipped as Leo sat on it. "My place."

"H-how? What were you doing there?" I couldn't stop my words from slurring. "In the...you know."

"Saving your butt. *Again.* I was in your neighbourhood when I clocked you storming down the streets with that up-to-no-good look. Figured I better tag along."

I blinked, repeatedly, and shifted my upper body, trying to lean on the headboard. If my head spun any faster the juices in my brain would turn to cream.

"I wanna go home."

"Yeah, I don't think so. We need to get you checked out."

"No, I'm fine!" I intended to grasp Leo's arm but ended up slumped down on his lap. Amused, he pushed me back.

"O-kay, as convincing as *that* was... I'm taking you to the hospital. Need to have you well enough for a telling off." Even with my blurred vision, his glare was a formidable force to be reckoned with.

"Do you really think there's anything a doctor can tell me that I don't already know?"

"Do *you* really think that attitude is going to work in your favour?"

Touché. "What I mean is, there's nothing they can do but make me rest and wait it out. Trust me—no need for a doctor. I'm just lightheaded."

I felt his gaze narrow on me as I allowed my eyelids to droop at will.

"We'll see," Leo said after a moment. "I'm gonna get you some water. You need to flush it out."

I slid down on the bed, sinking into it. Soft, soft bed.

A twisting feeling in my stomach stirred me awake. I swiped hair off my face as a tall glass of water appeared in my vision.

"You fell asleep." Leo nudged his chin at me. "Drink."

I took the glass but barely moistened my lips before placing it on the bedside table, the motion aggravating my stomach further.

"That's pathetic. Drink properly."

Who put him in charge?

I lifted a hand to hover over my mouth as another wave of nausea gripped me. "I need the bathroom." I hauled myself upright, my feet tumbling onto the floor. The world had turned into a carousel.

I flinched as Leo's arms came underneath mine. "What are you doing?"

"Taking you to the bathroom. I'd rather you throw up there than here."

"I don't need help." I pushed at Leo's general direction. "Get off!"

He backed off, hands in the air. His mouth twitched as if he was physically restraining his tongue.

I gave Leo's one-bed apartment a hasty scan. It was plain, non-imaginative; probably came furnished. The kitchen was a small square opposite the bed. The bathroom was a few meters away.

My stomach turned as I caught a whiff of the smell of blood and sweat coating my clothes. *Few meters too far.* The dizziness wouldn't let me make it.

112

I scrunched my face and head shaking, Leo hooked an arm under my right shoulder. "It's okay to ask for help, you know."

My balance steadied against him as he pulled me up. *Uh.* I pressed my lips tightly shut as my feet dragged along the floor like lead.

I lurched down to the toilet barely in time. Without a word, Leo held me steady as I pinned my hair back with my fingers.

Once the contents of my stomach were out, Leo let go and I clutched the rim of the sink, head hanging.

"I'll get you some clean clothes," he said as he left the bathroom.

I cupped water into my palm and washed with shaky hands, revelling as the tainted water disappeared down the drain. The dried blood on my knuckles needed a little rubbing.

This wasn't how I'd planned for the night to finish.

The mirror on top of the sink was as accusing as Leo's expression had been. My ashen skin emphasised the blackness of my hair. *Messy, messy hair.*

"These should do for now." Leo appeared from behind me and placed a pile of clothes on the floor. "I'll be outside the door if you need me, okay? Unless you want me to—"

"No!"

I waited until the door clicked shut before plopping down onto the floor, head seeking rest on my knees. Seriously, hadn't the night been bad enough without the humiliation that *this* was? Who handed me that drink in the first place?

I waited for the thumping in my head to calm before slowly changing into Leo's black sweatpants and a grey jumper. I tucked my tank-top under the trousers and pulled the strings tight. Snail-speed, I pushed up on all fours, onto my knees, and reached to the sink. I scooped more water, raking my hands through my hair. The good thing about dead-straight hair was that the knots fell out easily.

Now if I could just get out of here and fall into my own bed.

I pushed up straight, heavily relying on the sink, and called for Leo. It wasn't two seconds before his head popped in. His crooked smile irritated me.

"Don't you look like a million." He leaned against the door-frame, hands in his pockets.

"I'm ready to go home."

Leo's head cocked to the side. "Oh, really now? And who shall I ring to come take care of you?"

Ring? I patted my pockets instinctively, although the truth had already dawned on me. I'd left my phone at the fight club.

"You didn't happen to grab my phone when you brought me here, did you?"

"What? No, sorry." Leo's forehead creased from the sudden change of topic. "I'll get you a new one."

"I don't think so, *sugar-daddy*." I wafted a hand in the air; a lost phone wasn't the most pressing matter. "Anyway, I don't need anyone to look after me. I'm fine on my—"

"I'm not leaving you alone. You can barely stand."

"I don't *need* to stand." I took a laboured breath. "I need to rest. In *my* bed."

Leo's stare was intense, uncomfortable in its scrutiny. Again, he held his tongue.

"Fine. I'll make you a deal. If you can walk to the front door without tripping over, I'll take you home." Leo folded his arms in front of him.

My knuckles bulged from clasping onto the sink. Sadly, my 'gift' was never wrong: I could walk a few steps, and stumble over. My ego had suffered enough irrecoverable damage as it was.

I huffed and extended a hand. "Help me to bed?"

Using Leo as a human crutch, I wobbled over to the bed, climbed under the duvet and propped myself up. A glass of water emerged in front of me as I settled. This time, I drank the contents in small, audible gulps.

"You feeling any better?" he asked as he took the empty glass from me.

I shook my hand in the air, palm facing down.

"They must've given you too heavy a dosage. Or didn't take into account how skinny you are. When was the last time you ate?"

My thoughts flew to the hike with Jill. Was it still the same day? "I had some fruit for lunch."

"Some fruit?" Leo perched on the end of the bed and I pulled my legs in to avoid physical contact.

"I wasn't hungry."

He gave me a look of disbelief and—pity? "I have to admit, you're the hardest person in the world to look after."

"I never *asked* you to look after me. That's all you butting into my life unannounced and unwelcome." I noticed the tick on his jaw and regretted what I'd said. I was being unfair. He had saved me from ending up in a trash can *and* watched me throw up not five minutes ago. Even if I didn't like to admit it, this wasn't the first time he'd saved my life.

Leo lifted his thumb to his eyebrow and let it slide along the length of it. "Do you want some more water?

"Please. If you don't mind." I watched him head toward the kitchen. "Leo...?" I waited for eye contact. "What's your real name?"

A pleased grin flickered across his face. "Elikai. That's my real name."

"Well, thank you... Elikai."

"Anytime." With a wink, he walked into the kitchen.

Elikai.

Chapter 18

"What did those men want with me?" I placed the drink on the bedside table. The chair screeched along the floor as Leo dragged it by the bed.

"They thought you were playing foul." He slumped into the chair. "Fixing the fights. They wanted to know who you were working for, who was cashing in, that sort of thing. If you ask me, they needed to get you out before the crowd went crazy." Leo rolled his head back, inspecting the ceiling.

"Should've guessed. It's not the first time I've been accused of that."

"Somehow, I'm not surprised," he muttered. He intertwined his fingers behind his neck and tilted his head back again.

"So, were you there the whole time?"

Leo's head snapped upright to throw me a disapproving eyeful. "Yup."

I shrugged it off. "Then I'm surprised you didn't stop me earlier."

"I should've, but I thought you needed to blow off some steam and I figured if I kept an eye, you'd be okay. *My bad.*"

"Hey, if it weren't for being drugged then everything would've been fine."

"Yeah, taking drinks from strangers—not a stroke of genius," he admonished. "But that's not what I meant. If I'd known how sloppy you'd got at fighting I never would've let you start."

"*Sloppy?*" How dare he? Sure, I wasn't at the peak of my fitness level, but I knew how to fight.

"Yeah. Sloppy," he repeated.

"Excuse me, but I crushed three men—"

Leo burst out laughing. "*Crushed* is a little optimistic. Those guys had two left feet and technique like a pirate. Even then I bet you used your gifting to finish them."

"Oh, *please.*" *Great defence.* I flattened the duvet around me. Truth was, he was probably right.

An unwelcome cramp tightened my stomach. The drug would take some time to wear off.

"So," I forced the queasiness away, "not saying I agree with you, but what's so wrong with my technique?"

"To begin with" —Leo leaned forward, elbows on his knees— "you have to put weight on, and muscle. You're lacking in strength."

In protest, I launched a pillow at Leo. It flopped on the edge of the bed, hardly grazing his knee.

"Nice of you to prove my point."

I grinned involuntarily at my drug-induced arms.

"Anyhow, that's not all. Your reaction's slow, your focus needs improvement and you've picked up some *nasty* habits. Granted, the foundation is there but the last years have taxed. As soon as you're better, I'll start training you."

"Ha! Is that so? Why would I need to train if I have no intention of going back?" He didn't need to know I was trying to undo the Blood Debt.

"Because I don't think you want to lose the skills. You like the rush like I do."

He was right. Again. Annoyingly. "There's no real use for them here."

"You sure seem to find some." Leo scoffed, and I tried to hold back a grin. "It's really not something to be proud of, Rosebud." He lifted a foot on the edge of the bed, his face growing serious. "Plus, I want you to be able to take care of yourself. I think there are people out there after you."

"I'm sure I'm not that sought after of a partner," I said dryly. "Tony mentioned someone tried to mug you. Hope you went easy on them."

"Yes, I'm fine by the way. Thanks for the sentiment." Leo balanced on the back legs of his chair for a few seconds, and then let the chair slam back down. "It wasn't a mugger; I only said that to Tony. To be honest, I'm not sure who he was, but he was trained."

"What makes you think he was after me, then?" The corners of my lips pulled down as the off-feeling returned.

"It's not the first time I've seen people following you."

"You sure you weren't looking at your own shadow?"

Leo ignored the dead-pan. "Like I said, I get the feeling someone's after you, but I don't know why. Which is even more reason for you to sharpen your skills and get your head in the game. Let me train you."

"I hardly—" Saliva gathered in my mouth and I curled on the bed, arms hugging my stomach. "Bathroom. Throw up."

This time I accepted Leo's help without a grumble but insisted he leave me to it. Although clearly not thrilled with the idea, he let go, and I shut the door on his apprehensive face. I paused to gather composure, flicking the lock with my trembling fingers before bending over the toilet.

I flushed the toilet, feeling like my stomach had been carved empty. Rinsing had never felt better. I spat, holding my fingers under the running tap, my gut hurting from wrenching up nothing but water and air.

"Kalika, you okay? You don't sound good," Leo called through the door.

"I'm fine." I gestured at the door behind me for no one to see. "Stay there!"

I washed my face, rubbed toothpaste into my gums, and straightened up. Instantly, I realised I was in trouble. My vision faded, and it felt like a rush of wind swept me. Hopeless, my hands searched for a steady surface.

*

A loud racket brought back my consciousness. Someone was kicking and shoving against something.

"Kalika! Are you okay?"

I lifted my head from the floor. *Oops.* I had locked the door.

"I'm—I'm fine. I just...fainted." My limbs were sprawled in every direction. Based on the ache I had landed mainly on my right elbow and forearm.

The racket behind the door stopped. Only the door handle continued to move up and down.

"Did you hurt yourself?"

"N-no." *Nothing worth mentioning.*

119

A short silence fell behind the door. "Well, could you open the door, please?"

I scrambled to all fours and paused. The dizziness had eased but the rest of me resembled a jellyfish. I crawled to the door, reached for the lock and flicked it. The next second, Leo was inside, crouching in front of me. His facial muscles were wound tighter than barbwire.

"You locked the door." He clasped my sides. I held the whimper as his fingers dug into a bruise on my side.

"Sorry. Force of habit." I pushed his arms off and fell backwards, sitting half on my legs. I attempted a smile, but Leo snatched my chin, his thumb lodging in the dent on it, and glowered for several seconds.

"That's it. I'm taking you to the hospital." He scooped his arms underneath mine.

"No, no, no, wait!" I resisted with the little fight left in my body, as useless as the effort was.

"You need to be checked." Leo seized my wrists and gently twisted my arms down. "I should've taken you in straight away."

"No, *please*. There's nothing they can do in the hospital, trust me. You know I know my body better than they do." I dug my nails into Leo's shoulders, but he didn't even seem to notice. "I need rest, and I need food. That's why I fainted, I need some food." I searched his eyes, willing to find anything else than pure resolve.

Unforgiving, Leo forced me to my knees, making my face level to his. "They can feed you there." His grip tightened around my resisting arms.

"Leo, I'm begging you. I'll do *anything*. No locked doors. Please, don't take me in."

Leo's composure gave in a little, his thought-process flickering across his face. Then the spark lit up in his eye. "On two conditions."

"Sure, anything."

"You promise to stay here until *I* deem you feel better?"

I nodded furiously. "Fine." *Anything but the hospital.* I couldn't risk seeing Anita, or the other nurses.

"And whilst under my roof, you promise to do as I say?"

My nose crinkled. "Well, within reason—"

"*Anything*. Or the deal is off."

"Fine, yes, done."

Leo's chest widened as he inhaled his approval. "I gotta say, you sure don't sound like someone who's followed orders for most of their life."

Of course, he was right. I was a shadow of my former self. "Help me up?"

I joined my fingers loosely behind Leo's neck as he pulled me against his chest and lifted me in his arms with ease.

An awkward moment later, he lowered me onto the bed. "You really need to get some meat in you, young lady."

I was about to comment when I glanced at his face and took note of the tension in his jaw and the blazing frustration shining through his blue eyes. Guilt took me off guard. He wasn't as bad as I'd made him out to be and he deserved some manners if nothing else.

"I'm sorry, Leo. I've not been the nicest person to be around. I don't deserve half the things—"

Leo lifted a finger and left me staring at his back as he strode into the kitchen. After a quick rummage, he marched back, a bucket in one hand, water bottle in the other.

"If you need to throw up, use this." Leo placed the bucket on the floor, and the bottle on the bedside table. "Finish the water within the hour. Anything else you need, let me know."

I drew my shoulders in, unable to ignore the tugging in my conscience. It was the first time I'd seen Leo look—defeated? "Why do you bother with all this?"

"Because, believe it or not, I actually care about you."

I met his eyes, taken back. Before I had a chance to comment, he continued, "Anyway, you said you needed food. Fancy some Chinese? Can you hold it down?" He looked at me as if already second-guessing his idea.

"I'd love some. I don't feel sick anymore." I rested my head back; the pillow was a dream. "Just starving."

"Alright. There's one down the road." Leo tucked something into his pocket, pulled on a jumper and fastened his shoes. Keys jingled in his hand. "You going to be okay on your own for twenty minutes?"

"Of course." I turned my head to the side, sliding my cheek against the cotton as Leo vouched for his quick return. My eyelids were growing heavy as each blink drew longer.

I startled as Leo gently pinned my shoulders.

"If you get any ideas of moving from this bed while I'm gone, I swear I'll beat you up myself and then you *will* have a reason to go to the hospital."

His sense of humour verged on borderline.

"*Relax.*" I blinked lazily. "I'm not going anywhere. Your bed's too comfy."

Still pinning me down, Leo measured my face. He then let go, swiped his finger along my cheek and marched out as determined as he'd walked in a few seconds ago. Back to me, he lifted his hand in the air. "Just in case, I'm locking the door, Miss Rebel."

The sound of a key turning in a lock made me come to. I must've dozed off as soon as Leo left.

"I'm back! Too late to climb out the window," he called from the door.

I wiped drool off my chin. "What time is it?"

"Around one a.m."

The smell coming from the plastic bag hooked on Leo's finger took command of the room. I shimmied up and adjusted the pillow behind me. Leo fetched plates and cutlery from the kitchen and sat on the chair by the bed.

"Smells amazing." The one thing Narun had missed: Chicken Chow Mein. "I'm surprised they're open this late."

"Only on the weekends. I ordered beef. You want any?"

I shook my head. Leo scraped the contents of an entire tub of Chow Mein on a plate and handed it to me, a fork sticking up from it. It seemed days since I last ate a warm meal.

"Can I ask you something?" The forkful of noodles never quite made it to my mouth as Leo gestured me to go on. "What do you think of this world?"

He chewed, in no hurry to give his reply. "There are things I don't agree with, or that puzzle me. But there's a lot of good in people. I don't think we're that different from one another."

"Could you live here? Permanently?"

"If I had to. But my heart is in Narun."

"Then you should be doing what you love, not hanging around here, waiting in vain." The last word clipped off my tongue and an awkward vibe fell into the room. "You must have family and friends who miss you." I shoved a helping of noodles in my mouth.

"Sure."

"Then go back to them."

Finally, Leo lifted his eyes off his food. "We all have our callings." He winked as I silently questioned him. *What is he hiding?*

I prepared myself with a burdened inhale.

It was time for the discussion.

Chapter 19

"Why do they think we'd make a good team? It doesn't make sense. If you've always gone Solo, why send you on an impossible task to hunt down a...well, *me*. On top of that, I'm a Defender and you're an Attacker."

"The reasons aren't always clear."

"Oh come on, Leo. I'm not stupid. There's got to be more to it."

"Think about it, with your gifting and my reflexes... We're the perfect team." Leo grinned but it came across half-hearted. He stabbed a piece of meat, taking no notice of my dubious frown.

"Do you ever feel left out being a Solo?" During my time as Guard, I'd only met a handful of people who fought alone.

Leo laughed. "Am I supposed to?"

"I guess not. It's what you're used to, right?"

"Exactly." He continued to eat as if he'd already forgotten my prying. But I wasn't done.

"How long are you going to be waiting? For real?"

"Let's put it this way... I knew it wasn't going to be an easy task." Something flickered in his eyes, but I failed to catch its meaning.

"I know you're not telling me everything."

"Duly noted, inspector."

His cheek was asking for a slap—it was like he was proud of his secrets.

Leo set his empty plate on the floor. "So," he lifted his feet onto the bed and slid down on the chair, "my turn to ask the questions: what's going on with you and Sebastian?"

Sebastian's black eye came back to me. *That's right.* I had a bone to pick with Leo. Besides the usual.

"I can't believe you hit him! *And* went all third-degree on him. What's the matter with you?"

"I didn't hit him; I fought him. Fair and square. It's not my problem his skills aren't up to scratch, and there's nothing wrong with asking the guy a few questions."

125

I shook my head in disbelief. "Why on earth would you go see him in the first place?"

"I don't like him."

I waited.

"*Okay*, I was there to vet him," he confessed. "He gives me a funny vibe."

A funny vibe? He's one to speak.

"Stay away from him. Stay away from all my friends." I grasped the fork to eat some more, needing to occupy my hands.

"So, you're just friends? Nothing more?"

Selective hearing—and jealousy? "What's it to you? Who I spend, or do not spend, my time with is none of your business."

He moved his leg, making his plate rattle on the floor. I flinched more from the black look on his face than the sudden noise.

Robustly, I chewed a few more mouthfuls before placing the plate down on the bedside table. I avoided Leo's eyes like they passed on malaria.

"I think he likes you," he finally said, conceding. "You should be careful, that's all."

"I don't agree, but sure, I'll watch out for date rape drugs."

"Seriously." He pointed at the water bottle beside me. "If your jokes are so dry you must be parched."

I smirked and slid deeper under the covers. I appreciated how the heavy duvet acted as a shield.

"You're still in love with your partner, aren't you?"

I ground my molars, my defences instantly rocketing sky-high. "I don't wanna talk about it."

"You'll have to talk about it one day."

"Why? I definitely don't have to talk to you about it."

"True. But I'll say one thing and then I'll leave it, okay?" He waited until I marginally dipped my head. "You *have* to let him go. The pain won't stop until you do. And you won't be able to let him go if you keep bottling it up."

I fought against the stinging in my eyes. It was easy for him to say. He didn't know what it felt like having your entire world torn from you and being the one responsible for it.

I rolled to my side and forced my thoughts in line. Tomorrow was a new day, and everything would be back to normal.

*

"We won't win," I gasped as a battalion of Gorahites emerged from the tree-line. He was beside me, oddly calm, gripping two samurai swords in each hand.

"Stay focused. One battle at a time. It'll be okay."

I glanced at him. It'll be okay? Was he not seeing what I was seeing? We were about to be killed. Or worse— captured.

The thought sent shivers over my skin. Him captured, tortured...no.

I flipped my Sais nervously in between my fingers. The soldiers nearing us were strong, trained, ferocious. They came for blood. The blood of our kind.

"Kali, focus," he said again, much more sternly but I got the feeling it was him who needed to hear it. His mind was split.

"Get your head in gear," I snapped back, and he exhaled, giving me a glance. A longing glance. Did he want us to die? "Head in gear, now!" I shouted back as the first soldiers reached us and I turned my full focus on my inner voice yelling orders at me.

"Left side!" I voiced, and he reacted.

Chapter 20

A mix of scents hovered in the air as I woke up: stale Chinese food, slightly burned toast, cleaning detergent, and a hint of cologne. Flashbacks of the day before confirmed my whereabouts.

It felt late. Late in the day. Thankfully, the queasiness had passed; the foreign substance had cleared my system.

A new day.

Leo and I exchanged a few strained words, not sure where we stood after last night, and then he drove me home.

Outside my flat, one leg out of the car, I debated on the right thing to say. "This being drugged thing and the weekend in general... Can we keep it between us?"

"If that's what you want," Leo said curtly, one hand on the gear stick, eyes fixed ahead.

Come on, Kal, swallow your pride. "T-thanks for...helping me out, Leo. I appreciate what you did for me."

"This is it, then?" Leo angled himself towards me but looked slightly past me. "Everything goes back to normal, like last night never happened?" His voice was steady, but his eyes were so dark I struggled to unravel them.

I squeezed the door handle. "Nothing's changed, Leo."

"I see." He lowered his chin, and I slammed the door shut before he had a chance to give me a piece of his mind.

It took me a few attempts on the rusting lock before I could slip inside to my comfort zone. As soon as I had showered and changed, I headed to the park to train—I'd wasted enough time. I had a goal and now I needed to do something about it.

Day one of becoming a lean, mean, Gorahite-killing machine. *Again.*

*

The clock digits claimed 6:27 a.m. on Monday morning when I jumped out of bed, startled by a thump, supposedly coming from the hallway.

I pulled out a kitchen knife from my bedside table drawer and dashed to check the door in stealth-mode, only to stop short. A brown package lay on the floor, looking as if it had barely made it through the letterbox.

It was way too early for mail. Besides, had I ever received anything other than takeaway menus?

I placed the knife down and picked up the package. My name was written in neat, yet manly handwriting on the cover. It definitely wasn't from Tony—his scribbles were hard to decipher even with a code.

The wrappings yielded to my ferocious fingers and revealed the contents: a black mobile phone.

I stood still, phone in hand. *How…? Leo?* It had to be, no one else knew I had lost my old one. I rummaged through the paper and bubble wrap and came across a folded note.

'Hope this does the job. I added a few numbers. Leo.'

I re-read the words. He was being too kind, and I wasn't comfortable with it. Walking to the lounge, I pushed the start button and within a few seconds the phone switched itself on.

Fully charged.

I glanced at the note again and scrolled down to *Contacts*. All there apart from Sebastian. I saved Sebastian's number from memory and typed a simple *'Thanks'* to Leo. The phone pinged with a reply within seconds.

'It was worth it for that overwhelming show of gratitude.'

Whatever.

A few hours later, I walked into the lecture theatre, searching for Tony. Four rows back, he sat by himself.

I nudged his arm as I took a seat. "Morning."

Tony glanced up, dark circles giving away a late night. "Hey, what's up?"

"You tell me. I texted Jill my new number and she said she has big news." I pulled out a notebook from my bag and placed it on the narrow table. "She won't tell me until this afternoon."

Tony rubbed his eyes with his knuckles. "I hope she won the lottery."

"Come on, you must know what's going on. Apparently, she'd been calling me all weekend."

"Right, her...thing." Tony grazed his stubble with the back of his hand. "Yeah, no, if I say a word I'll die a slow, agonising death." He crossed his arms on his chest. "Speaking of yesterday, what you doing losing your phone? I worked hard teaching you how to use that thing."

"It must've fallen from my pocket. Sorry." I hated lying.

"Fallen out? Well, get one of those woman bags to keep it in... Honestly." Tony shook his head as the lecturer made her way down the stairs to the podium. A clatter of voices resumed as she fixated on the computer without addressing the students.

"The real question is," Tony lowered his voice, "how'd you manage to get a new one without me?"

"I'm not stupid."

"Well, let's see."

I protested as Tony beckoned with his hand but gave him the phone. *What is it with men and technology?*

"Not bad." He fiddled with it between his fingers and pressed a few buttons. "Suitable for you obviously: basic and old-fashioned."

I kicked Tony in his shin. Had Leo gone for simplicity for a reason? *Do I really care?*

"Did you get a good contract?"

Pants, hadn't even thought of that. "Good enough." I snatched the phone from Tony's hand. I'd have to ask Leo how much I was going to be paying.

As the lecture finished, Tony rushed off and I met up with Jill. Huddling into our jackets in the near-gale force wind, we walked to the café across the campus, surprised to find it nearly empty. I ordered drinks and returned with a cappuccino for Jill and a peach ice tea for myself.

"So, the news?"

Jill's hands disappeared under the table, and then she popped her left hand on top. It hardly took me a second to register the source of the bling. I'd learned what a ring on *that* finger meant a few months after arriving in England.

"You're *engaged?* Tony proposed?" I nearly knocked over my drink grabbing Jill's hand. She shrieked excitedly, drawing the attention of the few other customers. The white-gold band dressing her finger had a large, slightly angular diamond, neighboured by two smaller diamonds of the same cut. I shot up to wrap her into a hug, and a moment later sat back down, still eyeing the ring.

"I can't believe Tony managed to keep this quiet!"

"He was under threat of death." Jill sniggered.

"He mentioned. How'd he pop the question?"

Jill recounted the story of a midnight walk by a canal. By the arch of a bridge, Tony had bent on one knee and asked her to be his wife. The ring had been in a small, ballerina shoe-shaped box in honour of Jill's dedication to dancing in her growing up years.

"Have you set a date?"

"Not quite, but it'll be the summer we graduate." Jill wiggled her fingers, the light catching the bling. "We are, however, having a bit of an engagement party, well, two actually."

"Great. Am I invited?"

"Of course, silly," Jill rebuked, tongue-in-cheek. "We're having a party for friends on Thursday, and the week after we'll have a family meal with the bridal party, which leads me to a question... Would you be one of my bridesmaids?"

I choked on the ice tea, causing a coughing fit that made Jill's forehead knit.

"You don't have to if you—"

"No, no" — I was forced to pause for a cough— "I'd be honoured! You caught me by surprise, that's all. Jill, I'd be *honoured*."

Jill clapped her hands together, eyes sparkling, and then she grimaced. "I have to warn you, though... Tony is going to ask Leo to be the best man. Provided he can make the wedding, of course, but he'll be there for the parties."

I only guessed her worry was for my reaction rather than travel arrangements to and from Narun.

"Don't worry about that. Tony can have whoever he wants as his best man." Though seriously, why pick a guy you've only known for some weeks? Then again, I hadn't known Jill for much longer than that.

"We can coexist for a few nights," I assured her and shifted the focus back to Jill.

We talked for another hour or so until Jill had to go. I was strolling home elated by the news when a dinging text message brought me back to the grey pavements.

'Meet me in the park near you at 7 p.m. It's important.'

Chapter 21

"My, my, you actually came. I must be doing something right to tame the shrew." A well-humoured Leo leapt down from a park bench.

"Tone it down. If you value your life, that is."

"I'll take my chances." Leo grinned. "How are you feeling today?"

"Normal." I jerked my chin forward. "The phone—how much do I owe you?"

"Ah, I see you're back to your charming self." He motioned us to walk and I followed. "It was a gift. It's pay as you go, but I bought some credit in advance." He handed me an envelope. "Here's the fine print."

"Thanks, although I will pay you back." I took the envelope and rolled it into a scroll. "Was this why you summoned me?"

"No." Leo matched my pace as I walked down a slope. "Did you hear the news about Tony and Jill?"

"Yes." The slightly swaying trees drew my focus. "They make a good team. But seriously, why'd you want to see me?"

Leo veered off the path, starting towards an incline in the greenery.

I stopped. "Where're you going?"

He dipped his head to the side, beckoning me to follow. "Come. It's more private over here. Isn't that what you want?"

"Wait, what...?" I called but he disappeared in between the willow trees. Groaning, I followed.

Behind the treeline was a flat area, nicely tucked in, hidden from the paths.

"See?" Leo stood tall, hands on his hips. "Perfect."

My eyes darted around, searching for the punch line. "Perfect for what?"

"Training. You ready to start?"

I froze, rubbing my fingertips with my thumb as I drew a quick list of pros and cons in my head.

It *was* an ideal location and training with Leo would be great practice in getting back into shape. And boy, was I curious to go a few rounds with him. On the downside, I didn't want to give into him or let him see the eagerness detained just under the surface.

I rolled my eyes. I was blatantly going to give in.

"*Fine,* since we're here." I feigned disinterest. "Not for long, though."

"First, eat this." Leo tossed something—a protein bar, I judged as I caught it.

"I'm not hungry."

"Of course you're not. I do wonder… Do you actually have an eating disorder, or is this not eating thing just another way to get back at yourself?"

Blunt much? I gave him a dirty look but unwrapped the bar and took a bite.

"Anyway," Leo smiled, seemingly pleased I was eating, "if we're going to do this, we need to do it properly."

"Meaning?" I went for another bite. I was a little peckish.

"Meaning you follow my lead and do as I tell you."

I swallowed a chunk too big and coughed into my hand. "I have a problem with that."

"I know, Rosebud, you have a problem with everything, but you know how this works. If I'm going to teach you, you have to do as I say, like in real training."

I stuffed the half-eaten protein bar in my pocket. "Let's just get one thing straight—"

"Yes, *I know.*" The roll of Leo's eyes should win one of those shiny, golden men. "I'm no better than you. The only reason I'll 'teach' you is that you have been out of it, and *no*, this doesn't mean you'll hate me any less, et cetera, et cetera." Leo whisked a hand in the air as if bored of the words he needed to speak.

I suppressed a grin. "What makes you think I was going to say that?"

"I can see it on your face."

"How?" I challenged.

"It's smug."

"My face is not smug."

"Smug," Leo countered.

"It was suggestive at most."

"Fine, *suggestively* smug." Leo threw his hands in the air. Again, I had to stop the corners of my mouth from lifting. "So," Leo stood waiting, arms again folded, "can you manage that?"

"Whatever."

"Whatever...what?" Leo cupped his ear toward me. *He is loving this.*

"Whatever, *Bar'Elikai.*" I curled a lip at the honorific title and watched as he unleashed his fiercest crooked smile yet.

I thudded on to my back. For the sixth time, the thick bed of grass cushioned the blow. Frustrated, I went over what I'd done wrong this time, once again arriving at the same conclusion: Leo was too fast.

"Need help?" A hand appeared in my vision, along with Leo's face. His dark hair pointed to all corners of the world.

I held up a finger and spread my limbs, my joints relieved of the break. Leo sat next to me, knees bent.

"You're doing good. It's coming back to you."

"It never left me," I corrected. "It's just been a while since my opponent has been equally lethal."

"Wow. Was that a compliment?"

"No."

"You know, it's not easy switching your perspective from defence to attack, but you've got a knack for it."

"I like it. It's more... aggressive." *Gives me an outlet to vent.*

The birds chirped their lullabies before the night sought to tuck them in.

"Did Tony ask you?" I opened my eyes, instantly pulled in by the dusk of the sky.

Leo twirled a strand of grass between his fingers. "About being his best man? He sure did. And I hear you're a bridesmaid. Though you doing girlie things… That'll be a hoot." Leo blocked my feeble attempt at trying to hit him. "Apparently, it's customary for the best man and—"

"Don't. Just don't." I propped myself on my elbows.

"Tony's a good man." The corners of Leo's mouth twitched. "I'm glad I picked him."

"What do you mean you 'picked him'?"

Leo dropped the strand of grass and yanked a clover off the ground. "You don't think it was a coincidence Tony figured out you were the girl in a coma?"

I drew a blank for too long before the fireworks began.

Leo had placed the newspaper articles and police reports in Tony's path. He had fed Tony's curiosity and led his 'investigations'. He'd coordinated the whole thing; he'd caused me to reveal my identity.

Some nerve.

Much to my surprise, I couldn't muster the anger. In all honesty, he'd done me a favour. *Not that I'd ever admit it to him.*

There was, however, one thing I had to know.

"Did you orchestrate our whole friendship?" I partly feared the answer.

"Of course not. Tony seemed trustworthy and understanding, so I dropped a few hints." Leo threw the clover at me like a javelin; I flicked it off my cheek.

"You're lucky it all turned out well. Or you'd be paying." I flexed my joints, feeling my clothes sticking to my skin, courtesy of the slightly moist ground.

"Can I ask you something?"

I looped my arms around my knees. "You're going to anyway."

"Why don't you use your gifting anymore?"

"What makes you think I don't use it?"

"You're not using it on me," Leo reasoned. "And Tony mentioned you never talk about it."

"He did, did he… I'm not happy with you two being so close. He talks too much."

Leo snorted, confirming my suspicion.

"I don't use it, because that's not who I am anymore." *Or at least didn't want to be.* My gifting had mostly brought grief, anyway. Without it, *he* might still be alive.

"I hope you realise how stupid that sounds."

"I don't expect, or need, you to understand."

Leo cast his sapphire eyes heavenwards in frustration and jumped up, beckoning me to follow. I gathered my protesting limbs, not nearly as fast as I wanted to.

We practised for another hour before calling it a night and heading out of the park. The gates would be locked soon.

"Oh, I forgot your clothes," I said. "They're washed."

"Keep them. You could do with a wardrobe upgrade."

"Excuse me?"

"You do rise to everything, don't you?" he said flatly.

I pictured the contents of my wardrobe in my head before I realised he was right: I did rise to everything.

Leo hopped over a ditch filled with water and I followed, ignoring his extended hand.

"What is it about me that annoys you so much?"

For once he didn't hide his frustration, yet I gathered, it was only the tip of the iceberg.

"You know the answer to that, Leo."

"No, I don't, *Kalika.* I thought it was the whole partner thing and me reminding you of home, but you do genuinely hate me, don't you?"

A guilty conscience pricked me. Leo was giving up a lot, and the fact that I had changed wasn't his fault. I couldn't blame him for my mistakes.

"It's not like that," I said quietly.

"Then elaborate," he retorted much louder.

"Can we not have this conversation?"

"You'd like that wouldn't you, fleeing from everything that might involve emotion." If Leo's voice was a knife, it'd be the opposite of blunt.

"See, that's why! You go too far, you tease it out of me!"

139

"I see." His jaw was taut, pulsating from the pressure of his gritted teeth. I felt sorry for those who came against him in real battle. What surprised me more was that a part of me just felt sorry for him.

I pulled my jumper on tighter. "You're right. You're a reminder of everything I left behind, so it's easier to stay away from you. Plus, it's not exactly a secret why you're here. Any sign of a friendly word and you think you're closer to your cause! I don't want to give you the encouragement."

"So, you don't hate me?" Leo stopped across the road from my house.

"No, you doughnut, though you do rub me the wrong way."

"Likewise." His crooked grin was short-lived. "Where does that leave this weird thing we have going on?"

I twirled my house key in between my fingers, over and over.

"I can train you. If you like," Leo added.

"Why are you so eager to train me?" I searched for signs to read his mind, but his body language was as impenetrable as his fighting.

"I told you: I want you to be able to look after yourself, whether I'm here or not. Also, I could do with a punching bag to keep my skills fresh."

"Funny." Leo was forgetting even without him honing my skills, I was far more advanced than the average Jane when it came to self-defence.

"There's just one problem: why should I do anything that'll make you stay longer?"

"I'll stay in any case," Leo noted. "But I'll make you a deal. If you train with me, I'll give you some space. No more turning up on campus."

Interesting. "No stalking or hanging around my friends?"

"I'll ease off on…following you. *Our* friends, you'll have to share, but if you wish, we can ignore each other in public."

"And you're fine with that?"

"On one condition," he said. "Truce" —Leo extended his hand— "when it's just the two of us? After all, you're the only fellow 'foreigner' around."

I stared at his arm and fingers that waited perfectly still.

This could work in my benefit. If we trained together, I would get back up to shape twice as fast, which would speed up the process for resolving the Blood Debt. What was more, it would be the key to getting rid of Leo. If I was no longer under the Blood Debt, they would call Leo back, and I could get on with my life.

Win-win.

With a firm grip of his wrist, I shook his arm once.

Chapter 22

.

I fastened a black belt on top of a burgundy top Jill had bought for me. The diagonal neckline did wonders for the off-the-shoulder feature. Thankfully, the yellowing bruises from training were mainly on the other arm where the sleeve reached down to my elbow.

I slipped my feet into borrowed high heels and smoothed my palms down the front of the slim-cut jeans. Sebastian should be picking me up any minute for Jill and Tony's engagement party.

I hoped they didn't mind the plus one.

As we arrived at the party venue—Stan's parents' house—a bunch of people I vaguely recognised from university already filled the lounge and kitchen. Voices soared over the music. Jill was the first to spot us and question Sebastian's still blackened eye. He'd be getting that a lot.

Jill briefly introduced us to Stan's girlfriend who tidied a pile of shoes away from the doorway. Sebastian saw a mate of his and started chatting as Jill pulled me into the kitchen.

"I hope you don't mind I brought Sebastian." I tugged at the black cardigan Jill wore on top of her dress. "I double-booked."

"It's fine, don't worry," Jill chirped and stopped in front of two girls fixing drinks. "Camilla…meet my two other bridesmaids!"

The two girls—a blonde, Lana, from Jill's course, and Annie, a childhood friend—shrieked in excitement and jumped to hug me. I felt a twinge of remorse this was the first time I'd heard of either of them.

We exchanged pleasantries and I smiled along, a little windswept, as Lana launched into plans to go shopping for Jill's wedding dress. Annie, the chief bridesmaid, handed me a cup of lemonade and fell into a conversation with Jill.

Very quickly I gathered Lana liked to talk and did it with such speed I struggled to keep up. As she carried on, I glanced over my shoulder to see where Sebastian had disappeared, and instead noted Leo and Tony in the lounge.

I'd never realised Leo was a few inches taller than Tony.

"Camilla?" Lana burst me out of my bubble.

"Sorry, say what?"

Lana sucked in her already flat stomach. "I asked if you have a boyfriend." She took a bottle from the counter and topped up her plastic cup. "You want a drink?"

I lifted the half-full cup in my hand. "No, I'm not seeing anyone. You?"

"Nah, I've just got out of a relationship, so I'm not ready for *anything*." Lana giggled, biting the rim of her cup, and I noted the small gap between her front teeth. Her fringe was tangled up with her long eyelashes and she brushed the hair off with a finger.

I was about to attempt small talk when Jill hooked her arm with Lana's.

"Come on, let's get out of the kitchen and go mingle," she said, looking even tinier compared to Lana's height.

Annie smiled at me with her full lips and I started after them, only to wave them off as Sebastian caught me by the doorway.

"Hey—would you believe I actually know quite a few people here?"

"That makes one of us, then." I looked at the sea of faces. The number of people I knew was decreasing rapidly. "I'm not good with people."

"What are you talking about? You're not from around here but you already seem to have made close friends. *Bridesmaid-level friends.* That's rare."

That was all down to Tony and Jill taking me under their wings.

"Still." I pointed a finger to myself. "Anti-social."

"I find that hard to believe." His shoulder collided with mine. "Come on, I'll introduce you to some people." He roped his arm around my neck, letting it hang free from the elbow. I stumbled with him into the lounge, the music hitting me harder, and locked eyes with Leo.

It felt like someone pressed pause, and I registered several things at once: Leo's smile fading as he saw Sebastian, Sebastian's grimace

144

as he realised Leo was looking at him, and Jill's concern as she noticed the reason for Leo's change of expression.

Then, the party resumed.

"*Awk-ward*," Sebastian whispered in my ear. "I might've earned another talking to."

Me too. "Don't mind him. He won't bother you anymore."

"You talked to him?" Sebastian pulled his arm from around my neck.

"Oh, I sure did."

"You didn't have to do that. If he bothers you again, I'll send him packing."

"How chivalrous," I quipped. "So unlike you."

Sebastian caught me in the ribs, making an uncharacteristic squeal escape my throat. A few people nearby threw curious glances at us but soon lost interest.

"It's a good thing you have your looks, Milla. Your cheek could get you in real trouble." Sebastian feigned reproach, and I gave my best dramatic eye roll.

In the corner of my eye, I caught Lana jumping on Leo to give him a bear hug.

So, everyone did know each other—except for me.

*

It was past midnight when the last guests had left the party. Lana lay passed out on the sofa, breathing heavily, her arm hanging on the floor. Annie pulled a throw over her. Most of the tidying up was done, apart from the boys still moving chunky furniture back to their places.

Jill brushed her hair with the back of her hand, a duster scrunched in her palm, as she caught me by the kitchen door. "I thought the party was pretty successful."

"I'll say. How you know so many people, and still hang out with me, is beyond me though…" I kicked my heels off and gave my feet a quick rub.

Jill smiled, confirming she was all smiled out for the night. Her yawn backed it up.

"I hope it wasn't too awkward seeing Leo again," she whispered to me. "I know you haven't really talked since...forever."

My face twitched. In her books, my last proper encounter with Leo had been when I talked to him at Tony's flat. *I should just come clean.*

"Listen, Jill—" I started but sucked in the rest as Sebastian walked in the kitchen from the opposite direction.

"Are we ready to go?" He jingled keys in his hand.

"Go, go." Jill wafted the duster in the air. "We're all done here. Thanks for staying to help tidy up. You really didn't need to."

"Of course, our pleasure." Sebastian flashed a brilliant smile that quickly fizzled out thanks to the arrival of Tony and Leo.

I was pretty certain the evil eye Leo had been giving me all night hadn't gone unnoticed by Sebastian.

"You two heading off?" Tony shook Sebastian's hand. "Good of you to come, mate. I'll text you about footy."

Jill hugged me and I followed Sebastian out, ignoring Leo.

We walked to Sebastian's car which was parked on the far end of the street. As he reversed the car around, I glanced back at the house and witnessed Leo carrying a passed-out Lana to his car.

*

After work the next morning, I was relieved to find my seminar cancelled. I had toyed with the idea of skipping class, but at least now my attendance record wouldn't take another hit—and I'd have time for some over-due grocery shopping. My diet needed an update.

I walked through the sliding doors of the supermarket with a trolley and zipped up my jacket. The air conditioning must have been set for a heat wave.

I sauntered down the aisles, picking up nuts, vegetables, and high protein foods, aware I'd have to carry everything home. As I rounded the corner towards the chilled food, my trolley bumped into another.

In horror, I recognised the stunned face pushing the other trolley.

Chapter 23

We both froze, swung back in time to memories stored very differently in our brains.

"Hey." I questioned if my voice had been loud enough.

"Camilla. Hi," Anita replied after several seconds, almost visibly shaking herself from her thoughts. "This is a surprise. I thought—I thought I'd never see you again."

I squeezed the handle on the trolley, knuckles popping white. "I decided to stay. I thought the chances of us—"

Anita raised her hand, and I sucked in the rest I had to say. "I never had a chance to thank you for what you did for Aaron."

"Really, there's no need. After how I lied..." I trailed off, failing at basic vocabulary.

Anita lowered her chin and then lifted it with a faint smile. "I understand why you did what you did. I don't necessarily agree with the methods, but I get it."

"Anita. You should be angry at me, shout at me, insult me... Anything but *understand* me."

"Yes... David doesn't share my views." She lowered her eyes again, fixating on her shopping.

I only wondered what he'd say if he saw us now. "I don't want to cause a rift—"

"No, it's fine, don't worry." She rubbed her wedding band. "We've come to terms with not seeing eye to eye in regard to—to..."

"*Me.*"

Anita smiled, and I felt even worse. "How have you been?"

I flicked hair off my face, although none of it was in the way. "You don't have to do this."

"I meant what I said, Camilla." A frown deepened on her forehead as she said my name. "I believe you didn't mean to hurt me or my family. I did think of you as a friend; I want to believe that was real."

"It was. It killed me to lie to you."

147

"Listen," Anita pulled her trolley back an inch, "I need to pick up Aaron, but do you want to meet up one day, for a coffee or something? We could catch up."

"What about David?"

"Don't worry about David. Please, meet me, for me?"

Her brown eyes had always been impossible to resist and warily, I agreed. Anita dug out a pen from her bag and handed it to me. I scribbled my number on the back of her shopping list.

I gave back the pen. "I still…go by Camilla."

Anita covered the twitch on her lips with a smile. "Sure." She steered her trolley out of the way. "I'm glad I bumped into you."

I dove into the next aisle with my shopping and stopped. *What had just happened?* She wanted to catch up…?

There was no end to her grace. Somehow, I'd find a way to make it all up to her.

I hovered in the shop until it was highly unlikely Anita would still be there. It was only after I had paid for the shopping the obvious dawned on me: I wouldn't be able to carry everything home. I rummaged my purse and ruled out public transport. I'd blown my monthly budget on food, anyway.

I sighed, annoyed with myself. I needed a lift.

Jill was busy with Annie, so I dialled Tony. No luck. Sebastian's number did the same—voicemail. I hardly knew the others enough to call in a favour. I glanced at the trolley full of bags. Who buys five different types of cereal for one?

Idiot.

Reluctant, I dialled the one person who was sure to answer.

Leo picked up in no time. "Kalika, what's wrong?"

"Why does something have to be wrong?"

"Why else would you be ringing me?" he said, much calmer.

"Never mind, this was a bad idea—"

"What's up, Rosebud?"

I sighed and succumbed. "Are you busy?" I hadn't a clue what Leo did with his days. I doubted he was registered at the university. Did he work? How did he get money?

"Rarely. You wanting another session?"

"Not exactly. I kind of need a lift."

I didn't have to sit on the curb for long until Leo arrived. How he managed to always be near my whereabouts was astounding—or a little disturbing?

I swallowed my pride as Leo jumped out of the car.

"Thanks for coming, and sorry about this. You were the last resort."

"Exactly what a fella wants to hear..." He assessed the Mount Everest of shopping, amusement poorly contained in his expression. "How many people are you feeding?"

"I got distracted," I mumbled, embarrassed. In Narun, no one stocked up as it was selfish to hoard food. Everyone picked up only what they needed from the closest market, fresh.

We filled the boot quickly and I took to the passenger seat.

"Hope you didn't have to spend another night with a girl throwing up in your bed," I said as Leo turned the engine on.

"Eh?"

"Lana." I buckled up and Leo joined the main road. "She was pretty rough. I saw you carry her into your car last night."

"Ah. Yeah, I dropped her off on the way home." A sly smile crept up on Leo's lips. "Were you jealous?"

"Hardly."

"Hmm. I take it you got home safely, and Sebastian didn't—"

"Didn't what?" My head whipped toward him.

"Forget it."

"No, didn't what? Stay over? Steal a goodnight kiss?" For some reason, Leo came across uncomfortable and I liked it. "Is that why you looked like you could wring a deer when we left?"

"I told you, he bugs me." The car accelerated a notch. "He's all over you, all the time."

"You're one to talk."

I waited for a comeback, but it never came. Instead, we fell into a loaded silence. When he just gazed ahead, his jaw firmly clenched, I angled my head away.

I should've given the extra groceries to a homeless person.

Gladly, the drive wasn't long. Leo helped me carry the bags inside and I started unpacking as he ran to get the last ones.

"You must like your cereal." Leo placed the last two bags on the kitchen table.

"Like I said, I wasn't thinking. You want a box?"

"No, I'm good." Leo pulled a chair from the kitchen table and slouched on it.

I carried on with unpacking. "Are you waiting for a tip?"

"I'd be waiting a long time."

Got that right.

The bags rustled painfully loud in the otherwise quiet room. I noticed Leo take in the apartment.

"It's not a bad flat, similar layout to mine," he said. "How do you afford it?"

"I take part in human drug testing. Pays a bomb." I stuffed the empty bags in the cupboard under the sink and leant against the counter. Leo's eyes were narrowed on me menacingly. "*I'm kidding.* I work, remember? Gosh, don't take everything so seriously."

"When it's you, all bets are off," he muttered.

"What were you doing anyway when I rang?"

"I was at home. About to fix something to eat."

I threw him a banana from the counter. He caught it with one hand, gave it a quirked eyebrow, and laid it on the table.

"What do you actually do with your days? You're not really at university, are you?"

"I do temp covers and stuff," he said. "And watch over you, trying to keep you in one piece."

"Still unnecessary." I walked to the lounge, plugging my phone on charge. I wondered if Anita would actually contact me and if she did, whether I'd take her up on the coffee.

"You looked nice last night." Leo's voice came from nearby. I pretended I hadn't heard him. A floorboard by the entrance to my bedroom creaked as he paced behind me.

"Stop snooping. The clothes I borrowed are by the door."

"Is that a hint for me to leave?"

Was it? I bit a lip, hesitating. "If I ask you something, will you tell me the truth?"

He encouraged me to continue as he sat on the sofa. I ignored my common sense trying to pull the plug on the conversation.

"You followed me around during my... err, while I was—" I scrunched my face. "Not making the best decisions of my life." My throat was closing. Why wouldn't it cooperate? "What did you think of me then? As in, didn't you think I was a horrible person for doing what I did to people?"

"What did you do to people?"

"You know." I fiddled with my hands, unable to stop. "Used them, lied to them and then disappeared without an explanation, or without shedding a thought to the consequences."

"Honestly," Leo inhaled sharply, "I think you never meant to hurt anyone but yourself, like punishing yourself eased your conscience somehow. I think your mind was clouded and you thought you weren't significant enough to cause other people hurt."

"Come on, you must've thought I was a horrible person! Surely, I'd be the last person you'd want to be partnered with."

"You weren't yourself." Leo's voice came out soft like he was a different person altogether.

"Why does everyone say that? You all seem to find every explanation to justify what I did! Why can't people just be...disgusted with me!" I had to turn away; I was losing control. Everything inside me bubbled.

"Is that what you want?" The leather sofa made a noise against Leo's jeans. "Would that make you feel better?"

"Yes!" My hand flew to cover my face. *Fight it, fight it, fight it.*

Leo took his time. Part of me hoped he'd left me alone in an empty room.

"You have to forgive yourself, Kalika, and stop punishing yourself," he finally said, firm but kind at the same time. "I know you think it'd be easier if everyone hated you, that you'd feel better, but you aren't ever going to fit in anywhere unless you learn to live with yourself."

I let the air flow deep through my nose, into my lungs, and out my mouth in a steady cycle. With each breath, I gained more control.

"I saw Anita today, at the supermarket." I swear I could hear something click into place in Leo's brain.

"First time?"

"Since last time, yes." I paused, but as Leo remained silent I continued. "She wants to meet up, to catch up."

"And you think she shouldn't be so nice?"

"Why would she be nice? I lied to her and her family."

Leo exhaled as if working on his patience. "Give people some credit. Like Tony and Jill... They know you did what you did to hurt yourself. They wish you'd let them in, so they could help you, but you keep everyone so far away."

There was a personal note hidden loosely in Leo's words.

"Do you know why you get to me so much? Why I can't stand having you around?"

"You told me last time. I remind you of home."

"That's part of the truth." I walked to the window, my back to Leo, looking at the view that was all *England.* "The whole reason is that you're the only one who's seen me before coming here. I mean, you didn't really *know* me, but you said you saw me. And then you saw me do all those things, and you see me now." I paused to compose myself. "You're like a living reminder of everything I've done wrong. What's worse, I can't stop thinking what *you're* thinking of me and what I've done."

"Kalika." The voice coming inches from my ear startled me. "We all make bad choices. When you left Narun you didn't just lose your way; you lost *yourself* way before that." Leo swallowed, a little too listlessly, keeping something back.

I turned to search his eyes. I wasn't sure either of us could read each other.

"You can't fix me," I blurted.

"I know. Only you can do that."

We stared at each other until Leo swiped his thumb across my cheek. I flinched, and Leo dropped his arm, walking back to the sofa as if nothing had happened.

It felt like he drew out the warmth circling in my stomach as he retreated. "You hold your tongue when you're with me."

"That I do, Rosebud, that I do."

"Don't. As much as I hate to admit it, you know more about me than anyone here since we've grown up with the same set of beliefs. I'd rather you were honest with me. Brutally honest."

"You can't handle that yet, Kalika, and you know it."

I ate up his words, unable to make myself pursue the matter. *Once again, he was right.*

"Now then," Leo clapped his palms together, "are we training or what?"

Just like that my mood picked up, my eyes sliding to the chest of drawers by the sofa.

"How are your weapon skills?"

Chapter 24

"Bad idea. We don't have any protective pads. Besides, I don't exactly carry weapons on me."

"Oh, come on, it'll be fun."

"Are you telling me you have a sword lying around in your cupboard?" Leo narrowed his eyes on me as I held up a finger, walked to the chest of drawers and pulled out a hard, black case from the bottom drawer.

His interest piqued, he stepped over to me. "Are those what I think they are?"

I handed over the case and Leo took out one of the Sai daggers, sliding his finger along the pointed metal, down to the two curved prongs projecting from the handle. The metal glinted as it had on the day I earned them.

He let out a long whistle, picked up the other dagger, and gave me a dirty look.

"It's illegal to bring them here."

Oops. I had genuinely forgotten: weapons earned on the Guard were to be handed in upon retiring. Or becoming a fugitive.

"I—I wasn't thinking straight when I left. I thought they might come in handy."

"Where've you hidden them all this time?"

"I've had them in storage in Leeds since I left Narun. I picked them up when I decided to settle here."

Leo spun the dagger and wielded the air. "Wasn't my choice weapon, but these are nice—light, firm grip." The blades produced a familiar *'whoosh'* as they cut the air. My prized possessions pirouetted in Leo's hands, inches from his wrists. Choice weapon or not, he was familiar with the Sais.

"When was the last time you used these?" Leo pricked the sharp tip of one of the daggers and placed both back into the case.

"I haven't used them since I left Narun."

"Not even for a test drive?" He scoffed as I shook my head. "Then there's no chance we're practising. The last thing I need is you splitting your wrists before the engagement dinner. Jill would never forgive me." Leo was about to slam the case shut but this time my hands were quicker.

I grabbed the daggers and retreated a few steps. "Don't worry, she doesn't know we're on speaking terms. Let alone training. At least not yet." My fingers wrapped around the handles as I flipped them so the butt faced forward, my index finger straight along the handle. The feel of the cool metal, down to the weight on my hand, took me back years.

I spun the daggers from defensive to offensive hold, two fingers securing over the curved prongs, and back again. The rapid grip changes came easy.

Instincts were a marvellous thing.

"That's great. Now—put them away." *Spoilsport.*

"You're welcome to disarm me." I pictured blocking off imaginary attacks, speeding up as my coordination cooperated.

"Seriously," Leo growled. "Stop showing off. You're going to hurt yourself."

"*Please.*" I carved the air into beautiful figurines. "I know what I'm doing. Here." I tossed one Sai to Leo and he caught it. The next second, I struck, forcing his hand to defend. The metal clanged as the daggers clashed, the prong guards jamming into each other.

"Stop," Leo ordered. "We're not training with weapons."

I winked, drugged by the surge of power the Sais instilled into me. "Then *disarm* me."

Leo shoved against me and then pointed the butt end of the handle towards me. His other arm rose defensively.

"Seriously, I'm not doing this."

I stepped back, but struck again, plunging to the left, and then the right of him, my blade colliding with his.

Leo's reflexes were extra sharp with weaponry. I'd have to ask what his choice weapon was. Suddenly, something occurred to me, something so obvious I wondered if I had always known it.

I knew exactly how to win. *And oh, how badly I want to win.*

"I bet you twenty I can take you down." I swapped the dagger to my left hand.

"Great, you're one of those," he sighed, "thinking you're invincible with a blade. But I ain't game."

I ignored the underlying warning in his tone, rolled my wrist a few times, and charged at him. He dodged, and void of choices had to fend off my attack. I let Leo lock me in a grip, my Sai's sharp end twisted towards my arm.

"Happy now?" he snarled in my ear. "You lost your bet and I'm confiscating your blades, *psycho*."

Think again.

I pressed against the sharp blade. Leo's hold loosened as his dagger met resistance against my skin.

"What are you doing?"

"*Winning*." I thrust forward, barely grimacing as the fine blade cut into the skin on my upper arm. Immediately, Leo's arm went limp, and the Sai clang to the floor. I tripped him over and crouched on top of him as he hit the ground, pointing the dagger to his throat.

"Having fun losing?"

For once Leo's thoughts were clear as a summer sky. First, came the shock as his rounded eyes saw drops of blood fall from my arm onto his T-shirt; he thought he had hurt me accidentally. Then the penny started its downfall as the skin around his eyes tightened and his nostrils flared. Before the muscles on his face had turned fully livid, I quickly backed away.

Leo got up slowly—focused—causing a shiver to run through me.

I attempted a smile, aware it would not bend the tight line of his mouth.

Leo twisted my wrist, his thumb digging in. With a slight groan, I unclenched my fingers and let him take the dagger—barely smeared in blood—still in my hand. Leo picked up the other one and shoved the daggers on top of the drawer.

It was then the pain from the cut registered. Blood flowed in warm trickles down my arm, reaching my wrist. *Simple flesh wound, a small price to pay.*

157

I aimed for the bathroom, but a hand locked around my better arm, forcing my shoulder close to my ear.

"*You—*" Leo dragged me to the kitchen and yanked a chair from under the table. "Sit." The chair slid a few centimetres with a screech as he rammed me on it.

I assessed the bleeding wound. "It's just a cut, a scratch really."

"Don't—just don't," Leo bit out, his rising temper rolling off his shoulders in waves as he tried to control himself.

I pulled a face at his back as he marched towards the bathroom, returning with a hand towel. I winced at the heavy-handedness as he pressed the towel on the cut. Sympathy would be hard to tease out of him now.

"You think that was clever?" The pressure didn't give as Leo pulled a chair in front of me and lifted his leg on it rather than sitting down. His stare left little wiggle room.

"You're the one always telling me to use my gift. So, I did."

"Cheap. Shot. You ever do that again and I'm done training you." Leo's tone was more of an accusation than a threat, although I had little doubt he meant every word.

"It doesn't work like that and you know it," I stated calmly. "I don't make up other people's weaknesses; I just know them. Why you're so bothered if you hurt me, is your weakness, not mine."

Leo's teeth gritted, and it reminded me of a wolf snarling. He started wiping the blood from my arm.

"Don't *ever* do that again," he maintained. "You don't win a fight by letting go of your defences and hurting yourself! It should be common sense."

I bit my lower lip and pretended to examine the cut again.

This wasn't the first time I was having this conversation and he wasn't the first person to call me up on it.

Leo tossed the bloodied towel over to the sink. "Where's your first aid kit?"

I pointed at the drawer by his feet. As he rummaged it, I stepped to the kitchen sink. The water ran a faded red as the rest of the blood washed off. When I turned the tap off, Leo handed me some kitchen roll to dry off.

"Sit down so I can have a better look."

Bossy, bossy. How long was he going to stay sour?

"It's only shallow and *you're* overreacting."

"You might need stitches and *you* shut up." Leo pinched the skin to determine the depth of the cut. I whimpered more for protest than pain.

He disinfected the wound, fastened a bandage onto my upper arm and tapped it twice, ignoring my huffing. Then, he straightened up.

"I'm taking those daggers, *and* I'm booking you an appointment with a psychiatrist."

"This has nothing to do with the daggers. I can handle them."

He pointed a finger at me. "Consider it the price to pay for letting you off easy. You've also officially killed training for the rest of the day." *I figured as much.* "Which leaves me no reason to stay." Tight-jawed, Leo walked out of the kitchen. His slightly rounded posture stamped the guilt into my chest.

"Wait—" I went after him, and he stopped, only to turn his head to the side. I swallowed hard. "Don't be angry."

Leo's shoulders widened, lifting his posture. "What difference does it make? I thought we weren't friends."

"We're not," I hurried to say. "But...you're not intolerable either."

Leo faced me, keeping a hand behind his back. "Fine. I'm not angry." He faked a grin. "Happy?"

I racked my brain trying to come up with something to say, all the while wondering why I felt the need to make amends.

"Thanks for the lift." I dropped my gaze, feeling warmth rush to my cheeks. *What the heck is wrong with me?*

"Anytime, *partner*." He unleashed his signature smile.

"Don't ruin the *one* day I haven't felt an urge to chop your head off."

"So, you compensated by trying to chop your own instead?"

"I wasn't trying to..." The sentence wilted into a sigh as I realised it was pointless.

159

Leo backed up to the door, tipping an imaginary cap, and picked up the bag of his clothes and left.

Slight remorse for treating him unkindly gripped me until I turned to the chest of drawers.

He'd taken my daggers.

Chapter 25

"This looks amazing." I could nearly taste the main course—steak and roasted vegetables presented in a tower arrangement—based on the scent.

The restaurant for Tony and Jill's family engagement dinner was the real deal, chandeliers and lines of cutlery surrounding each plate. I'd been introduced to both sets of parents, grandparents and a bunch of relatives I'd soon forget, and sampled a starter that could only be described as a fishy mousse.

I was eager for the main course.

"Lana, you're missing out." Annie tutted next to me as she swallowed her first mouthful, disapproving of Lana's plate of vegetables and tofu steak. "You're not even a vegetarian."

Defensive, and obviously coveting Leo's steak by her plate, Lana patted her flat stomach and pouted her mulberry-painted lips. "This dress wasn't made to fit a steak."

It was questionable whether it was made to fit a person.

"So, Camilla" —I clenched my teeth as if on cue at the sound of Leo's voice— "what happened to your arm?"

Oh, no you didn't...

Leo's knife pointed to my upper arm, to the healing scar no one had noticed or cared to mention for the past hour, even though my gown was a halter-neck.

"What'd you do, Milla? Walked into a knife?" Tony chewed with his usual gusto, eyeing me from under his brow.

"Let me see." Jill reached over Annie to touch my arm. Her face said it all: on me, a cut was never just a cut. She assumed the worst and Leo knew she would. *Traitor.*

"It's nothing." I shot a warning to Leo. "I bumped into a shelf in a shop."

"I don't know." Leo sucked in a breath. I wished it'd been his last. "It sure doesn't look like a cut you'd get from a shelf. It's too neat."

What is he doing now? Payback? He was the one who stole my daggers. *I* was angry at *him.*

I kicked at his foot under the table—and made Lana yelp in pain.

"Sorry, Lana, foot cramp…." I rubbed my shin for even a pinch of validity.

"Leo's right, it looks more like you've been knifed." Jill leaned forward, pressing her elbows on the table, sounding concerned—and a little disappointed?

"Well, *detective*"— I pulled a face at Leo— "if you're that interested, it wasn't so much the shelf but a nail that stuck out of the shelf that cut me. At the supermarket." I flicked my hair back. "Really, it's not a big deal." I popped a carrot in my mouth in a hurry, accidentally biting my inner cheek in the process. I soothed the sting with my tongue, wishing for the conversation to die down.

I almost had my wish.

"Hmm, prone to accidents, then? Bit of a klutz…?" *The man cannot take a hint, can he?* "You know, bad balance is often the cause of clumsiness. I could teach you some exercises that would help," Leo said, perfectly composed with a twinkle in his eye he hid nearly too well.

Tony choked out a laugh, curiosity and amusement playing for prime position on his face.

"*Thanks*, Leo. How…considerate. But I'll be okay." I plastered on a smile.

"Maybe you could teach me, Leo. My balance is shocking!" Lana ran her fingers along Leo's forearm. If steak wasn't such a rare luxury I would've puked.

Leo recovered from his coughing fit.

"Speaking of balance, Lana. You sure you should be drinking all that if you're driving?" Annie—who I was beginning to like for her call-it-as-you-see-it honesty—pointed at the empty wine glasses in front of Lana, taking the heat off me.

I downed a glass of water and poured more. I wasn't sure what Leo was trying to achieve with the little episode but keeping our truce must not be on top of his list.

I dug my head down and tackled the main course. Gladly, I was left to it until everyone had finished and Tony announced a little break before the dessert.

I excused myself.

"Milla, wait up." Jill's high heels clicked against the stone floor as she grabbed me by the elbow on my way to the bathroom. Annie bypassed us with an acknowledging smile.

"What's up?"

"That's what I wanted to ask you." Jill lowered her voice, ushering me next to the large plant that brightened up the otherwise plain hallway. "What's going on with you and Leo?"

I'm going to break his neck, that's what.

"Uh, I don't follow."

"*Come on.*" The end of Jill's earring folded on her collarbone as she tilted her head. "I'm not stupid. There's something going on, I can see the looks. Besides, he can barely take his eyes off you, even with Lana jabbering in his ear all night." Jill straightened the white ribbon interrupting her deep-red dress at the waist. "Have you guys come to an agreement of some sort?"

"We've" —I wished the gown gave a little more breathing space— "had a chat."

Jill's eyes lit up like a sparkler on bonfire night. "Really? You guys are friends now? We can stop walking on eggshells?"

I traced the wall with my fingers to busy my hands. "We can co-exist. No big deal."

Jill beamed, clearly dying to tell Tony and ask more questions, when her mum interrupted us by wrapping her arms around Jill's teeny waist. She needed Jill for something and ushered her back to the dining room.

"It's amazing how much they look alike, isn't it?" Annie whispered into my ear, making me jump. *Can everyone sneak up on me these days?*

I followed her gaze to Jill and her mum walking along the corridor.

"You'd never guess she was adopted," Annie thought out loud.

My jaw dropped. "Jill's adopted?"

163

"You didn't know?" She took my blank face as a no. "Oh—she was adopted when she was four. Sorry, I thought you knew. She's pretty open about it." Annie swayed her head as if dancing to a tune.

"I guess it never came up." What did I expect? I hadn't exactly been an ambassador for all things open and honest.

I smiled at Annie and excused myself for some fresh air.

The restaurant's decked patio was lit by large, metal pillars shaped like a candlestick. There was a circle of granite benches, periodically interrupted by flower arrangements, in the middle of the space.

I wasn't the first to arrive.

Leo greeted me with a nod as he perched on one of the benches, his legs straight in front of him.

"Where's your groupie?" I claimed a seat on the bench next to him.

"I'm assuming you're referring to Lana?" He quirked his lips. "She's… somewhere."

I reached forward enough to slap the back of Leo's head. "Thanks a lot for the scar. I thought we'd agreed on a low profile."

Leo revealed his pearly whites again. "You had it coming."

"Says you, *thief*. I want my Sais back." When his only reply was a half-hearted eye-roll, I let it go and turned my focus to the surrounding windows. The rest of the restaurant was quiet, with only a few people dining in the main room. I ignored the nagging feeling that I was actually glad to talk to Leo alone.

The steak must've been more wine-infused than I thought.

"Will you stop that?"

"Stop what?" Leo's voice was velvet.

"Staring at me like I'm a traffic light. It's weird."

Leo chuckled to himself and retracted whatever he was about to say. "You look happy," he said after a moment.

I lowered my chin, choosing to ignore his comment.

Leo's gaze still burned my face. Hadn't anyone ever taught him it was rude to stare?

"Did you know Jill was adopted?" I asked, shifting his attention.

"Yes, of course. Why?"

"No reason." I balanced my feet on the heels, staring at the faint scuff marks on the tips of the shoes.

"You only just found out?" Leo cottoned on.

I lifted one of my bare shoulders. "Annie mentioned it in passing." I wasn't sure why it bugged me. "Guess I'm no good at this friendship thing." I made a face to deflect the topic and again we fell quiet, bar from Leo tapping his shoes against the tarmac.

"If I asked you something would you promise to say yes?" he said, serious this time.

I declined, obviously, but eased my expression when I saw Leo looking foreign in his own skin.

"Kalika, I need to tell you something."

Air filled my lungs. It wasn't news Leo was hiding things from me. Was I ready to know what it was?

A shiver crept up my spine and suddenly, I was brutally aware of how little protection the silky dress offered in the light breeze. Or was there a breeze?

"This is not the place, though," Leo added after a while, and I felt like I'd dodged a bullet. "I wanna take you somewhere. For a day. Away from here where we can talk without distractions."

"I don't think that's such a good idea."

"Please. I *need* to tell you something. Something I should've told you a long time ago, but—" Leo buried his head into his hands.

I was sure my heart was going to thump its way out of my chest. Leo, still hunching, looked as if he was weighed down by a physical burden that was getting too heavy to carry.

"Le—"

"*Leo!*" Lana shrieked as the door to the patio burst open. "There you are! I was beginning to think you were hiding from me on purpose!" Lana's tipsy brawl felt out of place in the cocoon I had thought we were in. Tony's cousin, whatever his name was, stumbled in, hanging onto Lana's hooked arm. Within a nano-second, Leo's face airbrushed back into party mood.

"Just getting some fresh air; trying to make room for dessert." Leo slid sideways on the bench and Lana sat next to him. "You alright, Dave?" He knuckle-punched Tony's cousin, who took a seat by me.

"Camilla, is it?" Dave slurred so close to my cheek the alcohol on his breath made me a little drunk.

I shuffled further from him, trying to keep it inconspicuous.

"Now, how Tony manages to befriend such fine-looking people is beyond me." Dave's eyes lingered a little too long, a little too low. "Your boyfriend's a lucky guy."

"Don't have one." I rose from the bench; the fresh air had turned sour.

Lana giggled for no obvious reason. Yes, bringing her car tonight was plain idiotic.

"Aw, where you going, love? I only just got here."

I smiled politely, reminding myself Jill wouldn't appreciate her dinner guests leaving with a broken nose.

"I think it's time for dessert." I brushed the creases from my dress.

Dave got up to follow me and took support from my shoulder as he lost his balance. I staggered in my high heels as his weight pressed down on me.

In a flash, Leo appeared next to Dave, placing a firm hand on his shoulder. "Alright, bro, time to switch for coffee."

Dave said something incomprehensible but didn't seem to mind Leo's subtle direction. Lana, still tittering, followed us indoors.

"Oh, Leo," I called behind him. "I hear the forecast is looking bright for next weekend."

Chapter 26

Palpitations. Sweaty hands. If I didn't know any better, I'd say I was nervous.

As the boxing gloves hit the corner, several gulps of water were already down my throat. The punching bag swung from side to side, easing itself into a gentle rhythm.

"Stressful morning?" a man on a cross-trainer panted.

"Sorry?" I tossed the paper cup in the bin.

"Just saying," —he gestured towards the punching bag— "I'd hate to be on the receiving end."

I smiled, threw in a lame joke and headed for the dressing rooms. Leo was to pick me up soon.

My pulse refused to settle. I'd have to hear Leo out. I had to know what he was hiding, but at the same time, could I handle what he had to say?

I angled my face up to the showerhead, the water cooling my cheeks. I had a feeling I'd soon be facing past demons.

There weren't many I could handle.

*

The knock on the door came. Though expected, it still startled me, accelerating my heart to heavy, short thuds. I took a moment to prepare myself before unlocking the door.

An expressionless Leo stood on the doorstep and we stared at each other for several seconds, passively mimicking each other's body language.

"Come on, then. Let's get this over with," I finally caved, breaking the spell, and followed Leo to the car a pace behind. "Where are you taking me, anyway?"

Leo opened the car door for me. "I rented a cottage in the woods about an hour away."

"Please tell me you're joking."

"Why would I be joking?" he returned.

"*Seriously?* A cottage in the woods?" I was sure I looked as unimpressed as I sounded.

"What's wrong with that?"

"Nothing." I laughed dryly. "If this is a romantic mini-break or the site for my brutal murder."

He locked the doors for effect as he slid me a lazy look. "You'll just have to wait and see then, won't you?"

After fifty minutes of driving, Leo turned onto a path barely wide enough for a car. We slowed down to a snail's pace, jolting in our seats thanks to the bumps on the road. One pothole away from my limit, a small, wooden cottage revealed itself behind a bend. Past the run-down exterior, I suspected the cottage had heart.

We stopped on the unruly bed of grass, a few metres from the porch, for a moment listening to birdsong. I admired the large, rounded logs weathered by time. There were two small windows facing the front. Three slightly slanted steps led to the porch, which was a square decking decorated by a dead potted plant.

How Leo had found out about the place was, well, not something I really cared about.

"Is this when the murdering takes place?" I muttered.

"If you keep up the sarcasm, it might." Leo got out and pulled out a bag from the back seat. "Come on. I'll fix us up some lunch."

Of course. The guy was obsessed with me eating.

The last bite of the sandwich yelled at me from the plate. One bite, one tiny bite that could've easily been consumed with the last one.

But it wasn't just a bite of a sandwich. It was the only thing standing in the way of knowing and not knowing. It was the excuse to postpone the inevitable. It would take less than ten seconds to chew it, swallow it and wash any remains of it down with a drink. Then there'd be nothing to do with my hands, nothing to occupy my mouth, nothing to…distract.

Leo pretended to busy himself behind me. The charge in the air was different from usual. The smell of stale peat and varnish would now forever be associated with this moment: the moment when one last bite of a sandwich screamed at me on my plate.

"Are you going to eat that?" Leo's hand hovered over the plate.

I narrowed my eyes at the offending piece and popped it in my mouth. *Stop being a chicken, Kalika.*

I pushed my chair back and walked from the kitchen area to the open-planned lounge. Two armchairs faced each other by the fire, separated by an Ikea coffee table. A neon green vase on the table added a stroke of colour to the otherwise brown-dominant room.

"How much longer are we going to drag this out?" I swiped a finger along the mantle; someone had been to dust.

Leo took position by the kitchen table.

"You should sit down."

"I'd rather stand." My gaze flirted with the woodwork on the doorframe, and the freedom it led to.

"Kalika, this isn't going to be easy to explain, so I need you to listen until I'm finished. I need to tell you the *whole* truth before you go AWOL on me."

"Who says I'm gonna leg it?"

Leo grimaced half-heartedly. "Your track record."

"Just say what you have to say."

"You need to promise to hear me out fully," Leo insisted.

"*Fine.*" The irritation stemmed from my nerves. I perched on an armrest. "What's this about?"

Leo leaned against the table, palms gripping the edge. "I lied to you before." He slid his thumb along his eyebrow. "I never wanted to, but I thought it'd be best. Otherwise, you'd never have listened to anything I had to say."

"The truth hasn't exactly been the cornerstone of our oddball relationship, so if you think telling me whatever is bugging you is going to make me roll over and come back, you're wrong." My jaw jutted forward as I watched Leo sigh. His shoulders were sunken with the weight of the world; his eyes reminded me of someone else's...*his* eyes. Near the end, *his* pupils had been as Leo's now were: oceans of unexplained mysteries I wasn't allowed to dive into.

169

My shields shot up as if from a press of a button. I wasn't ready to venture down this road.

"Why are you really here?" I asked regardless.

"That much I never lied about. The purpose was always to bring you back to re-join the Guard as my partner."

"Why?"

"To fight the Gorahites," he stated. "There's a force stronger than before rising in Gorah. They have slowly infiltrated our lines, and now many live among us, spreading their evil from within."

Narun under threat didn't sit well with me.

"I meant, why you and I? What could possibly make *us* so special?"

"There was a prophecy."

Oh.

The tension started easing on my shoulders. "You should never build your life on prophecy, you know that. They change with…choices. What the Council foresaw must've been before I left. The Council must've been mistaken."

"It wasn't the Council who foresaw it."

I scoffed. "Great, you're telling me all this is based on some—"

"It was Kailen."

The name knocked me with the force of a sledgehammer. The pain flooded in from the hole in my chest, spreading with each pump of blood further into me. Like fire it burned, taking life as it consumed and roared into larger, hungrier flames.

Someone pleaded for my attention, but the ringing in my ears was too loud, too demanding.

My Kailen.

Chapter 27

Death. Pain. Torture. Capture. Fear.

My insides wanted to crawl out of me, out of the moment, out of the fate they were faced with.

Kailen was on his knees a few feet from me, his head bowed, arms tied behind his back. Blood trickled from a wound in his forearm and dripped in heavy drops from his mouth. The soldier behind him kicked him in the side and I tensed up as if feeling the stab in my ribs.

"Stop it! Stop hurting him!" I shrieked, before taking a hit in the face from a soldier in front of me. The man behind me, holding me still, tightened his grip. "Let him go!"

"Useless." The ginger-haired soldier in front spat on the ground. "Don't waste your breath. The only thing waiting for him is a long, agonising death. Unless he tells us what we need to know."

My whole body shook out of fear. The thought of them torturing him was excruciating.

How did this even happen? It had been a standard mission, minimum risk. Yet here we were faced with the unspeakable. Faced with...

No, they couldn't take him away from me. Not him. I couldn't breathe without him.

The ginger-haired soldier laughed at me. "Aww, little girl, shaking in her boots... I thought they raised warriors in Narun."

The other soldiers joined him in laughter and I screamed and thrashed as the soldier behind me licked my neck, sliding his hand up my stomach.

"Kali...don't—" Kailen started, but his captor kicked him again.

The Ginger placed a hand on my throat, squeezing it until I couldn't scream even if I wanted to. "I have a proposition for you, Kali..." He pulled out a knife, letting the cool blade rest against my temple.

I gagged for air.

"Renounce your King and join us"—the soldier's breath was offensive on my skin—"and your boy won't suffer anymore."

Kailen struggled against his captor and shouted something at me, but I could only focus on the oxygen draining out of my lungs and the tiny blood vessels popping in my eyes.

I gasped loudly as the soldier released my throat, and I swallowed chunks of air at once.

"What do you say, little girl?" He pulled on my hair, tilting my head, so I could see the blade on Kailen's throat, his eyes in anguish. I felt everything inside of me crumble. And I cried. Like a little girl.

The soldier was right. I wasn't a warrior.

"Please... let us go," I sobbed. I was weak. Everything about me screamed 'weak'. How had I not known all this before? Kailen had been the strong one and the thought of losing him—I'd be nothing.

"Join us and he won't suffer." The ginger soldier repeated with a nasty drawl in his voice. "Simple as that."

Kailen shook his head. But he knew.

No one could save us. They had us. They would decide our fate. They would make Kailen—

"I'll join you," I heard myself saying. The voice of reason was bound and locked up in the back of my brain.

"Kali, no, don't listen to them!" Kailen's orders were muffled by an elbow smacking his mouth. I ripped myself free, only to be caught by the ginger soldier.

"A-a-a," he tutted. "Not so fast, little girl. I fear I can't simply take your word for it, no more than you can mine." His eye twitched at every other word while his fingers dug into my jaw. "Renounce the King...by killing one of your own. Or your partner and yourself will watch each other writhe in pain for a very long death." He jerked up his chin, and the soldier behind Kailen forced him to stand.

Kailen's swollen face met mine and the pieces that were already shattered inside of me pulverized. I felt the pain he felt. I felt the sorrow burdening him. Yet his greatest weakness was me.

He feared for me.

The soldier picked up Kailen's sword and wrapped my fingers around its handle. "Kill him. It's the only way to guarantee he won't suffer in our hands."

172

There was no hope left. I couldn't watch Kailen suffer. I couldn't handle the knowledge that he would suffer.

But I could never take his life.

"Kill him and I'll believe you have renounced the King of Narun," the ginger soldier whispered by my ear. "The King of Gorah will welcome you and no harm will come to you. You can end your partner's sufferings now."

To my surprise, Kailen stood still. Without objection, he looked at me with eyes that tried to communicate an ocean of emotions. Maybe he wanted me to do it. Maybe he was begging me to do it.

I swallowed, tasting blood, loosely holding the sword, its point touching the ground. My eyes flickered to the soldier holding onto Kailen and I saw my chance. The soldier was distracted—unprepared.

I had to try.

I tightened my grip and turned to the ginger-haired soldier. "With this kill," I said in a voice that sounded too robotic and pitched to be mine. "I renounce the King." I grabbed the sword with both hands, swivelled, and plunged the blade into the soldier's stomach.

"Kali..." Kailen spluttered, blood dripping from his mouth.

My breathing stopped as my eyes shifted from my arm, along the sword, and into Kailen's pierced stomach.

A noose tightened around my heart.

I pulled the sword out, causing Kailen to drop to his knees. The sword fell to the ground with a thud.

What was happening?

I staggered back, struggling for breath, desperate for a thought that made sense. How? How was it possible? How could I...? I hadn't...? Had I...?

NO.

I lurched to grab a hold of Kailen's arms, his warm blood soaking my clothes. I couldn't speak, I couldn't hear, I couldn't see what my eyes were seeing.

It could not be true.

"Kali—"

And then there was nothing.

Chapter 28

Hands shook me, cupped my face, forcing me to look past *his* beautiful face in my mind's eye into a face that was...*not his.*

"Kali, listen to me, you *need* to listen!"

The sweet smell of peat brought me back to reality. I was on the floor, not sure how I ended up there.

"Look at me." The voice, *Leo's* voice, beckoned me, and then reason dawned. As quickly as it had gone, it returned.

"How dare you speak his name?"

Leo's fingers dug on my shoulders, his eyes desperate to lock into mine. "You need to listen to me carefully," he said. "It wasn't just the Council who sent me here, it was Kailen. He asked—*begged* me to find you! He made me promise I wouldn't give up on you no matter what."

I shook myself free from Leo's hold. How could he feed me such lies? "This is low even from you." My teeth ground against each other. "Using *him* to persuade me? Have you no shame?"

"You're not listening! This was Kailen's plan! He saw the future, he saw what was coming, and he took it to the Council and convinced them too. He'd seen his destiny, and yours. *It had to happen.* For the sake of Narun, for your sake. You were everything to him."

My chin quivered as I fought the stinging in my eyes. "You're lying."

"I'm not, I ca—"

"You're lying, and you know how I know? Because he's *dead*! He's gone because of me! I killed him, I ran a sword *through* him." The tears flooded, spilling down my cheeks salty and warm. My muscles shook, unable to control themselves.

"You didn't kill him, Kali! I know that's what you think, but—"

"You don't know what happened that day. You don't know *anything*!" I swung my arms, but Leo caught them into his firm grip.

"I know *everything*, Kalika." He sounded forlorn. "I know because I was there. Since the day Kailen had his vision, he took me under his wing and convinced me to spy on you two training, so I'd learn how you fought." Leo took a quick breath and lowered his voice. "I was there for *years*, Kali. I saw how you loved him and he loved you, how he protected you, how he would've done anything for you. I was there because he was preparing me to take his place. He knew what the outcome of the battle was going to be that day and he knew what it would do to you, but he'd seen there was no other way. He made me promise—" Leo's eyelids closed, the crease between his eyes deepening, and then he looked at me again.

"He made me *swear* to watch over you and I did, because he was like a brother and I would've done anything for him—just as I would for you." Leo's voice crumbled until it was nothing but a pained whisper.

"For years, Kali, I've looked from the side-lines, torn by the desire to be with you and the agony of knowing what would have to happen if I ever were to be with you."

I was numb to his confession. How could I even begin to digest his words?

"Kali, you didn't kill him." Leo was still on his knees in front of me, gripping my wrists. "He went to the battle knowing what would happen. He even knew you would blame yourself and it tore him apart, but he couldn't tell you the truth; you would've done everything you could to stop him and get yourself captured by the Gorahites. He'd seen the road you both had to walk."

"It was by my hand he died from—my sword, my mistake," I croaked barely audible.

Leo released my wrists and pressed his fingers to his temples. "No, it wasn't." His arms dropped to his sides. "He pushed the soldier aside and *ran* into your sword because he needed you to *think* he was dying. It was the only way to…to stop you from following him. He couldn't fool your gifting, he had to be wounded, *lethally* wounded."

"What are you saying?"

176

Leo's chin lowered. "He didn't foresee he was going to get killed that day. He saw his *capture* by the Gorahites."

The sledgehammer pounded into my chest a second time. I couldn't move lest my skin shattered into millions of pieces.

"I watched him dying; he lay on the ground, life ebbing away from his veins." The memory was fresh in my mind. It had never left. "He couldn't have survived it."

"You saw what he needed you to see. What you didn't know was that one of the soldiers was a Healer. As you know, Kailen would've known that. He told me he was gifted with the ability to pick up on people's skills." *He had picked up on mine straight away.*

"The soldier knocked you unconscious, so he could heal Kailen for interrogation in Gorah. They wanted him alive—it was all a part of their game." Leo let out a pained grunt. "Kailen had seen me coming, ready to attack, but I couldn't reach you until they knocked you out. Kailen demanded I take you to safety first, and I did. But when I returned, they'd taken him. They were gone. The body you saw burning when you came to wasn't his."

The smell of burning flesh returned to me, making me physically nauseous. None of it made sense.

"Why are you saying these things? He died that day and I am responsible for his death! *Me*, only me. I was his partner, and it was the sword in my hand that killed him—" My fingers wrapped around my neck, pulling at an invisible rope strangling me. "I couldn't even face his funeral. I had to get out of there, I had to leave."

"No, Kali," Leo said gently. "Kailen died sixteen days later, in Gorah, by the hands of his captors."

I closed my eyes, but it didn't help. I couldn't shut myself away from this. I couldn't silence the questions. I couldn't fight the doubt. I couldn't shake the image of my dripping sword as I pulled it out of Kailen's pierced stomach.

Sixteen days. I could've saved him. Instead, I was fleeing like a coward.

No. It couldn't be true.

"Stop messing with my head!" I held my skull as if to stop it from exploding into pieces.

"I realise this is overwhelming to take in, but Kailen was adamant everything had to happen as it did, for the sake of the future. It's the truth," Leo said quietly.

The truth? What was the truth anymore? There had been so many lies the truth would've got tangled in their web long ago. Whose truth mattered anyway? Mine? Leo's? Would either change anything?

It would change everything.

My breath paced itself to the thud in my temples. This had to be a dream. Some strange, parallel reality. A fantasy. A figment of my imagination. Anything, but the truth. The truth could not be *this*.

"Kalika, please, I know this is hard..." *Hard?* Had a word ever carried such meekness to it? "Try to understand. Kailen only wanted to protect you and the future of Narun, and so did I. I still do. It took him a long time to convince me to go along with his plan, but once he had won the Council over... I didn't know what else to do." Leo shook his head like it would undo what had been done. "Kailen kept saying it was for the greater good. Eventually, I began to see the bigger picture, and believe in it."

"Leave me alone," I snarled.

"Kali—"

"Stop calling me that!" I pulled my shoulders in. "That was *his* name for me."

"I'm sorry, I'm so sorry..."

Lifeless, I stared at Leo. "Leave me, Elikai."

"I don't think you should—"

"Go away, *now*."

Defeated, Leo retreated outside as my head buried itself into my hands.

Too much.

*

It was dark when the door opened, bringing in a gust of wind. I recalled little of the light retracting from the room. I hadn't moved.

How could I? Where would I have moved to? What reason was there to move? What place was there to go to that could change how I felt?

I was a statue, cemented to my faith.

Yet my mind stormed furiously, as it had ever since Leo left the room. It ached physically from the vastness of my thoughts.

Could it be true? If it was, everything I had believed in had been turned on its head. The past, every memory and every feeling with it, had been changed, snatched from me and exchanged for something...much crueller.

Could the man I'd known since I joined the Guard—who I'd grown to love, who I'd fought along with, and shared life with—have hidden such a secret? Could he have deceived me? Had he ever even loved me? Had *anything* he'd said been true?

A floorboard creaked nearby. Leo kneeled close to me.

"How do you feel?"

How did I feel? Betrayed. Wronged. Used. Confused. Guilty. Angry. Furious. Numb. Hurt. Lost. Every emotion under the sun and then some.

"What do you think?" I croaked, staring at my open palms.

"Do you want to talk about it?"

"What's there to talk about? How do I even know you're telling the truth?"

He didn't reply. I wasn't really expecting an answer anyway. Half of the 'confessions' hadn't even started to process through my brain. First, I needed to establish whether to believe him or not.

"When did he...when did Kailen see the—?"

"A year or so before he was captured."

I blinked rapidly to shun away the tears. *A year.* "That's when you first met him?"

"No," Leo admitted. "I'd known him for a little longer."

"How come he never mentioned you?"

Leo wavered. "Kailen wanted to keep it that way. Maybe he knew on some level—"

"*Knew?*" I glanced at him, my fingers curling. "You're saying that when we talked about our future together he was never even gonna go through with it? That all along he was actually preparing you as my next partner? That's *sick,* Leo."

"It's complicated." Leo rubbed the back of his head. "He didn't see us like that. He just saw the bigger picture—purpose."

"But that's not how *you* saw it." I shot back, my insides being wrung out to dry. At least I now had an emotion to channel on: anger.

"I never meant to fall for you, Kalika."

"I can't bear the sight of you." I angled away from him, staring at nothing.

"I know you'll need time to think this over, but—"

"No. No buts. I don't want anything to do with you. *Ever.*"

"In time—"

"*No,* Leo, don't you see?" I spat, Leo's dejected face doing nothing to melt the ice in my eyes. "I love Kailen. I'm responsible for his death and it doesn't matter what you say. I could've saved him. *You* should've saved him! You should've fought for him, gone after him, or at least, *told me* so I could follow him. Instead, you left me with a charred corpse—"

"I did follow him! That's why I left you because no matter how many times Kailen told me not to interfere, I couldn't leave him! I needed to try, but I was too late. I only caught one of the soldiers. That's how I know what happened before I found you."

So he knew. He knew I was a coward and a traitor.

"Then answer this: how could I possibly return and start over after all this?"

"Because that's what he wanted! It's your destiny, your calling. You can't turn your back on everything you are and who you're meant to be! How do you think he'd feel if he could see you now? See who you've become? See that his sacrifice was for nothing?"

The arrows punctured through my skin like I was made of feathers. I slapped his cheek. He took it. I slapped him again and picked myself up from the floor.

"I've nothing more to say. Either drive me back, or I'll walk home." I felt the burn of Leo's stare on me; a spot on the wall received my full attention. Waves of silence continued to hit ashore.

"I'll take you home."

Chapter 29

Somewhere between week two and three, I decided I had to leave the flat. The kitchen cupboards lay empty, the air cried for ventilation. The only conversation I'd had was when I informed work I quit for personal reasons.

The phone had rung without me caring to see who was ringing and knocks on the door had been pleading and concerned. After a few days, the phone battery had died and brought some peace.

The days rolling into another had passed with tears, fits of rage and numbing stillness. Reality and nightmares had blurred, and I had often wondered when I really was awake.

I turned off the shower and dried myself off with a scratchy towel. I was literally driving myself crazy. The mirror witnessed my hollow cheeks and rebuked me. I had to find a way to get over this. I had to. Here or there, I could not let his sacrifice be in vain.

Damn you, Leo.

I dug out clean clothes and mechanically brushed my hair back. Slowly, I was looking more like a human. At least, the shell of one.

I plugged in my phone and laid it on the bed. Calls from Leo, Jill, Tony, Sebastian, and a few unknown numbers, and messages from the same. I gathered Leo had filled Jill and Tony in as the messages soon changed in tone from clueless to concerned. Sebastian wondered where I had disappeared to. University informed me of a missed deadline and shocking attendance.

Then there was a message that brought a trickle of life into me, received over a week ago.

I read it, and read it again: *'Camilla, I wondered if we could meet for coffee? Let me know. Anita.'*

It might be exactly what I needed.

I texted back, apologising for the delay and querying when she was free. Then, I slid the phone in my pocket. The others could wait.

I had to get some air.

Warily, I slipped outside and stood with my back glued to the front door, devouring the oxygen for a few minutes. It was oddly warm, and a little too bright, yet the world stood annoyingly unchanged, clueless to the earthquakes in my life.

I ventured down the street, welcoming the blood starting to pump in my veins. Step by step, I was waking from the dead.

I was at the corner store when a text message beckoned my attention. Anita suggested lunch the next day. I confirmed, and then, basket in hand, stood still in the centre of the shop corridor, trying to second-guess Anita's motive, until a curious cashier came to ask if I was okay.

Quickly, I paid and walked back to the flat on autopilot. I was at the door, inches from my comfort zone when faint steps drew closer to me.

"Kalika," a strained voice said. I froze, pinpricks creeping up my scalp. "It's good to see you."

My arm fell to my side, the key remaining in the lock.

"I've been so worried...Will you please talk to me?" Leo's brokenness was unveiled, each word bearing witness to it.

Hardening myself to it, I faced him.

Dishevelled, emotionally tortured—that was the man in front of me, not the Leo with a crooked grin. In fact, he reminded me of myself from this morning. I had a feeling his car had been his bed for the last few weeks, parked in front of my house.

I dodged his bloodshot eyes the best I could.

"There's nothing left to say."

"I'm sorry, Kalika, so sorry. I never meant to—it wasn't meant to..." Leo ran his hands through his unkempt hair, settling them to the back of his head.

A sting of guilt started to pierce me. Not bearing the distress on his face, I whipped around and pushed the door open.

It was all too messed up.

*

Anita sat by a table next to the back wall, glancing at the menu, putting it back, shifting in her seat. I watched her through the coffee shop window, giving myself a pep talk. She looked well, that much I could tell. Her face was bright, excited even.

Why she wanted to meet me, was unclear.

I focused on the faint reflection on the glass. She could see I wasn't well. No amount of makeup could hide it.

I pulled a face at my own reflection and focused back to Anita as she checked her watch. *Time to go in.*

"Hi, Anita."

She smiled warmly, trying to hide both her relief that I had come and her worry for my worn face. "It's good to see you again. Please, take a seat." Anita motioned to the chair, her gaze never leaving me. I apologised for being late. "Don't worry—I was early. Anyway, how are you? You look...well?"

I fixed my eyes down at the table. "Anita, we both know that's the last thing I look like." I struggled not to tear up. I needed to unload onto her but there was no way I could pull her into any more drama.

"Oh, *honey.*" Anita reached her hand across the table but lowered it palm down inches from my hand. "Is everything okay?"

I swallowed, afraid I couldn't hold it together. "I've been going through some stuff. It's my own fault, really. I'll be fine."

"I'm sorry to hear that, Camilla."

"Actually, my real name is Kalika." I couldn't face any more lies, especially when it came to her.

"Ka-lika. It's pretty."

A waiter came and we both ordered soup, the first thing on the menu.

"Do you want to talk about it?"

"I-I'm sorry... I can't. Let's just say I'm—I'm doing some soul searching." I raised a shoulder and let it drop, hoping Anita would accept the answer.

She examined my face and pulled her hand back. "Ironic you'd say that." Anita fixed a strand of hair back to her bun. "That's actually why I wanted to see you. Ever since we *parted ways—*" I grimaced apologetically, but she flourished her fingers. "Water under the bridge, love. Anyway, you never left my thoughts. I understand you had your reasons for doing what you did and well, that's your business, no one else's."

I attempted to object, but Anita continued, "What I'm trying to say is that for someone going to the extent you went to, you must be really trying, and struggling, to find your place."

I held Anita in even higher esteem for not asking the questions most people would be dying to know.

"I take it since you're still here you're wanting to stay and start over?"

"That was the plan." My chin quivered. "Now I'm not sure if I can. Everything's so complicated."

"Well," —Anita stopped to thank the waiter as he brought out the food— "maybe I could help you."

I stirred a spoon in the soup; it smelled comforting. "I'm not sure I follow."

"Have you ever considered taking up medical studies?"

I jolted as the soup burned my tongue. "Medicine? Become a doctor?"

"Yes! Cam—*Kalika*, think about it. You need a plan for the future and the reason you're finding it hard to settle is that you're trying to turn your back on who you really are." Anita placed a napkin on her lap. "I don't really understand how but what you did with Aaron…it's a gift. You saved his *life*. Just think how many lives you could save…!"

"It's not that straightforward. I can't heal people, I only see what's wrong with them."

"Yes! What an advantage that'd be!" Anita pushed her bowl of soup aside.

"Really, it's not that simple."

"But it *can* be. I believe there's a reason you have this gift. You were born to make a difference, and deep down you know it."

I squirmed, her words hitting a spot. I hated feeling useless.

"Mull it over. You don't have to decide anything now." Anita buttered her bread roll before dunking it in her soup. "Mmm, this is delicious."

186

After we finished lunch I hugged Anita goodbye, and headed home, walking slowly along the streets.

What Anita had suggested sat right with me. For the first time in weeks, I held a glimmer of hope that there might be a way out of my imaginary prison cell. That there might be a way of making a difference, of righting wrongs, of...repayment.

Once I resolved the Blood Debt, I could start afresh—for the last time.

I swallowed the lump in my throat.

What if this was what I was meant to be doing all along? Maybe, just maybe, Kailen had been wrong?

Prophecies are conditional. They—

I jumped as a car cut into the pavement.

"Camilla! You're alive!" Sebastian shouted through the rolled-down passenger window, his face a beam of light. He reached over to open the door. "You lost your phone again?"

"Something like that." I placed a hand on the edge of the door, attempting at a casual expression. "I've had a lot going on."

My effort must've lacked conviction as Sebastian push out his bottom lip. "Sounds like you need some cheering up." He patted the passenger seat with his hand. "Hop in. I'm taking you out."

Without a second thought, I climbed in.

Chapter 30

Jill squeezed the air out of me and dragged me through the door to her flat.

"Are the doughnuts a peace offering?" She took the twelve-pack of iced doughnuts from me, still holding onto my arm. She looked as she had the last I saw her: as if nothing had happened.

"An attempt at one, at least." Bribery didn't seem like such a good idea anymore.

"Tony should be here any second," Jill noted and gestured for me to take a seat.

"I'm sorry I dropped off the grid again. It's not intentional, I swear." I sank into the sofa, elbow grazing the armrest. I should get them a recording of my apologies for Christmas.

Jill curled up on her usual armchair.

"Did Leo tell you what he told me at the cottage?" I asked carefully.

"Not really." Jill scrunched her nose. "He said it was between the two of you, which is fair enough. I gather it was a big deal, though."

Relief nudged the weight off my back. I wasn't sure I would've felt comfortable with Jill and Tony knowing everything. *I* wasn't even comfortable.

"He's pretty upset, you know." Jill fiddled with her sky-blue T-shirt. "Leo, that is. He's hardly left your street for the past weeks." She lowered her chin. "He wasn't too happy seeing you with Sebastian last night."

The thought of Leo being there when Sebastian had dropped me off—after we'd spent a few hours at the beach—hadn't even crossed my mind.

"That's what you get for spying on people."

"What were you doing with him?"

"Sebastian? I bumped into him and we hung out. I dozed off in the car, so he helped me inside."

Jill examined her nails. She had no intention of letting me in on her thoughts and I wasn't particularly eager to be in the know.

I slid my hands along my thighs just as a relaxed knock sounded from the door.

For some reason, I was nervous of seeing Tony, like it was the first time meeting my friend's boyfriend.

"Milla-Kalika! Whatever your name is…" Tony sauntered in and threw his arm around me as he joined me on the sofa. "I see you brought bribes!" He squeezed me for a few seconds, let go, and took the doughnuts from the coffee table. "Wise move."

"It's good to see you too, Tony."

Pink icing painted Tony's lips from a bite too big. He picked up another doughnut with his free hand, put the box down, and swung his legs on the coffee table, only for Jill to instantly whack them down. "You okay?" He frowned.

I pounded my fist once on Tony's knee. "I will be."

"Good. Now," he narrowed his eyes, "what you doing to my best man, though?"

"Tony!" Jill rebuked.

"What? She needs to know." Tony angled towards me. "He's a mess—worrying about you and kicking himself for doing this to you."

I stared at the corner of the table, elbows resting on my knees, fingers intertwined. *I was the mess.* "It's not that simple, Tony."

"Nothing ever is, Milla, but you gotta do something. And being whisked into your flat late at night by Sebastian doesn't help. Poor guy didn't know what to think."

"I never asked him to sleep outside my flat!" I stood up and paced to the window, feeling a flush spreading on my cheeks. I traced the line of my eyebrow with a finger, staring aimlessly.

I wasn't angry at Leo or Tony. I was angry at myself.

"I'm not trying to be harsh." Tony's tone had softened, probably from the effect of Jill's stern looks.

I jumped as he placed a hand on the back of my neck; I hadn't heard him walk over.

"Look, kiddo, I'm not saying you gotta become his partner, or even go back to Narun. But you need to talk to him, clear the air. Whatever this thing is between you, you have to sort it out. We want you to be happy. Both of you. So, figure out what you want."

What I want? Did it matter what I wanted? Kailen had made too many decisions for me. He'd taken away my choice when it really mattered. *Then I had taken his life.*

And now I was ruining Leo's.

"I'll...talk to him."

"Great." Tony swivelled me around to face him. It must've been my glistening eyes that made him pull me into his chest. "It's going to be okay, Milla."

I met his hug, drawing comfort from it. I didn't have a biological brother, but Tony came close.

"I owe you—a lot." I pushed myself back. "You too, Jill." I threw her an unusually coy smile.

"Of course you do, kiddo. At least three more boxes of doughnuts." Tony rocked my head gently from side to side with his palm, let go, and slapped me on the back of the head.

"What was that for?" I smoothed my hair down.

"*That* was for not returning my calls, *little sis.*" Tony scowled before throwing himself down on the sofa. "Don't do that again. If it wasn't for Leo keeping us updated, I would've kicked in your door."

"Sorry." I winced. "And FYI, I'm still older than you."

He ruffled my hair. "Whatever you say, little sis."

*

I peered through the window. Leo's car was still parked in the same spot as last night when Jill dropped me off home. The figure inside appeared to be asleep on the lowered driver's seat.

The figure moved, pulling its arms closer to its chest in a restless sleep. I watched for a couple more seconds as the wind orchestrated a battalion of leaves to pummel the windscreens of the other cars parked on the road.

Feeling confident I was doing the right thing, I pulled on my coat as I exited the flat, crossed the road and tapped on Leo's car window.

He jerked, scanning his surroundings whilst bringing himself to. As he saw me, he bolted upright and unlocked the door. I opened it but didn't climb in.

"Want to take a walk?"

Leo nodded and scrambled out of the car. For once he lacked his usual sleekness of movement. I took in his crinkled clothes and weathered face. The realisation that I was the cause for his unkempt state filled me with remorse. No matter how much grief I thought he had caused me, I had no doubt directly contributed to the worst past years of his life.

"How are you doing?" His voice panted with emotion.

I took a moment, surprised I didn't feel more uncomfortable with his presence. "I've had time to think things through." I walked along the narrow pavement. Had Leo not opted for the road by the curb, we would've walked shoulder to shoulder. "You?"

Leo took a stab at his signature grin. "I'm okay."

I wasn't convinced.

Stiff as robots, we headed to the park and settled into a pace slow for both of us. I hugged myself to keep the wind from blowing through me.

Either Leo was out of words out or he was waiting for me to take the lead. I held on until we were on the park path.

Finally, I sucked in the damp air and said, "Leo, I owe you an apology."

"You don't owe me anything."

"I do" —I touched his arm and regretted it, pulling my hand back swiftly— "I've been so self-centred I haven't really considered your side of the story. I'm sorry about that."

Leo lifted his eyes from the path to the horizon.

"I also need to tell you what I've decided to do, and it's only right I don't prolong it." I inhaled courage and exhaled it at the same breath. This time when I grabbed his arm to stop him, I let my hand stay, forcing composure.

I have to do this right.

"Leo, in spite of everything I now know, I've decided to stay here for good. And I want you to go back home, rebuild your life and do

192

something that will bring you… purpose." I was locked in his stare, ignoring the subtle changes in his face.

"Kalika, you know I won't—"

"No. Listen to me." I blinked slowly. "I sound like an old record, but…*I know now*. I know why you did what you did, and I know about Kailen. I've thought about this *a lot* and I feel my place is here. I can do something with my life, start over again, but this time do it right. I can use my gifting *here*."

Leo remained unfazed, his exterior icing over. "Your calling is in Narun."

"Not anymore." I gestured to a bench to dodge a pair of runners passing us on the path. Neither of us sat on it. "You know as well as I do that visions are conditional. What Kailen saw was a long time ago."

"Doesn't matter."

"Leo, there's nothing left for me in Narun, nothing but pain and regret. I was never a warrior! I renounced the King because I was a coward, and whether you think I killed Kailen or not, I will always hold myself accountable."

"You *didn't* kill Kailen!" His anger harshened his word. "Anyone would agree, and if you need the King's pardon, he will grant it."

I sucked in my lips and raised my fingers over my mouth. *How can I get through to him?* "I've made up my mind. I'm not going back."

"I'm not going to give up on you. I promised him. I promised myself."

"You're not giving up; I'm releasing you from that promise by telling you that my place is here and yours… Well, we both know you still have a future in Narun. You can still fight for the King. It's just not me anymore." I ignored the twinge in my gut.

Leo remained rigid. His blue ocean-eyes were packed with so many emotions it ached to look at them.

"You don't know what you're saying." His voice changed like it did when his exterior became a mask. "You're choosing the easy road because you're so lost it seems like the only alternative. You're wasting your life running after something that will bring you no purpose, and with it, no fulfilment."

193

I rubbed the back of my neck, letting it hang. I took a step back, and forth, and back again. Leo's jawline pulsed as he gritted his teeth.

"I talked to Anita a few days ago. She suggested I study medicine to help people with my gift. She said I could make a real difference and I believe her. And I have friends who—"

"Like Sebastian?" Leo scoffed, catching me off-guard, but I managed to internalise the surprise.

Instead, I shrugged at his biting tone. "Yes, he's a friend." My lips searched for words until I'd considered everything possible to say and decided against it.

It turned out the silence spoke more.

Leo's composure wavered. His eyes were both fierce and hurt, and they held mine captive.

It was Leo who broke the connection.

"I wish I could make you see what you're giving up," he started slowly. "I wish I could stop you from making the biggest mistake of your life. I wish I could—" Leo looked down, face twisting with emotion. I swallowed, throat dry. When he lifted his chin up again, it was a different person in front of me.

"—but I can see you've made your choice. I'll go back. Alone. You won't see me again after today." Leo turned and walked off before the extent of his words had sunk in fully.

"Wait!" I jogged after him and stopped as he did. Without giving me a glimpse of his face, he raised his hand.

"I've waited long enough. Goodbye, Kalika."

Shivers crawling up my spine, I could but stare as he walked out of my life. As soon as he was out of sight, I buried the memory of his crooked smile into the hole gaping wide open in my chest.

Chapter 31

He was gone. Leo had held true to his word.

I pressed the phone close to my ear, shocked at the suddenness of the news.

"You still there?" Jill queried on the other end of the line.

"Yes." I gathered my bearings. "Just surprised he actually left. So soon." Had it not been merely two days since I talked to him? What had I expected?

"I know." Jill breathed heavy. "He came by yesterday to say his goodbyes. He couldn't stay another day from the sound of it. I was kind of hoping he'd change his mind."

I stood at the centre of my bedroom, at a loss for words. He was really gone?

"—but he rang to say he's on his way home, wherever that is."

I barely registered what Jill was saying.

"He just left," I stated, mainly for myself.

"Isn't that what you wanted? Him getting his life back?"

Had that been what I wanted? "Of course. I want him to be happy." *Was I happy?*

"He wasn't sure if he'd come back for the wedding," Jill said. "Tony's been pretty bummed out."

"I'm sorry to hear that." The weight of blame nearly caused my knees to buckle.

"It's not your fault."

Except that it was. I sighed and kicked the bed.

"Anyway, I thought you'd want to know." The line rattled, and I pictured Jill puttering around her flat. "I'm actually on my way out. My mum's over for a few days."

"Yeah, sure. Thanks. Have a great time." I failed to sound upbeat.

I tossed the phone on the bed. *Leo was really gone.* The room suddenly felt pressing, the walls inched their way closer. I needed space—fresh air.

It was grey outside; the whole day had been overcast.

I crossed the road but steered away from the park; too many memories to be thinking clearly. Instead, I jogged towards the industrial area. The factories would have closed and emptied of workers.

Even though I'd finally had my wish, something bugged me. Maybe it was the slightly eerie evening, or that I had lost a training partner and sort of a friend.

I rounded a corner, leaving the housing estate behind. I took a step off the curb, but my foot never hit the ground. An arm wrapped around my neck and yanked me back. A smell familiar somehow engulfed me as a cloth was pressed tightly over my mouth and nose.

My arms flung to fight, but it was too late. The force behind me had the upper hand. I was slipping, fading…. Darkness.

*

A motor purred, steady and monotonous. I was moving, but not of my own will. My eyes blinked open, but it made little difference; the dark refused to subside.

This must be a dream.

I struggled to breathe as if the light was my source of oxygen. My arms didn't cooperate, my legs wouldn't move.

Hold on. The smell—pungent and overpowering—lingered faintly in my nostrils reminding me of something.

My muscles trashed. I wasn't asleep. I was drugged.

Clarity of thought overtook the haze and I became aware of thick tape restraining my wrists behind me. My ankles shared the same fate. I attempted to roll on my back, only for my head and side to collide against the limits of the space. With force, my thoughts met each other: I'd been kidnapped.

A scream rose in my throat, but it never made it past the strip of tape fastened over my mouth. Futile, I wrestled against the ties but soon surrendered. Whoever took me had wanted me to stay put.

The darkness was thick but judging from the small space and the humming, I was inside the boot of a car, helpless in having any say of my destination.

I relaxed my muscles to save the fight in them, and instead focused on the most important question: who was behind the wheel?

196

After what felt like hours, the car stopped. Although stiff and aching, I stayed still to listen.

A door opened, and weight shifted from inside; there had only been the driver. The footsteps sounded too heavy and wide apart to belong to a woman, and quickly they distanced until there was little of any other sound—had I heard a cricket?

Infrequent traffic and the bumpy last kilometres had confirmed I'd be where there were few to nose around.

My heart skipped a beat as noises—multiple this time—returned from outside: voices, male, low. I couldn't make out words or recognise the speakers. I held my breath as the lock clicked, and suddenly cool air flooded in. I had to blink several times to aid my eyes to adjust to the lighter darkness.

A shape appeared in the air and I studied it, forcing my eyes to meet my captor. Gradually, the form became clearer, changing from a shape to a person. I knew the face, but I didn't understand it. A vile smirk distorted the familiar features.

It could not be him.

"Hello, Kalika."

A shudder shook me as Sebastian's hand reached to pull me out of the boot.

Chapter 32

Was this a prank?

Sebastian's firm grip, forcing me to stand up, told otherwise. Three other men, all dressed in black, stared at me, on alert. I calculated my odds.

"Surprised to see me?" Sebastian's voice was a drawl, thick with arrogance. Swift, he ripped off the tape, causing my lips to tremble from the sudden onset of pain.

"What's going on, Sebastian?" I strained against the ties, wanting to deny the truth.

"*Aww*, still not so witty." A raucous laugh echoed in the open space. "Do you not know your friends from your enemies?" Sebastian pinned my chin.

I attempted to free myself from his grasp, luckless. His appearance was no longer that of a laid-back student I had called a friend. Before me stood a fighter: poised, confident, menacing. His eyes were now darkly brown, his shaggy hair shaved to a buzz cut, and even his mouth curved differently.

"What do you want?" I glowered.

He sneered. "Well, I want you, Kalika."

It was only then it hit me: he knew my real name.

I froze, taking in Sebastian's tanned face, the bridge of his nose and the lean muscle over his body. Had I not seen it before, or not wanted to admit it to myself?

"That's right." Sebastian lifted his chin. "We're not so different, are we, now? After all, I was your kin...*before* we were banished from our homes, sent to the other side of the river, and forced to start over so your King could have his precious people stay on his lands." Sebastian spat on the ground and pushed my face away from him. My eyes flickered to the three soldiers standing by. I noted the single line of crimson paint on the side of their necks—a symbol of their devotion to bringing Narun to ruin.

"You're from Gorah."

"Born and bred."

I breathed in deep, refusing to let him intimidate me. "What do you want from me? How'd you know who I was?"

"Oh, we've known about you for a long time. Finding you, now that was the tricky bit, and frustratingly, that stalker leech of yours found you first so we had to get creative. But in the end, you took care of him quite nicely by yourself."

Leo.

"Now that he's out of the way..." Sebastian trailed off meaningfully, drunk on the sound of his own voice.

I jutted my chin forward. "What are you after?"

"Same thing we were after years ago: you and your special talent."

Years ago? Goosebumps covered my arms. What was he talking about?

"Don't worry, I'll explain later. Let's get you inside, don't want you to catch a cold in the night now, do we? Big day ahead tomorrow." Sebastian's face reeked of arrogance. The darkness inside of him wasn't veiled anymore.

Drops of panic infiltrated as the reality sunk in: this wasn't going to end well.

Sebastian flicked a knife from his pocket and cut the tape around my ankles. My attempt to kick at his jaw fell short: his arm blocked my leg, his elbow smacked into my gut. I stumbled as he forced me forward, his fingers locked around my arm.

"Oh, and one more thing." He dropped his grip on me. "Since you know my weaknesses, let's even the playing field."

While the last word still hung in the air, I felt a blow between my ankle and knee. I registered the crack before the pain struck like a bolt of lightning. Agony took me to the ground, but no one tried to silence my scream.

"That should deter any escape plans for now," Sebastian said.

I was barely aware of the men coming on either side of me, pulling me up, and dragging me across the gravel towards a large, grey building. I couldn't tell if Sebastian followed.

Absorbed by the pain, my only resistance was a groan.

The ache in my leg became bearable. I was on the stone floor of my assigned prison cell, —a cobweb-ridden cellar—legs resting at full-length, back leaning against the rough, slightly moist concrete wall. An older man with shaky hands and darting eyes had come in to place a make-shift splint on my leg. *A well-bribed vet, perhaps?* But, as long as the bone remained aligned and supported, the healing process would be on the go.

I drifted between sleep and consciousness, trying to make sense of what was the dream and what the nightmare of reality. My head jerked as I slipped in and out of sleep.

Sebastian's face haunted me, all memories of him now marred. Why had I trusted him so blindly? Why hadn't I doubted him? Instead, he'd been my haven from the drama that was my life.

Dumb and dumber—yours truly.

What did he even want with me? He'd dedicated the time to gain my trust, and waited for Leo to leave before...before what? What could he want with me that was worth the effort? There were others more valuable.

I rubbed my ear against my shoulder and stretched my neck. The more awake I became, the more the horror swelled inside. Not only was I in trouble, but I was also alone in it.

*

At least no one could sneak up on me unnoticed...

I angled my head towards the door as it whined open.

"Rise and shine."

Passively, I met Sebastian's condescending smile. Why give him the pleasure of getting any emotion out of me?

"Friends tend to greet each other, you know. It's polite." Sebastian squatted in front of me, savouring the state of my leg.

"It's also good manners not to break each other's legs."

A scoff parted behind Sebastian's pursed lips. "You know—" He patted my bad leg as he straightened to standing. I held in the whimper. "It doesn't have to be like this. If you cooperate, we can make you much more comfortable."

"I like it cold and damp. What do you want with me?"

"Not your charm, that's for sure." I saw a glimpse of the Sebastian I knew in the face of my captor. He walked across the room, lifted his foot against the wall behind him and crossed his arms on his chest. "So, what's it going to be? Are you going to help us willingly or—"

"I really don't see how I could be of any use. If you're after names you—"

"*Names?* Of the Guard?" Sebastian sounded as if I had offended his intellect. "*That* we can get anywhere."

"Then why me?"

"Don't act stupid, Kalika. Surely you realise what an asset your gift is?"

"My gifting?" I dragged my palms back along the floor until my wrists hugged the wall.

"If you're trying to buy time it's pointless. We're in no rush," he said. "Yes, your gifting! You know the weaknesses of every member of the Royal Guard, past and present. Now that in itself is priceless, but we believe with the right training you can do even better."

Shivers ran from my neck, down to my tailbone. "What do you mean?"

"Think about it." Sebastian lifted his chin. "Think of how much power you could possess if you extend your gift to not only seeing the weaknesses in people but in gates, defences, walls, towns, Kingdoms, even battle strategies. You would be—"

"It doesn't work that way," I cut in, a little relieved.

"Not *yet.*"

"No, *really*, it's not something I could do even if I wanted to. Not that I'd ever do anything to help you."

Sebastian tutted. "That's because you haven't had the right teacher. Your king wants to keep your talents to a level that suits him. He's afraid you could become more powerful than him, so he keeps you on a short leash. Yet with us...you could be invincible." Sebastian's eyes—black-brown without the contact lenses—glazed over.

Goosebumps spread from my spine to my arms. I stared him down, fixated by, and uneasy with, the darkness in his gaze.

"What makes you think I would do anything to help you?"

"Isn't that what traitors do? Jump ship?"

I fixed my glare on the other side of the square room. A single shelf interrupted the otherwise grey wall.

"Ah, touchy subject. They do say the truth hurts the most... That is the truth, isn't it?" Sebastian pushed his foot off the wall and took a step, then another towards me. "You're a traitor, a coward, a runaway...*a killer*. What reason could you possibly have to go back? Would they even take you back?" He nudged my foot with the tip of his boot as if kicking a lump of rubbish.

"See, with us you can start a new life; you can be someone powerful. You could have a life in the king's courts but be free to do whatever you like. Imagine, if just the mention of your name would invoke fear." Sebastian's words seeped with a lust for his own desires.

My bottom lip rolled underneath my top teeth. "I may be all of those things and I might not be able to ever return home, but I would never, *ever*, turn against Narun and the King."

"Haven't you already renounced the King once?"

My neck tensed up. He knew? How did he know?

"I will never become one of you," I said much quieter.

Sebastian retorted with a dismissive wave. "We'll see about that." He gave me one final look before leaving me alone with the echo of his subtle threat.

I will not make the same mistake twice.

I rested my head against the wall, plotting my options for escape.

A few moments later, the lock turned again, and a man built like a tank appeared in the doorway.

"Get up," he growled with a bass voice.

"I have a broken leg."

"You still have the other." The stone face remained; he was doing his duty and he wasn't going to stray from it. "Get up."

What chance does a crippled antelope stand against a lion?

I sighed and sucked in my lips. With the help of my arms, one leg, and the wall, I propped myself to standing. Eventually.

"That took time. *Good.*" The man stepped over, scooped my arm behind his neck and dragged me out too fast for my limping leg.

He took me along a narrow, all-stone corridor that led us deeper into the ground. The humidity made me quiver and the stench of stale air disagreed with me heavily.

We took a left turn; the corridor narrowed, and the ceiling lowered. Light diminished with each step, but the lack of it hardly bothered the man dragging me.

We stopped as my sight was adjusting. The man lit a hanging lightbulb fastened next to a metal-framed door. The rusty hinges squeaked open, revealing a small, oblong room—low ceiling, damp stone walls, uneven concrete floor. A simple bed lay at one side, toilet and sink at the other.

"Welcome to your new home." The man shoved me in, and I stumbled, slamming my palms against the floor. Dirt embedded its particles under my skin thanks to the scraping motion.

The door locked behind me. It would've been pitch black had a narrow trickle of light not protruded through the hinges of the door. I heaved myself up to the bed and sat down on its thin, worn mattress.

It could be worse. I think.

Chapter 33

Day 8. (I presumed.)

It was getting harder to keep track of time. I hadn't seen or heard from anyone since I was moved to the dungeon. My only interaction, if you could call it that, was a daily plate of porridge pushed through a hole under the door which I shoved back after it was empty. At first, it was my means of tracking time, but I could swear they kept changing the time of delivery as another way to mess with my head.

Once I had received an apple cut into slices. What that was about, I didn't know, but I'd savoured each bite.

I had briefly considered that they had changed their plans, moved on and left me to die. But that would be pointless. Truth was, I had heard of their tactics during my years as Guard.

First, they wore their hostages out physically and mentally by denying human contact, providing only enough food to survive *and* make your flesh crave for more, and by keeping you in darkness to emphasise loneliness and to cause you to lose track of time. And of course, give you too much time to think.

Yes, ultimately, boredom was the worst, even before fear or anxiety of what was to come. My mind had gone over the past, current, and future with a fine-toothed comb. I had cursed, cried and regretted my actions. Rethought what I could have done differently. Kicked myself for not seeing who Sebastian was, and then mourned for the loss of a friend. Planned an escape, and realised it was impossible with a broken leg. Planned another and arrived at the same conclusion. Worried about whether Jill and Tony were thinking I'd run away from them. Fumed over my current situation. Convinced myself Leo would come to my rescue, and then admitted he was long gone and out of my life.

Bottom line, my future looked bleak.

*

Day 11 in the Damp Dungeon Lock-up.

Or twelve. Maybe fifteen?

Why hadn't anyone come in? Shouting through the door had only amounted to a sore throat. I had hoped to even hear a 'Shut up' to keep me sane and give some indication that someone was actually there. To just hear another voice...

Would somebody please come in already? Green Martian men could've taken over and I wouldn't have known.

Who would have noticed I was missing? Tony and Jill would be looking for me. Or would they? How long until they'd give up?

If only I had a clock to count minutes to keep some track of life.

My stomach was eating itself. Where was my food tray for the day? I crawled to the door to peek under it but there was nothing but more shadows. When had I had it last?

My tongue slid in between my lips. The burn on it felt raw. *Oh yes.* I had had porridge today, and burned my tongue on it, shovelling it in before it had cooled down.

On my hands and one knee, I dragged myself to the rusted sink, splashed water on my face and took a few gulps. The metallic taste was still cringe-worthy, but at least the water was clean. I washed my hands, feeling futile of the action. Soon they'd be filthy again, like the rest of me.

I needed to get out of here.

I'm really not built for this perseverance thing, am I?

*

Day...?

It must've been at least a month.

Frail—that's how I felt. Hope for escape diminished the weaker my body grew. Even with full strength, it would've been a challenge to get away.

I curled on the bed, constantly cold from the lack of nutrition, hugging my stomach. Was my destiny to die in a cell in the hands of my captors?

Just like Kailen.

He had died in a cell somewhere, protecting me, believing I would one day fulfil a higher purpose. And this was how I repaid him: a meaningless death, a wasted life. I had let him down in life and now also in death.

Could he ever forgive me?
Could I ever forgive myself?

Chapter 34

"Boo."

A whisper next to my ear startled me to near heart failure as I lay on the bed. The gasp would've been a scream had I more energy. Sebastian's face glowed with satisfaction as he assessed my physical state. How had I not heard the door open?

"Sebastian." My voice sounded foreign and cracked. It would offer little cover.

"The one and only." He placed an electric lamp on the floor. "Of course, it's not my real name, but it'll do."

Shielding my eyes from the light, I manoeuvred up, to the furthest end of the bed. Sebastian looked down on me, his frame taunting as if he was a vulture, deciding if the carcass was worth it.

"I see you haven't even tried to claw a tunnel yet. How disappointing." He scanned the floor level. "I thought you had more fire in you."

"What do you want?" I asked, not sounding menacing in the least. Part of me wanted to grab his arm and thank him for coming to see me.

I slapped that part of me right on the nose.

"Same as little over three weeks ago." *Three weeks?* Was that all? "Have you considered my offer?"

"I won't join you." I never realised speaking took such effort. "Or help you. Or—"

"Yeah, yeah, blah, blah. You're not the only captive to have said that." His cruel eyes unsettled. "I think your partner spoke something similar once upon a time."

I hugged myself tighter, doing nothing to stop the tremble. The last shred of bravado I was clasping onto was about to crumble.

"Kailen, I believe his name was," Sebastian mused, hands behind his back.

Any other day, any other place, I would've jabbed his throat for defiling his name.

Sebastian swiped a finger along the wall, rubbed it against another, and placed his hands behind his back again. "I saw him in prison, you know." He was visibly intoxicated by the effect he had on me; I felt sick. "Not a nice way to die. Shame he—"

"Stop." I covered my ears. "Please, stop." The vulnerability I so openly portrayed took Sebastian by surprise. A wicked edge dominated his face.

"Not so confident now, huh? I didn't even have to mention the limbs he was miss—"

"Stop, *please.*" I pressed against my ears harder, knowing full well I was giving him exactly what he wanted, but I couldn't bear what I was hearing. It would set my thoughts in stone.

Sebastian's laughter bounced off the walls, amplified by the echo. I tried to shut myself out and think of anything else than what he was suggesting.

"Suit yourself," he finally said. "We'll save that for later." He swivelled around and marched to the door. An ear-piercing wolf-whistle made me jump. Two soldiers filed in on cue; one I recognised from before. "Take her to the house and start packing up."

Instantly, the two guards grabbed me from either side and yanked me up, only to let go as Sebastian came to stand in front of me. He raised his arm, and I fell onto the bed from the force of the back-handed slap across my face.

"*That*" —he cracked his knuckles— "was for the time I had to take a hit from that stalker leech of yours, so I wouldn't blow my cover." Sebastian crouched by the bed, pinched my chin between his fingers and stared into my half-open eyes. "Prepare to see your new homeland."

My head slumped as he let go. I didn't get back up.

I squinted as soon as the blindfold was taken off. The light hurt from weeks of darkness. From what I could see of the room, it was definitely an upgrade.

"There's a change of clothes on the bed and a bucket in the corner if you want to wash. I'll bring you food later on," the younger of the two guards stated as if I were a paying hotel guest. The other guard shut and locked the wooden doors on the windows, blocking the view from outside, and left.

I assessed the remaining guard curiously. Although laden with muscles on his tall body, he looked barely sixteen.

"You were born in Gorah?" I winced at the stinging on my face from Sebastian's slap. The boy glanced at me, not sure whether to entertain the conversation.

"Yes," he finally admitted and strode to the door.

"Wait!" I beckoned him to stay, not even sure why. Against the odds, he stopped, and I struggled to get my words out. "When do we leave?"

"The day after tomorrow."

"You don't have to do this," I blurted. *Granted, lame attempt.*

"I know." The boy winked which seemed out of place. "But I want to." He then tilted his head towards the bucket. "Get cleaned up. It's a long journey and you stink." He left me to it.

I took a quick inventory of the room. The bed was made with white linen and a grey duvet cover. Although void of other furniture, a square, blue and white rug filled the floor space. A large metal bucket rested in the corner with an empty bowl next to it. A towel hung on its brim. My eyes drifted to the white door slightly ajar next to the wash area—a toilet.

The property had an old feel with its high ceilings and walls that had seen many a turn of a century and several coatings of paint. Maybe I was in an old farmhouse.

Using the wall for support, I staggered to the bucket. My shrinking muscles ached for protein and my body for nutrients. Feeling weak was exhausting.

I washed eagerly, minding the sore side of my face. It would blacken the skin around my eye. As quickly as possible, I changed into the clean clothes: ill-fitting trousers and a simple black, long-sleeved, buttoned shirt which I was sure was from the men's section.

Drained of energy, I sat on the rug in the middle of the room, threading my fingers through the thick wool. Just over three weeks of capture. And what was to come? Three years? Thirteen years?

Thirty years? Once in Gorah, there'd be no escaping. My options were to die in a cell or turn against my home.

No Guard feared death; it was capture we never spoke of. Some had been forced to turn to the other side. Nobody knew how much they could take until tested. We had rescued some over the years, but it was preferably done in transit. There were only a handful of times an elite group had gone beyond enemy lines to rescue captives.

They had often been too late or never returned.

Chills multiplied on my skin. I had never been to Gorah. Soon, I'd see it first hand, just like Kailen had.

Steps halted behind the door. The boy soldier entered with a tray.

"Settling in, are we?" He looked at me strangely, as if wondering why I had chosen the floor over the bed. He placed the tray in front of me, never taking his eyes off me.

"Do you really think I'm going to jump on you with a broken leg?"

"Lesson one: never turn your back on your enemies."

"What have I ever done to you?" My tone was more rhetoric than questioning, as my eyes consumed a plate of boiled potatoes, carrots, two thin strips of chicken breast, a pear and a cardboard cup of milk. The plastic fork struggled to pierce a potato.

"You were born on the wrong side of the river," he stated in reply. "Don't worry, you'll be one of us before you know it."

Potatoes had never tasted so amazing. "What makes you so sure?"

"Let's just say I've read your file." Again, he winked and then left.

Peculiar young soldier.

I forced myself to eat slower, chewing several times before swallowing. I took three gulps of the milk and hugged the paper cup against my chest in thought.

The day after tomorrow.

That wasn't a lot of time. The door was the only feasible exit from the room and I had no idea what was on the outside. I remembered five different faces plus Sebastian, all trained soldiers with skills to match mine. Except that I had a broken leg and a feeble body. And even if I did manage to get out of the house, it had been a long car journey to get here. *Here.* Where was here?

I swallowed the well-chewed piece of chicken. There wasn't much hope in getting out, was there? Which meant in a few days I would be in Gorah. And then... How long would it take until I'd give them what they wanted? No one based much on my conviction. What if Sebastian was right and my gift could be developed? Would I be the downfall of Narun?

Fear rolled in like a landslide. All this because I ran away. Because I was a selfish *coward* rather than a warrior. I struggled to swallow the lump forming in my throat. A slideshow of faces flashed in my mind. For their sake, I couldn't afford to be weak anymore. For their sake, I couldn't risk being taken to Gorah.

I knew what I had to do.

I snapped off a piece of wood from the splint on my leg. Biting my cheek, I cut my left wrist.

Chapter 35

"Well done. You've earned yourself twenty-four-hour supervision."

I came to, slowly, staring up at Sebastian's eyes so black it was hard to separate his pupils. He stopped his slow-clap as I turned my head. The room was the same, except for an uneven, red patch adding pattern to the rug.

I lay on the bed with a sensation of heaviness on both wrists: restraints, skin-digging restraints. My left wrist was wrapped in a cloth. Underneath, the cuts ached, and I suspected amateur stitches.

I see my idiotic escape plan flopped like a fish gone belly up.

"That really was a stupid thing to do, Kalika, even for you." Sebastian shook his head. "Good thing our young soldier never lets his guard down. Even when you're faking an attempt on your life." He tutted. "Do I need to take your fingers out of the game too?"

"My head hurts. Could you talk a little quieter?" I mumbled, feeling the effects of blood loss.

Sebastian laughed and stood up from my bedside. "It's a shame. We could've got along well under different circumstances." He squatted, dabbed the blood on the rug, and rubbed his clean fingers.

I must have been out of it for a while.

"We did," I noted. "Before you went arch-enemy on me."

"We're not so different, you know. We too fight for what we believe in and want to protect our land. We love and lose just as you do." The floorboards creaked under Sebastian's combat boots.

Drowsy, I stared at the yellowing ceiling.

"You think we're all evil and you're some superior race." Sebastian stopped by my feet, brushing a finger along my bad leg. "I bet you don't even know how many families your Guard has broken over the years. How many children left fatherless and homes you destroyed? There you live in a land abundant in produce when across the river, we toil for our food until our fingers bleed."

"You started the war." I struggled to keep my eyes open.

"We were banished from our homes!" I jolted as Sebastian bellowed. "But we'll have our revenge, and you're going to be in the front of our ranks claiming back what is rightfully ours. I promise you that." His nostrils flared, mouth distorted into an ugly knot.

My faith was in the hands of a man who despised me for my birthplace.

Sebastian stormed out and another soldier stepped inside to stand guard. I struggled against the restraints, rubbing and twisting my wrists. The top layers of my skin rubbed off, but I didn't stop. Somehow the pain was comforting; I was in control of it.

What felt like several hours later, the door opened, and I was collected. Hooded and hands bound, they carried me out of the house and into the crisp air. Outside, orders were shouted, footsteps went back and forth. In the middle of it all, a bird chirped.

I focused on the bird.

I was shoved into what I assumed to be the back of a truck. I winced as they thrust me onto the unforgiving floor. Heavy boots retreated, the doors slammed shut and soon the truck roared into life.

I was alone, in all senses of the word. I took the hood off with my tied hands, and there I sat, deserted in pitch black once again, heading to the last place I wanted to go.

Dead in a coffin, on my way to the crematorium.

I didn't even try to keep track of how long we'd been travelling. Physically and emotionally drained, I dozed off and woke up to my head banging against the side of the truck. We hadn't stopped since setting off, but we'd have to eventually; it'd take at least a couple of days, depending on where we were to begin with, to travel to Gorah.

I quivered, feeling uncomfortable and thirsty. The skin on my wrists burned from trying to loosen the ropes.

Are they afraid I'll punch a hole through the truck?

I nearly fell on my side as the tires screeched and we came to a halt. The engine shut down seconds later. The driver's door opened and closed, and I tried to make out the conversation outside.

Petrol. We'd stopped for petrol. I stretched my spine and rested my head back. The driver soon returned, and the engine kicked to life, shaking the vehicle.

Instinctively, my head whipped to my right as the back door opened and closed. It was dark outside, but a street light illuminated the container enough to take in the surroundings—aluminium boxes stacked and secured with ropes—but that was not what made my heart skip. I could've sworn someone had slipped inside the truck.

I held still, listening, peering into the blackness. Why would anyone sneak inside?

Eyes darting frantically, I searched where the shape had vanished, but it was too dark and the motor too loud to distinguish any additional noise. The truck accelerated but I was on pause, waiting for someone to grab me or stab me. I didn't have a preference.

Nothing. Not even a peep. The tension released in my neck. I was imagining things.

I eased—and jumped within my skin as a hand covered my mouth.

"Shhhh, it's me, it's me," a voice whispered.

The scream got trapped in my throat. My good leg kicked out, thrusting my back against the wall. Eyes hurting from bulging, I ordered myself to calm down.

Just another one of their tactics to scare me.

The person lit up something that gave enough glow to turn the darkness to dusk. I evened my breath and as I relaxed, the hand eased, and let go, still holding up an index finger.

"Easy, it's okay. It's just me."

Head tilted as I stared into the eyes eating up mine.

"What are you doing here?" I asked, my teeth chattering ever so slightly.

"I'm here to save you, you muppet."

I heard the words, but it wasn't until Leo positioned his hands on either side of my face that they registered.

I burst into tears and buried my face into his shoulder.

Chapter 36

The tears leaked out, dampening Leo's jacket. He shushed and stroked the back of my head, in no hurry to let go and I was thankful. I was overdue a breakdown. Leaning on Leo, I shifted everything onto him. His strength flowed into me.

"How did you find me? How did you know?" I doubted Leo could even hear my voice from the rattle of the truck.

"I'm sorry I took so long." He eased me off his shoulder, his palms cupping my face. "Are you okay?" His thumb skimmed across the bruise on my face, his hands falling to my shoulders, and down my arms until they reached the ropes around my wrists. His eyes feral, he pulled a knife out of his combats and flung the cut rope into a corner of the truck. Palms up, my hands rested on my legs.

"I'm so sorry I took so long," he repeated. "I never should've left you."

"No, it's all my fault." I stared at my hands. "I've made so many mistakes." My voice cracked as fresh tears ran down my cheeks.

"Hey, it's all right." His thumb wiped a tear rolling down to my jawline. "You're going to be fine. I'm gonna get you out of here."

"I can't—"

"You don't have to. I'll get you out." Leo pulled a flashlight and scanned the insides of the truck.

I dried my cheeks. "I can't walk without a crutch. Sebastian broke my leg."

Leo went rigid, and as he shone the light down, I hitched up the trouser, revealing the makeshift cast. Shadows hid his expression, but the laboured breath was hard to miss.

He backed away slightly and continued to search the truck a beam of light at a time.

"You left," I said under my breath. "How did you know they had me?"

"I never should've left," he said, strained as if struggling to control himself.

"I told you to go."

"But it was my decision to leave," he countered as he went to pick up a metal rod lying half under a cardboard box. "I'll never forgive myself for it." He tried bending the rod, and it gave away easily. He placed it back on the floor.

"How'd you know they had me?" I asked again, feeling useless in my sorry state.

Leo stood with his hands on his hips, half listening to me, half searching for a plan. I gathered my broken leg had annihilated his escape plan.

"I was travelling home when I remembered something about Sebastian—a fighting technique he used when I sparred with him in his class." He shook his head dismissively. "I could never place it until at that moment I realised where I'd seen it before. It was a hunch, but I had to make sure. When I came back, you'd disappeared into thin air, and I couldn't track down Sebastian. So, I did some digging and my leads led me to the old estate Sebastian took you to. But I was too late."

I lowered my chin into a nod. "They're taking me to Gorah."

"I figured. I heard them talk about a ship." Leo worked his jaw, his mouth a thin line. "How did they…did they…did they hurt you?"

"Other than the leg, it's just bruises and a black eye."

"Phase one—weaken the captive by starvation and isolation," he said as if quoting a manual. "You don't look too great."

"I don't feel too great."

Leo's face distorted at my honesty and he gave up searching the truck. He sat next to me, knees bent, hands over them.

"They're likely to stop overnight. That's when we'll make our move."

My insides tied into knots. How could we get away from multiple skilled fighters with me not only being useless but needing support to walk?

"Don't worry, I'll take care of it." Leo read my mind, nudging his shoulder into mine.

"I'm not sure I can fight."

"Leave it to me. Now get some rest, it might be a while still."

I pulled my arms across my shrunken waist. Leo's shoulder tensed as I rested my head on it. I adjusted my position a few times until he relaxed, and wriggled closer to me. His arm wrapped around me, and I fell asleep leaning on him.

I came to as the truck hit a pothole.

Neck stiff, I rolled my head up and stretched it both ways.

"How long was I asleep?" I straightened my back, arched it and slumped.

"An hour or so. I have a feeling we'll be stopping soon." He moved away from me and stood up to stretch. I shivered as his body heat left me and tugged at my sleeves.

"Do you think they'll leave me here for the night?"

A frown creased Leo's forehead. I doubted it had left in the past hour.

"No. Someone's going to check on you. They won't leave you here overnight, the temperature's dropping." Leo took off his jacket and tossed it to me.

I wore it like a blanket.

"But they'll find you." A wave of foreboding crept in. "We can't win fighting from the back of a truck; they'll have a huge advantage. They'll end up capturing you too!" I panicked at the thought of Leo getting caught.

"They won't," he said, calm as ever. "I'll hide." He left the end of the sentence hanging, waiting for me to read between the lines. As I stared at him, he picked up something from the floor, playing with it between his hands, untangling.

"You want me to go with them."

"It's the only way." Leo avoided eye contact. He disliked the option more than I did, but I knew he was right: outnumbered, and me useless, it was too much of a risk.

I wanted to say I understood. I wanted to focus on the logic. Still, I couldn't stop the tears from pooling.

Quickly, I lowered my head, hoping Leo wouldn't notice.

In a flash, he was in front of me, lifting my chin up. "Kal, hey. Do you trust me?"

I nodded as much as his hand allowed.

"Then don't worry. I promise I'll get you out. I'll be close. As soon as the opportunity comes, I will get you, okay?"

I sniffled, wiping my cheeks with the back of my hand. *I'm pathetic.* "I'm sorry. You must think I'm absolutely useless."

"I don't think that at all. If anything, I prefer this to the constant bickering about everything I do." A slanted smile appeared on his face and I appreciated the attempt to lighten the mood.

The truck slowed down a gear and veered off to the left.

"We're getting off the motorway," Leo noted.

I took in a shallow breath as he picked up the rope.

I handed back Leo's jacket, instantly missing the warmth. "Make it real."

Leo's fingers grazed the broken skin where the rope had dug in, touched the bandage a little higher up on my left wrist, and stopped.

"What happened here?"

"Just…a deep graze." This was not the time to get into my ill-considered escape attempt. Hopefully, it never would.

Carefully, Leo tightened the knot and I checked his work. He managed to hide the fact the rope was once cut.

"What if they find you?"

Leo smirked, checking that the surroundings hadn't been disturbed by his presence. "Then I'll roll over and wave a white flag."

"I'm serious! You can't get caught because of me."

"*Relax*, I'm not exactly a rookie."

Of course, he was right. But my heart still thudded.

Whining, the truck slowed further and turned once again. It crawled for a few more metres and then came to halt. I propped myself straight, bracing for what was to come. I failed to see which shadow Leo vanished behind.

I waited, painfully long, for the back doors to open.

Thankfully, the street lights only illuminated parts of the back. The night air brought shivers all over my body, and I tensed up as if to lock in my body heat. The boy soldier, as I called him, jumped in, marching straight to me.

"Where are we?" I kept a keen eye on him.

"Motel. We're staying for the night." He grabbed my arm and helped me up on my stiff limbs, gentler than before. "If you play nice you might even get a soft bed tonight."

"I wouldn't count on it."

The blood in my veins iced over at Sebastian's voice. He stood outside by the back entrance, arms on the floor of the truck. I held my insides from turning. What if they found Leo? What if they empty the truck? What if they get rid of the truck?

Too many things could go wrong.

Much to my dread, Sebastian jumped inside.

"Did you enjoy the ride?"

"Best ever." The cold, or the fear, was making my teeth clatter.

Sebastian scoffed amused as he came to stand within my reach; the boy went rigid next to me. I turned my head to the side as Sebastian stroked a strand of hair behind my ear, and leaned in.

"You cause a scene outside and I'll take out the other leg too, along with a few civilians."

I nodded my understanding, and he moved out of my way. I wondered if Leo had heard the threat.

"Take her to my room," Sebastian ordered.

The boy pulled on my arm, rougher this time. We were a few steps from the doors when a foot swiped under my good leg, and I stumbled, taking weight on the broken leg. Pain like a bolt of lightning coursed through me. I couldn't suppress the scream. I swung half out of the truck before the young soldier steadied me by the arm and yanked me back.

"Just making sure you're not faking that leg of yours," Sebastian said, pleased, and jumped down to the ground.

The boy shrugged as our eyes met and lifted me out of the truck.

I didn't dare glance back for any signs of Leo.

Room fourteen was a typical motel room—two single beds, a wall-mount TV, desk, armchair, and an all-white, ceramic bathroom. I was placed on the floor next to a bed and tied to a radiator. The boy helped me drink a glass of water.

"You hungry?"

I'm near starvation. What'd you think?

"A little."

"I'll see if you're allowed something from a vending machine."

The boy's features were sharp: high cheekbones, narrow chin and nose, forgettable eyes. His neck and shoulders were nearly too big for his head, but regardless of his bulky frame and crew-cut hair, there was an innocence about him the others didn't have.

"You're nicer than the others."

The boy hooked his fingers on his belt. "My uncle once said to treat every captive as a future brother. You reap what you sow."

My stare trailed him as he went to peek through the window.

"What's your name?"

"Call me Kol," he said as he shut the blinds. "The others have arrived. Someone else will watch you now. It's been a pleasure."

As soon as Kol left, Sebastian and another soldier—the Tank—walked in, not even acknowledging my presence. The Tank tossed a duffel bag on the floor and crashed on the bed furthest from me. Sebastian turned on the TV, and sat on the end of the bed, flicking through the channels. I waited for him to throw a meaningless comment, or at least remind me I wasn't invisible, but when the Tank started snoring and Sebastian settled into watching sports, I relaxed by leaning my head against the wall.

They must not have found Leo.

*

I stirred from restless sleep—annoyed how difficult it was to stay awake—wiggling my fingers to bring life to a dead arm. The TV was on, but muted, shining an eerie light into an otherwise dark room.

Sebastian's bed was empty. The Tank snored on his back, arms folded behind his head. *Probably dreaming of white, sandy beaches.*

My limbs ached, and I inched away from the wall to get a glimpse around the corner. The bathroom was dark, the door ajar. Where was Sebastian and how long would he be gone?

I dropped my chin and closed my eyes as a shadow passed on the other side of the window.

Stealthy, Sebastian entered. He stopped in the middle of the room, perhaps assessing if I really was asleep.

A hand came over my mouth.

Chapter 37

My eyes flashed open and widened in relief as Leo placed a finger to his lips, then held up three fingers and flicked his thumb to the door: we had three minutes to get out.

He cut the rope, and I held a grunt as he pulled me to my feet. His focus flickering on the sleeping soldier, he scooped me up and I clung to him as tight as I could, holding my breath until we were out of the room.

It was quiet outside and I couldn't see anyone standing guard or otherwise loitering under the night sky. Leo carried me past the other motel doors to the side of the L-shaped front of the building. As we cleared the corner, he put me down and checked if we were followed.

"Sebastian," he whispered, barely audible, and pressed his back against the concrete wall.

"We'll hide in the woods."

"No. That's the first place they'll check." Leo's gaze flickered to my leg. "We'll be too slow and leave a trail."

"But it's dark. Hiding is our best option."

"It's my call." He didn't wait for my approval but turned to take another glance. I heard hasty footsteps, then banging on doors.

A few weeks ago, Leo would've had to physically restrain me from lunging at them. Now, I wished nothing more than to flee the scene.

Seconds later, Leo turned and picked me up, taking me to the back of the building. The treeline was a few metres down the grass-covered slope. Large metal bins decorated most of the back wall, illuminated by the light shining through windows. Leo would have disabled a security camera or two prior to our Great Escape.

As we reached the second set of bins, he carefully put me down.

"Someone's coming; I'm going to take them out. *You*—stay there."

I didn't get a chance to object before Leo vanished in the shadows. I crouched down, glueing myself to the side of the bin. Soon enough, I heard faint rustling and a beam of light growing larger as it neared me. My instincts geared me for a fight: shapes formed from the shadows, grass folded under combat boots and even through the rubbish, I smelled a hint of testosterone closing. It wasn't Sebastian or Kol. This one was hard of hearing in his left ear.

I closed my eyes to sharpen my other senses. Leo was close.

A rustle, a faint groan and a thud.

I crawled on the ground for a glimpse. Leo lobbed the guard over his shoulder and off-loaded him in a ditch by the border of the woods. He tied the man's hands and knees with something he pulled out of his combats and gagged him.

I pulled myself up and waited for Leo.

"Once he wakes up they'll know you had help." Leo came next to me and hooked his hand around my waist. "Sebastian will figure out it's me."

The thought unsettled me.

"There's a door at the back that leads to the reception." Again, Leo lifted me up to his arms.

"You're taking me back inside?" I questioned but cottoned onto his strategy the same instant. We couldn't outrun them; we'd have to outsmart them.

We snuck in from an unlocked back door to a tiny entrance hall, leading to kitchen storage. Leo placed me down next to the wall, aiding my hobble past the kitchen entrance and into the hallway. He must have memorised the corridors earlier.

I struggled to keep up, the past weeks leaving a strain upon my body. Movement, even though heavily assisted, exhausted me.

On cue, Leo's arm tightened around my waist. "You okay?" he mouthed.

I reassured him and took a laboured breath.

"Almost there."

'Almost there' was the manager's private room, around the corner from the reception desk and small entrance foyer. Leo used a key card to open the door; he'd been well prepared.

The room was like the other bedrooms apart from having a small kitchen area and supporting a nicer finishing touch.

Leo pulled a chair over for me, and strode to the window, parting the curtains just enough to see through.

I could tell why this was our hideout: it had a view directly to the front yard and three escape options.

"This wasn't exactly 'plan A'," Leo admitted. "I heard Sebastian talking with another soldier. They were going to…hurt you. I had to get you out, there and then."

I caught my breath in long but shallow breaths. "What were they going to do?"

Leo's neck tensed, and I knew that was all the answer I was going to get. He took another glance outside the window. "They're doing a perimeter check. Sebastian's running the show."

I clasped the armrests, feeling the effects of weeks of damp, dungeon air in my lungs.

"I'd say in about five, ten minutes we can go. How are you doing?" The direction of Leo's hushed voice had changed. He was currently pressing his ear to the door.

One day I would have to ask him the secret to his kitten steps.

"A little weary but fine."

"Here, eat this." He handed me a protein bar from one of his trouser pockets. I took it and devoured it. Leo was back by the window.

"In case we don't make it out of here, I wanted to thank—"

Leo's head snapped in my direction. "You don't think I can get you out?"

"That's not what I meant. I trust you. *But* there are a lot of them and I'm useless when it comes to…well, anything." I motioned at my leg although it was only part of the problem.

"Hey, I don't want any of that. I'm going to get you out even if it kills me." Leo sounded casual, but he meant it. He also struck a familiar chord: he was not the first to have said so. Kailen had given up everything to save me, and for what?

A tidal wave of suppressed emotions crashed against me. I felt every inch of my sorry state, physical and emotional, weighing down

229

on me. Threateningly, my chin trembled. I had wasted the past years doing nothing but trampling Kailen's memory. I had turned my back on everything I believed in, everything that mattered, and created a self I could barely face in the mirror.

My finger trailed the smeared bandage on my wrist. And what was worse, I may be the death of Leo, who gave up years in the hope to set me on the right path. If only I hadn't left to begin with but faced my demons like a true warrior.

I slumped forward, burying my head in my hands as guilt imprinted its thumbprint on me.

"Kalika, what's wrong? Are you hurt?" Leo was on his knees in front of me in a second, grasping my shoulders.

I pushed against his hands. "I'm a mess, Leo. I've done so many things wrong!" I swallowed the rising lump in my throat. This was not the time for this.

"Shh, it's going to be okay." Leo brushed my cheek. "We just need to get out of here and then we can start over."

My head shook. "I don't deserve another chance."

"So you made a few bad choi—"

"A few? *A few?*" I faced Leo. "I ruined everything! I'm responsible for Kailen's death, I deserted the Guard and ran away" —I ignored Leo's attempts at trying to shush me— "I abused my gifting to harm myself, lied to those who helped me, fled from those who trusted me, treated you like rubbish, *and* I risked the King's life by getting caught. If that's not enough, I might get you killed trying to rescue me." I squirmed away from Leo, away from lack of judgement on his face.

"Listen." He placed two fingers under my chin and lifted it. "We've all made mistakes. The important thing is where you go from now. Let the past go." His fingers moved to my wrists, hovering over torn flesh, and instantly retreated. "I'm so sorry I left."

I pulled my arms back. "This was all me, Leo."

"Sebastian will pay for this."

"*No.* Don't take him on, he's strong and he's smart."

Leo laughed dryly. "You still don't have much trust in my abilities."

"I can't have you risking your life, no matter how small a risk you think it is. I *will* not." Determination took over the emotions. I would make sure Leo got out of the mess I got him into.

"Shh, did you hear that?" He lifted a finger. "Someone's coming."

I dropped onto the floor and army-crawled under the bed, with Leo on my heels as soon as he'd put the chair back by the desk. The door opened, and a pair of black dinner shoes appeared. *The manager.* He puttered around as if looking for something, pausing at times. Soon enough, he left. We lay silent for twenty seconds, listening, until Leo shuffled out, pulling me behind him. He went to check the window, tight-lipped.

"We should go."

I dusted myself off. "What's the plan?"

"Make for the woods further down the road." Leo adjusted the strap holding up a knife against his ankle. "We'll find cover and stay put for the night. Tomorrow we'll head for the town centre for a car. It'll be easier to blend in when the town's up."

I considered my appearance—bruised, ragged and malnourished. I might as well wear a sign begging for attention.

I reached my arm out. "Let's go, then."

Leo checked the corridor and beckoned for me to follow. I hopped along behind him, taking support from the wall. By the side exit, Leo suddenly paused, fingers hovering over the door handle.

Impatiently, I watched him staring at the door, then the corridor behind me, and the door again. Finally, he locked eyes with me.

"Do you trust me?"

"Of course," I said in a hurry but meant it wholeheartedly.

"Good. Remember that." Leo inhaled and opened the door.

Outside, not two metres from the door, stood Sebastian.

Chapter 38

"Well, well, well, look who it is. Mr Saves-the-Day has finally shown up." Sebastian blocked the way, Kol a few steps behind him.

An invisible rope tightened around my neck.

"Sebastian. I can't say it's a pleasure." Unfazed, Leo took a step outside, standing directly in front of me.

"Lucky for you, I'm in a good mood." Sebastian smirked. "Hand her over and we'll let you walk away in reasonable shape."

Statue-like, Leo and Sebastian stood staring each other down, not missing a blink.

"I'll come with you if you let him go unharmed." I inched out to Leo's side, but he pushed me back against the doorframe.

"No."

Sebastian tutted. "Bad call. I only offer a deal once. I guess we'll make room for one more passenger."

"Over my dead body!" The door slammed shut behind me as I attempted to bypass Leo again, but his arm pressed against my chest.

"Let me handle this, Kali," he said with a stern look.

"Aww, look at you two... How cute," Sebastian mocked, unfolded his arms, and placed them behind him. "I'll make sure you'll get cells next to each other in Gorah."

"She's not going anywhere with you." Leo took a step forward and I prepared myself.

Sebastian whistled, and five guards emerged from the darkness, forming an impenetrable wall behind him. Our odds diminished. We couldn't win.

Leo glanced at me; he knew the same.

"It's up to you. You can come with us peacefully or with a few more broken bones. Either way, you're coming with us," Sebastian said.

"You lay a finger on her again and I will kill you," Leo bit back.

I balled my fists, my fingernails sinking into my skin. I wouldn't let them take Leo. I would not sign his death sentence.

"Wait—I'll do whatever you want if you let Leo go," I pleaded.

"Too late, love." Sebastian motioned for Kol. "Take her, I'll deal with him."

Kol had hardly taken a step forward when Leo's arm shot up.

"Stop. *I* will come with you and I'll cooperate, but I want her escorted back to Bridleton to Tony's flat unharmed, and I want your word you'll never go after her again."

Sebastian's laughter echoed in the night sky. The others didn't seem to know what to do with themselves.

Whatever Leo was trying, sounded dumb even to me.

"You really are something else!" Sebastian shook a finger at Leo. "First of all, why would we want you? And secondly, why would I even consider a deal when I can take you both? Even if Miss Hop-Along *could* fight, you wouldn't stand a chance."

I had to give it to Leo; nothing seemed to shake him.

"You know I'd kill at least half of you before you'd even get close to her. Starting with you." Leo lifted his chin, not breaking eye contact with Sebastian.

"Well, aren't you awfully sure about yourself. No wonder Kalika found you obnoxious." Sebastian spat on the ground as if needing to make his point any clearer, yet much to my surprise he stalled.

"You know I'm right."

"Tell me then, why would we trade you for her? You might make a nice addition to our front line, but we both know Kalika is worth much more."

"Because," Leo said simply. "I have information that no other Guard has."

"Oh yeah, and what's that?" Sebastian's patience was wearing thin, but he must've seen Leo as a threat to have entertained him for so long.

Speechless, I observed, equally curious about Leo's play.

"I have the information you need to capture the son of the King of Narun."

My eyes bore into the back of Leo's head. *The Lost Prince?* Only the King's closest advisors knew anything about the Prince; he hadn't

234

been seen since the Queen was murdered. Leo couldn't have any information worth bargaining with, nor would he ever give it up.

Could he? Would he…?

My brow furrowed. He must be buying for time.

It was a pointless play.

Sebastian folded his arms in front of him again as the other soldiers waited for his lead. "Why would I believe you?"

"Can you afford not to?" Leo dismissed Sebastian's condescending tone. "I know the reward for the Prince's capture. You'd be bathing in gold for the rest of your life. Not to mention everyone would know who you are; everyone would *remember* you."

Sebastian licked the corners of his lips. He couldn't possibly be buying into it.

"The King's son in exchange for *her*? Maybe you're more like me than I thought." The night fell quiet as Sebastian mused to himself.

My pulse accelerated. This wouldn't end well for anyone when they found out Leo was lying. *He is lying, right?*

"I'll humour you," Sebastian said abruptly. "*If* you take us to the alluding Prince, we will let Kalika go. For good. She can live the rest of her little life as she pleases. I'm a man of my word."

"This is ridiculous—" I was quietened by Leo's raised finger.

"And you'll escort her back home, unharmed?"

Sebastian rolled his eyes. "As you wish, but *you're* still coming with us."

Leo extended his hand towards Sebastian. "In that case, you have—"

"What? Wait, no—*no!*" I grabbed Leo's arm and hopped a step forward so that I was by his side, seeking eye contact. "I'm not okay with this. I won't let you reveal his location or let them take you! Leo, I'm not worth it!" I shoved at Leo and started towards Sebastian. "Take me to Gorah. I'll come with you!"

Leo yanked me back and steadied my balance with an iron grip.

"Well, cutie," Sebastian put on a casual voice, "You're more than welcome to—"

"No. She goes home, that's the deal." Leo let go of me but kept a solid arm in my path.

Sebastian lifted his hands, palms facing us. "Alright, alright, let's kill the drama. My deal is with you, Leo. Quite frankly, if you *are* telling the truth, we won't need her. But if you're lying" — Sebastian's eyes narrowed menacingly— "you both pay for it. Especially her." Sebastian winked at me and I noted the veins on Leo's neck bulging.

"Deal." Leo stretched out his hand, and Sebastian shook it firmly.

My objections went to deaf ears.

Sebastian's hand departed with a grin, and a second later his face grew stern. "So, where is the heir to the throne?"

Leo placed his hand on top of mine to stop me from shaking him. The hardness in his features melted for a brief second, and then he faced Sebastian.

"You're looking right at him."

Chapter 39

"You expect me to believe *you* are the King's son? Heir to the throne? *The Lost Prince?*" Sebastian looked about as vexed as I felt. Did Leo actually think Sebastian would buy it?

I sucked in the crisp air. *Might as well stock up on it for the rest of my life in prison.*

Leo sighed, heavy, but unalarmed. "You can believe what you want, but it doesn't change who I am."

A sense of trepidation clawed up from the pit of my stomach. I narrowed in on his features and scoffed. *Of course he's bluffing.*

"You have three seconds to prove it, *Prince.*"

I was about to end the ridiculous play when Leo dug something out of his inner jacket pocket. A small brass like object flashed between his fingers. He opened his palm, dangling a short pendant in front of Sebastian. On the end hung a small, brass crust of a moon, or at least that's what it reminded me of. Its outer lining was smooth while the inner curve was uneven, broken.

Sebastian stared at the small thing catching a glimmer in the night light, fully transfixed. He took a step forward, reached out for the object, but didn't touch it, and flicked his gaze back to Leo.

A triumphant sneer spread across his face. "My, my…it is you."

My head whipped between the pair. "What's going on? What is that thing?" I slapped Leo's chest. "What is going on?"

"All this time the bigger prize was right in front of me." Sebastian's eyes were slightly glazed. "She didn't know, did she?"

"Know what? *What* is going on?" I was beginning to think I'd been muted.

Sebastian flashed a grin in my direction. "Who would've guessed your personal stalker would turn out to be the only heir to Narun?"

He believed Leo?

Whatever that thing was—Leo tucked the pendant back into his inner pocket—it meant something to Sebastian. It meant that he believed him.

Shivers sprinted up my spine as terror gripped me from inside.

"Leo? Is he right?" My face twitched, and I forced Leo to look at me. He peeled my hand off his face gently.

"I trust you'll hold onto your end of the bargain, Sebastian," he said, looking at me.

Sebastian came out of the victorious haze he was already wrapping himself into. "Of course." He beckoned with his finger. "Kol, take her, escort her back and make sure she gets to her friends before you return."

Kol melted into action. I went for Leo's arm, but he stepped aside, leaving me with a handful of his jacket instead.

"No, no, no! I'm not going without you! Leo, don't do this!"

Kol grabbed my arms, trying to pry my hands off Leo.

Panic fuelled my veins. "I won't let you do this, *I won't*! I'm not worth it, Leo, don't do this!"

Sebastian laughed in the background, my resistance bringing him some kind of sick pleasure. Kol pulled me, lifting me from the waist.

"Leo, please, you can't sacrifice everything for me. You have to run! I won't let you do this!" With my free hand, I tried to release myself. "Let me go—Kol, let me go!"

I drowned in hysteria as the magnitude of what Leo was doing hit me. He would reveal his identity for me, be taken away and possibly sacrifice the future of Narun *for me*.

No. No way.

I evened the weight on my legs and swirled to hit the unsuspecting Kol. He stumbled enough to lose his grip on me and the second he did, I pushed against Leo.

"Get away from here!" I yelled, desperately willing him to flee.

Calmly, without hurry or care in the world, Leo took my wrists, brushed his thumbs against the torn skin, and pushed me down, all too easy.

"It's my choice," he said softly. "And you are worth it."

I screamed as Kol tore me away.

While I was still shrieking objections, I saw Leo smile at me before Kol dragged me into the darkness. One of the other guards placed a gag in my mouth, stifling my screams. I struggled against

Kol with everything I had until he forced me into the backseat of a car, tied my hands and feet, and locked me in.

I hammered against the door as the engine purred and Kol set off.

How could Leo do it? The King's son's identity had been sealed, even from the Guard, since he was a child so he would be safe. So that one day he could take the throne and continue in his father's legacy. Narun's legacy.

Now the Gorahites not only knew who he was, but they had him.

And it was all my fault.

I pounded at the door again, only to stop abruptly as the realisation hit me. All this time, I had treated the heir to the throne like something to be disposed of. I winced at the thought of how I'd disrespected him.

Kol hit the brakes abruptly and I skidded on the seat, grabbing the seatbelt behind me so I wouldn't roll off. He apologised and accelerated.

Would they kill him? Interrogate him? Use him for ransom? The already once-worn skin on my wrists moistened, but the ties wouldn't give in.

I had to stop them. I had to alarm the Guard, the King… I had to do something. I wouldn't be the death of him or the downfall of Narun. I couldn't be.

Please, I couldn't be.

"Hope you're comfortable back there. We have a long drive ahead of us."

I strained my neck to see Kol's face from the rear-view mirror. By the time he'd let me go, Leo would be far away, and so would the chances of getting him out.

*

The long drive back was unbearable; every mile added a pound of guilt and tore me further from Leo. The effect of hopelessness was searing.

Though desperate to bring him back myself, I had finally concluded that I needed help. The best thing for Leo would be for me to return to Narun and tell the King everything—and beg for his forgiveness. He would send an army out straight away.

If it wasn't too late.

"Where does this friend of yours live?" Kol asked.

Treetops had changed to high buildings, some I recognised. I gave simple directions to Tony's flat.

I'd been gone for a lifetime. What would Tony and Jill think? Mind occupied with Leo, I hadn't thought of what was waiting for me. Did they know of the past weeks? Had Leo been in touch with them?

"Guess we won't be kin after all." Kol's eyes flickered across the rear-view mirror. I refused his gaze. "Shame. We could've got along well."

"Will they kill him?"

"Not today." Kol stopped for a red light and pulled a knife from the seat next to him. The ropes around my wrists separated, same with feet. He holstered the knife into his ankle strap.

I sat upright, sliding to the right-hand side of the backseat. "Tony might not be home."

"It's not even seven in the morning. He'll be there." Kol took the turn to Tony's street. "And if not, we'll wait."

The familiar surroundings belonged to a different time. They stood for a season that had passed, a 'me' that had once again changed.

I was nervous to see Tony. Nervous of all I had to explain.

"Here we are. Time to say goodbye." The engine silenced. Kol jumped out and opened my door. "Let's go. If Boy Scout's home, my job here is done."

No one could fault Kol on fulfilling his duties.

Behind the familiar door, Kol knocked twice. We waited— nothing. Kol knocked again, louder, adding a knock to his rhythm.

"He must be out," I reasoned.

"Or fast asleep." Still holding my arm, Kol pounded again. This time the door swung open before he could finish, leaving his fist in the air.

Tears clouded my vision as Tony's sleepy face and bare chest appeared in front of me. He rubbed his neck, staring at us blankly. It took him another glance to fully wake up.

"Milla, are you okay?" Concern stamped on his face, Tony took my arm as if to pull me in for a hug. He stopped as he registered Kol's presence, and his arm on me. "Who's this?"

"Just the driver." Kol released his grasp, nodded to me and flew down the stairs.

I fell forwards into a hug. "I'm so sorry, Tony. I can explain, I didn't—"

"I know. I know everything." Tony cupped his hand on the back of my head. "Leo told us you'd been taken and that he was going after you. Where is he?"

Tears spilt over at the mention of his name. Shushing, Tony pulled me inside and closed the door.

"Tell me everything," he said, unusually solemn.

I didn't wait to sit down. "He found me, and we escaped but...but they caught us and, oh, Tony, they have him. They took Leo! They're taking him to Gorah and it's all *my* fault." My eyes darted around, unfocused and helpless. "He made a deal with them: my freedom for his capture. I tried to stop him, but—" I gathered myself, wiping my face with the back of my hand. "He made them bring me back here."

"Wait, that guy was one of them? I should—"

"No, Tony." I placed my hand on his chest, only pressing lightly. "He's a trained soldier. He'll be long gone now."

Tony read between the lines, and seemingly let the matter go, moving onto scanning me from head to toe. Grimacing, he shook his head at the sight.

What a sight I must be...

"What did they do to you? You look awful." Tony helped me further in.

I cringed as I sat down. I only hoped I wouldn't ruin his sofa. "I'm okay. My leg is broken, but it's healing, slowly."

"You need to go to a hospital."

"No, too many questions. I have to get Leo back. They'll—Tony, I've ruined everything!" I wanted to lie down, face down.

"I want to hear everything, but before that, can I get you anything? Water? Food? Painkillers?" Tony picked up a T-shirt from

241

the back of a chair and pulled it on. "I really think you should go to the hospital."

I shook my head. "Just water, please." Although starving, I wasn't hungry.

Tony rushed into the kitchen and returned with a pint of water. He waited as I emptied it through chapped lips in erratic gulps. I noticed he was eyeing my wrists as I handed the glass back. Dried blood painted lines on the skin of my wrists, hands, and forearms.

"Tell me everything, from the start."

I recounted what Tony needed to know and he listened solemnly until I came to a pause.

"I don't get it. If they went through all that trouble to get you then why'd they let you go in exchange for Leo?" Tony rubbed his jaw.

Of course, that was one crucial detail I couldn't leave out.

"To cut a complicated story short, the Queen of Narun was assassinated nearly twenty years ago and because of it, the King decided to place his son in hiding to keep him safe. To this day, only the King and a few of his advisors knew of his whereabouts." Leo's familiar features played in my head. Had there been a resemblance to the King?

"Anyway," I shook off the image of Leo's signature smile, "since then the Gorahites have wanted nothing more than to find him." I swallowed, struggling to continue. "Leo... He made a deal with Sebastian that he would reveal the location of the Prince in exchange for my freedom."

"Leo gave up this Prince for you?" Tony blew out a lung-full. "He really does love you." The words shocked but didn't surprise. "So, they'll let Leo go once they have this Prince in custody?"

"No," I said. "Leo *is* the Prince. *He* is the only heir to Narun, the son of the King."

"Come again?" Disbelief danced around his features. I repeated myself and Tony placed two hands behind his neck, slumping back in his chair. "Well, I'll be darned...You two sure keep having aces up your sleeves." He blew air, cheeks puffed. "You didn't know?"

"No, of course not! Had I known he was the King's son, well, *none* of this would've happened."

"You do know, it was his choice. It's not your fault they've taken him. He'd do anything for you."

"I have to get him back," I retorted, staring at my hands.

"What can we do? You're a mess and I'm, you know, *normal*."

"I have to return to Narun, in hope that it won't be too late to send a team—an *army* out." I got up to stand on my good leg, feeling futile but needing to do something.

"Woah there!" Tony gave me little choice but to sit back down. "You can't go in your state!"

"I *have* to. They already have a head-start and it's a long way to Narun." A sense of urgency gripped my stomach.

"Can't you just ring someone?"

"No network."

"Right. Still" —Tony eyed my cast, now visible since I'd scrolled the trouser leg up to my knee during the drive— "you gotta get that leg sorted."

I licked the corners of my lips. He was right. I needed a real cast for the leg to heal properly. Yet, a trip to the hospital would raise too many questions. I was poster quality only for hostages kept in a dungeon.

I'd have to get someone to make a house call.

"I'll ask Anita." I sighed and tugged down the sleeves of my shirt. I wanted to burn the shirt.

"Good call, lass. I'll ring Jill and she can bring you some clothes and stuff." Tony crinkled his nose. "Um, did you want to take a shower first?"

"Sorry, I must stink." It was the faintest grin, but after the last weeks, it felt freeing.

"It's not that, but it would be better if Jill doesn't see you like this, or Anita." Tony lifted a finger, walked to his bedroom, and returned with a wall mirror. He raised it, and I caught my reflection.

"I see your point."

I had to touch my cheek to make sure the reflection really was me. Aptly, I looked like I had spent weeks in a dungeon, void of light and nutrition. My left eye and cheek were multiple shades of purple, my hair buttered flat. The clothes hung off my frail frame as if I had taken part in an extreme version of the Biggest Loser and won.

Tony took the mirror back, stopping still on his way back to the lounge.

"What's wrong?" I asked as he slammed his palm on the side of his head.

"I forgot. I completely forgot!" Tony dashed back to his bedroom, and I heard him rummaging through drawers. He returned with a piece of paper in one hand, phone on the other.

"Leo, when he rang, he gave me a number. He said if he doesn't come back, I need to ring this number." Tony wafted a piece of paper in the air.

"Dial it."

Tony held the phone next to his ear. A glint of hope sparked up inside—

"It's a dead line."

Hope belly-flopped. Tony dialled again, with the same result. Frustrated, he tossed the paper on the sofa. It floated off it and landed on the floor.

"I must've written the number wrong."

I tried to reach the paper. "Did he say anything else? Who, or what it was for?"

"Nope." Tony picked up the paper and handed it to me. "He just said to ring it."

I didn't recognise the number and I wasn't willing to waste time on it.

"Forget the number." I folded the paper neatly between my fingers, stroking the fold. "Leo can explain it when we get him back, right?"

The doubt Tony tried to conceal from his eyes twisted the knife already piercing my gut.

Chapter 40

With Jill's assistance, I lowered myself to the sofa, pen and paper in hand. A plate of mash, chicken and vegetables waited for me on the coffee table. I wolfed down half a plate and had to stop, my stomach stretched to its max.

I pulled at the top Jill had brought me. I wished the sleeves would've covered the marks on my wrists a little better.

"Right so," I pushed the plate aside and took the pen in hand, "I need to get some supplies for the journey—"

The doorbell startled me.

"That'll be Anita." Jill bolted for the door.

Tony had warned me Jill had been on the phone with Anita as soon as Tony had rung her to come over.

"Camilla." Anita hurried over, gave me a hug, and knelt beside the sofa. "How are you?" Her expression told me loud and clear she knew the answer to that question—anyone could tell I didn't exactly trip on a lamp post.

"Thank you for coming." I twisted on the sofa. "I'm not sure how much Jill told you—"

"She said you were hurt and needed some *discreet* care." Anita assessed my state; her frown deepened. "You're very pale, sweetie." She grazed my cheek. "And thin."

Only Anita could see beyond the big, black bruise on my face.

"It's complicated. As always." I bit my lower lip.

"Hmm. Let's have a look at you. Tony, would you mind getting my bag from the door, please? It weighs a ton." Anita took her coat off and rolled up her sleeves.

I took a raspy breath. "My leg needs attention and my wrists bandaging. The rest is nicks and bruises. No infections so far. I'm a little malnourished, dehydrated—vitamin levels and iron are down—and generally run-down, but I can handle that," I recounted out of instinct.

"Well" —Anita unzipped the duffel bag Tony brought in— "leave something for me to diagnose."

I flashed a coy smile. I was itching to get back on the road but after weeks of emotional torture, it felt comforting to have someone care for me.

"So, the leg..." Anita pulled her gloves on. "Jill said it might be broken?"

"Yes. Minor tibial shaft fracture, no damage to the fibula."

Anita squeezed my leg lightly. "You'll need X-rays if that's the case. We need to see if—"

"It's aligned, and stable," I confirmed. "It needs a cast but it's healing. As you can see the bruising and swelling have mostly gone down."

"But—"

"The fracture is precisely here. Spiral fracture." I drew a line on the skin of my leg and stopped as I saw Anita stare at my exposed wrists. Her mind followed the breadcrumbs and found the gingerbread house.

She gave me one of those looks of pity and shock wrapped with a questioning frown. I didn't bother with an explanation.

"I suppose there's no point telling you to call the police," she said quietly, the sound I made confirming her hunch. "Who held you hostage?"

"People who the police have no power over. It's under control," I lied.

She gave me a disbelieving look. "I have the kit to put a cast on and I brought you some crutches, just in case." Anita finished taking my blood pressure and took out a needle from her bag. "I'll run basic bloods; you look anaemic. You need to drink a lot of fluids and eat, but start slowly." She pushed the plate of mash further on the table. "Soups and that sort of thing. Food easy to digest. And of course, stay out of harm's way, okay?"

I pressed on the cotton wool on the crease of my arm as Anita looked for a plaster.

"The results will take a few days," Anita added.

"I'm leaving—"

"Absolutely not. You're not going anywhere until we see that you're all right. It'll take up to two days for the cast to harden fully, anyway. Anything else, and I'm marching straight to the police."

I would be long gone before the police arrived.

"I don't want to lie to you, Anita. My friend's life is on the line, so I'll be leaving as soon as you're done. You'll be wasting the police's time."

Anita assessed the level of determination on my face, shared a look with Tony, and realised I wasn't going to budge. With a defeated nod, she turned back to my wounds.

"Man, I can't believe Leo's like...royalty," Tony voiced his thoughts, breaking the silence.

Who knew I'd had a Prince as a personal stalker. He'd seen it all. Yup, the son of the King had once even watched me hurl—and cleaned up after. *Terrific.*

"He'll always just be *Leo* to me," Jill said. "Royalty sounds too snobby."

The irony: we all knew a different side to Leo, yet none of us had known the *real* him.

His absence was growing into a planet orbiting my thoughts. Not knowing where he was, how he was, or if he was alive made everything worse. By now he would've realised what a horrible mistake it was giving himself up for me.

I hoped he blamed me.

Once Anita had given me the best home care possible, she gave me a firm hug and pressed an envelope in my hand. Before I had time to object, she was gone. Inside I found a wad of cash. She had come thoroughly prepared.

I would pay her back one day.

"So, what's the plan?" Tony asked behind me as I shut the front door, balancing on a crutch.

My brain shifted gears. "I need to get to a shop." I nodded towards the list resting on the table I'd finished while Anita placed the cast. "Get supplies and go." I'd wasted too much time already.

"So, what do we need to pack with us?" Tony said.

247

My head tilted. "We?"

Jill appeared behind Tony. "Yes, to come with you."

My depleted muscles tensed. The thought of Jill or Tony ending up on the bad side of a Gorahite soldier shook me. I couldn't handle the risk.

"That's not a good idea." I sounded stern. "Sebastian might have his men keeping an eye on me. Plus, the closer we get, the more soldiers we might encounter. It's a risky time for strangers to be entering either land." I lowered my chin. "With my credibility, I'm not sure my word could vouch for you guys."

"We'll be fine—"

"Hang on." Tony raised a finger, and Jill swallowed the rest of her sentence. "You think there's a chance something could happen? That Sebastian's men might…?"

I nodded, and Tony turned his head from side to side.

"Okay. *Okay*," he said after a moment. "In that case, Jill can hold the fort here." Tony shook his head at Jill as she tried to object and turned back to me. "It'll just be you and me, buddy. I might not be much of a fighter, but I'm a darn good chauffeur."

Leg broke and in poor health, I could do with his help.

I gave Tony a sharp nod.

It was due time to rescue a Prince.

Chapter 41

Jill disappeared behind a row of shelves, list in hand. The crutches gave some independence, but the speed they reduced me to was infuriating. Hence, Jill was the go-getter, Tony the man with the trolley, and I, well, the annoying one telling them to hurry up.

"Do I need a jumper?" Tony stopped with the trolley abruptly.

"I'm sure you have one at home," I said as I bypassed him.

"Shouldn't I get a black hoodie?"

"Yes. And some pantyhose and you can be a ninja ballerina," I remarked irritated.

Tony pretended to run me over with the trolley. "I'm serious! Don't I need to blend in in the dark?"

I pushed at the trolley with a crutch. "Tony, *seriously*, and with all my love, you need a lot more than a black hoodie to hide from these guys." If he was any more chilled out about our mission, he'd be all out frozen.

Tony scoffed and mumbled something about crutches and ninjas. Jill returned and unloaded two handfuls into the trolley, before carrying on down the aisle in search of another item on the list.

I limped behind.

"Excuse me, miss?" A man brushed my elbow.

He was well-shaped, average height with a white shirt—sleeves rolled up—and navy trousers. My guess was he was in his early forties.

"Can I recommend a book?" He held up a children's novel. "I thought you might enjoy it. You can purchase it outside." He smiled, placed the book on a shelf near me and walked off.

I took turns in staring at the man's back and the cover of the book. He walked to the end of the aisle on the other side of the shop, still within my sight, and stopped by a shelf.

The cover of the book was of a boy riding a donkey. The title was written in large, colourful font: *The Unusual Prince*.

Was he serious? Did I know him? He looked like a businessman on a lunch break although his poise was particularly strong.

My jaw tightened. *It had to be.* I gripped the crutches and raced towards the man. He picked up an item to investigate closer.

"Milla, Jill's asking if there's anything else you need," Tony said nearby. "She's got everything on the list." I hopped past him. "Oy, Milla, what's up?" Tony caught my arm, making me nearly stumble over.

"That man. I need to follow him." I freed my arm, focused on the stranger slowly making his way forward.

"What man? What's wrong?"

"I think…" *Was I imagining things?* "I think he's going to take me to Leo."

Tony's trolley swirled around with him as he tried to see where I was looking. The man gave a subtle glance and disappeared around the corner.

I have to follow him fast.

"I don't have time to—" I started, but Tony's face convinced me I had to make the time. "The man in the white shirt, he passed me a book and recommended that I read it, but I think he's going to take me to Leo, which is why I have to follow him before he disappears!" I sounded obsessed—or possessed. *Same difference.*

Tony gave me the look one gives a toddler after they've victoriously put on their shoes—on the wrong feet.

"Milla, I know you really want him back—"

"What's going on?" Jill joined us, tuning into our body language.

"She thinks this man she saw is going to take her to Leo," Tony explained, a little condescending. I tried to move forward but Tony yanked at my arm.

"What man? One of Sebastian's soldiers?" Jill quieted her voice, her hair whisking from side to side as she took in the surroundings.

"No, no. I don't know." I eyed the area where the man had gone. "He—he gave me a book...*No*, I'm not crazy, it was called *The Unusual Prince*! It was a children's book."

I took my opportunity when Jill and Tony shared a glance and went after the man. They soon followed.

I ignored the hushed conversation behind me. I rounded the corner but couldn't see him.

"Excuse me?" an elderly shop assistant called from the till. "Miss, excuse me." She smiled as I faced her. "Your uncle asked me to tell you he's waiting for you outside."

The stirring in my gut reached boiling point. *I was right.* I left the woman with a hasty thank you and hobbled towards the exit, my entourage not far behind.

"What about the shopping?" Tony still hung onto the trolley like he owned it.

"Leave it," I snapped. "If it's him, we won't need it."

Tony grumbled, but I no longer heard the spin of wheels behind me.

"What if it's a trap?" Jill rushed to my side—not that it was very hard with my pace.

"It's not. It has to be him. I don't know how, but it *has* to be."

Frantic, I searched the parking lot, narrowing on each male loitering or walking. Cars, people, women with prams. Where was the man?

"What did he look like?" Jill scrunched her face in the low-hanging sun.

"Average height. Short, dark hair. Clean-shaven. He looks like a marketing manager," I described.

Jill frowned. Tony lifted his shoulders.

A taxi pulled up next to us. I waved it off desperate to find the stranger's face.

"Hop in."

My heart fluttered. The man sat on the driver's seat of the taxi, reaching to open the passenger door.

"I can only take you," he said to me softly.

"Sorry, mate, but we're a package deal." Tony dashed for the backseat, closely followed by Jill, in the time I got my crutches in the front.

"He thought you might say that," the man said with a sigh. "Okay, then."

"Leo?" I whispered, afraid of the answer.

251

"He's safe."

My pulse doubled its tick. "Are you serious? He's really okay? You have him?" I wanted to let relief take over, but I couldn't, not until I'd lay eyes on him.

"See for yourself in about ten minutes." The man helped me fasten my seatbelt.

Tony popped his head between the front seats. "Who are you?"

"I'm one of *Leo's* personal guards." The man glanced at the rear-view mirror.

"How did he escape? Did you save him? How did you know he was taken?" I squeezed both sides of the seat, knuckles white. *Please, let this be real.*

"I'd like to know where you were to begin with," Tony butted in. "Sure weren't 'guarding.'"

"Tony!" Jill pulled him back, disapproving.

The man joined the traffic on the main road, paying more attention to his mirrors than our hunger for answers.

"I'll leave it for him to tell you," he said plainly. "Right now, I need to do my job."

My senses were instantly awakened. Of course, Leo wasn't safe yet. Leo wouldn't be safe from now on: his identity was out. Sebastian and his men, not to mention every Scout, soldier, Hunter, and citizen of Gorah, would be looking for him, doing everything in their power to stop him from crossing the borders into Narun.

I had cost him his freedom, maybe for the rest of his life.

I checked for cars possibly tailing us; every passer-by became a suspect. Tony and Jill shouldn't be here. If anyone saw them in the car with us…

Jill cleared her throat, several times. "Can you at least tell us your name?"

"Sure, Jill. You can call me Joe."

Jill's eyed popped. "How do you know my name?"

"It's my business to know who Leo associates with." Joe threw Jill a quick smile.

"That's not your real name though, is it, *Joe*?" Tony certainly wasn't going to give the guy an easy ride.

252

"Knock it off, Tony. You should be used to fake names by now." I meant it as a joke, but it came out like an insult. I added a scoff to lighten the tone.

"Tell me about it." He paused before adding, "Where're we headed, anyway?"

"We're almost there."

We fell silent. Leo would have the answers. My fingers tapped the cast impatiently. Could this be too good to be true?

I kept a keen eye on the wing mirror. We were near the shore at the tourist end of town, passing hotels and B&Bs. Joe took a turn towards a several storeys high hotel. Confident, like he had done it a thousand times, he pulled up in front of the entrance and left the engine running.

"I'll meet you in the lounge in five," Joe said to me. "Keep an eye out, will you?"

I agreed and took Jill's hand as she helped me out of the car.

The entrance was impressive, but the real wow-factor was the lounge. Marble statues created aisles to the right and left, one leading to a seating area with leather armchairs. Lifts, a stone reception desk that was grand in its simplicity, and a seemingly empty bar were on the left. The foyer was scattered with families, the elderly, and businessmen.

A little boy ran towards me, slowed down to stare at my black eye, and then dashed past me. On his heels was his flushed mother calling him to stop. An older couple sat closest to us at the seating area; the man napped while the woman read a novel. Two men in pin-striped suits sat on the other side—one reading the Financial Times, the other on his iPad. A suited lady sat near them, talking on the phone.

"Shall we sit?" Tony rubbed his neck, slightly disorientated.

"There, by the window, near the door." I motioned with a crutch.

It only took a couple of minutes for Joe to walk through the gilded entrance. Clocking us in an instant, he beckoned for us to follow.

The lift doors slid open as we reached him. We piled in, together with two young women. They took in Joe's frame, impressed, rubbing their lips together meaningfully behind his back. *Men in suits.*

Six illuminated numbers later we reached our floor. Joe cleared the hall and led us to a door.

My heart raced a marathon as he swiped the key card.

Chapter 42

My eyes were drawn to the three duffel bags on the floor as the door opened. Not far from them, a pair of black, clean combat boots dug into the carpet. Rashly, I took in the unfamiliar frame of the man wearing the boots. His bulky appearance filled most of the entrance.

He exchanged a look with Joe and moved out of the way.

It was then I saw him. At the far end of a rather large room, sat Leo, talking to a man his age who was eating an apple.

Leo's attention flew to the door; one of my crutches fell to the floor. I shoved past the others and met Leo's arms half-way in the room, barely registering the black eye decorating his face.

I clasped onto him as tight as if Kol was still behind me, taunting to pull me away.

"Glad to see you, too." Leo sounded as relieved as I felt, yet I caught a strain on his voice that instantly didn't sit right with me.

"How did you escape?" I breathed into his neck.

"Easier than trying to get out of your grip," he quipped, but I wasn't ready to let go. "Kal, some air."

Gently yet firmly, Leo unclasped my arms. I cringed as my bad leg thudded to the ground. I hadn't realised my feet were a few inches off the floor.

Leo mouthed an apology and turned to the others. "Good to see you, guys." Leo gave both Jill and Tony a hug. "I figured you might be joining us."

"Try and keep us away, *your Highness*." Tony did a little bow and pulled a coy Jill under his arm.

"I don't want any of that from you three," Leo warned, a little weary.

"Are you hurt?" Jill pulled a face at Leo's black eye, searching for any other obvious signs of injury. Thankfully, I already knew there was nothing seriously wrong with him, although he had several hidden bruises on his body.

"I'm perfectly fine. Thanks for asking," Leo replied, and gave Joe a glance.

"So, how—"

"Did you escape?" I finished Tony's sentence. "I thought for sure... *Wait.*" I shoved Leo enough to get his attention and slapped him lightly on his better cheek. "Don't ever do something like that again! Why didn't you tell me who you were?"

I heard the apple drop onto the floor a second before the youngest of the three men placed a hand on my shoulder. Tony mumbled something. Joe held the arm of the well-built man guarding the door.

Leo rubbed his cheek, a little taken back, and told the guard to let me go. He gave me a questioning look I had seen all too many times. I ignored it.

"Why did you do it? Why did you risk *everything* for me?" My voice reflected how I meant it: desperate rather than angry. Leo touched my chin with a knuckle and embarrassment settled on my pale cheeks as I remembered who he was—and became painfully aware of everyone staring at me.

"You know why," Leo remarked softly, and strolled over to Joe. He whispered under his breath, and Joe signalled the other guards.

Instantly, they cleared the room.

"Well trained." Tony whistled, his posture easing noticeably at their exit. "Are they your personal gofers?"

Leo placed a hand on Tony's shoulder. "Something like that. They're my bodyguards, of sorts."

"Leo, I'm so sorry for getting you into this mess." I struggled not to tear up. The dungeon hadn't been kind to my hormones.

"Kal, it was my time." Leo went to pick up the apple that had fallen from the guard and tossed it in the bin. "Besides, I'm in charge of my decisions, not you."

I didn't buy his smile; something gnawed at him. *Was it me?*

I was too scared to ask.

I perched on the bed, next to Jill. She hooked my arm into hers.

"So, what happened, mate?" Tony enquired.

Leo motioned for him to sit as he pulled up a chair. "Sebastian and his merry men were taking me to Gorah when my men found us. Three of his men were killed, a few captured, but Sebastian and one other got away. My men insisted they take me to Narun, but" — Leo's jawline tightened— "Sebastian won't give up, and he knows what to use as leverage." Leo's gaze flickered to me. "Plus, the word will be out; Sebastian won't make the same mistake twice. He will have notified the King of Gorah. There are Scouts everywhere." Leo ran his hand through his hair. A line formed between his eyes as things unmentioned weighed on his mind.

The guilt inside of me was becoming a boulder.

"How did your bodyguards know you were taken? Milla said we had to get word to Narun."

"It's complicated," Leo said. "Since I've been in hiding, I've always had my men with me, except when I came to find Kalika. It would've drawn too much attention, so I talked them out of joining me, though I updated them on a weekly basis. They were always nearby. When Kalika was kidnapped I told them I was going after her. There was no time to wait for them, so I put in place a signal in case I was captured." Again, his eyes refused to stay on mine for long.

"The phone number you gave Tony." It made sense now.

"But it was a dead line," Tony grunted.

"It served its purpose. Dialling it activated a device on me that my guards were able to track—by that time Sebastian had finished searching me for trackers." Leo straightened up, wincing slightly. The bruise on top of his ribcage bothered him. "They were already on their way anyway as I told them of the possibility of me revealing my identity."

I sniffed angrily. "And they *let* you do it?"

"They weren't thrilled, but it was my call."

"We're so glad you're back, Leo," Jill hurried to say before I had a chance to answer back. "We've been so worried."

Our attention shifted as Joe appeared in the doorway. "Sir, fifteen minutes." He didn't wait for an acknowledgement before leaving us.

257

"Fifteen minutes for what?" I verbalised everyone's thoughts, although I was pretty sure my hunch was correct.

"Until I have to go." Leo sighed. "We've already stayed in one place too long. Bridleton will be their first port of call."

"You're still leaving?" Tony and Jill said in unison.

"I have to." Leo stood up. "It's not safe for me to stay here. For anyone's sake."

"That sucks. Big time," Tony mumbled.

Jill skipped over to embrace Leo. "Will we ever see you again?"

"Of course, you will." Leo released her from the hug. "I just need to go back home for a while and once things cool down, I'll send for you. How's that sound?"

"You won't be able to come back, will you?" Tony sulked.

"Not for a while, bro."

I had taken away his freedom.

Jill wrapped her arms around Leo once more. I never realised how close they were.

Joe popped his head in to give a ten-minute warning, now more pressing. I stared down at my hands, perched on the edge of the bed.

"Actually, you guys, do you mind if I have a minute alone with Kalika?" Leo said, causing my pulse to beat out of sync.

It was only Leo. Why was I nervous?

Tony and Jill stepped outside without objection. I waited for the door to click shut before glancing at Leo. He stood there watching me, edgy.

Goosebumps made their entrance and for a second it felt it wasn't Leo in front of me; it was the heir to the throne.

I cleared my throat. "I'm truly sorry for the situation I've cau—"

"No," Leo cut me short, unapologetically blunt. "Don't talk to me like I'm the Prince. Talk to me like you know me." He took a step forward but then hesitated.

"But you *are* the Prince and I need to apologise for how I treated you all this time. If I'd known who you were, I never would've been such an idiot." I dropped my hands to my lap, internally cringing at the things Leo knew about me. "If that wasn't enough, I've messed up your life and compromised the future of Narun. You should have me arrested."

"I should, shouldn't I."

I bypassed the sarcasm. "Leo, *why* didn't you tell me?"

He paced over, and sat next to me, placing his fingers on the handle of the crutch beside me.

"I wanted you to come with me because you *wanted* to, not because the Prince of Narun asked you to."

"You should've told me."

"A title doesn't change who I am. I'm still the guy who drives you off the wall. And this—" Leo stopped short. "Look, we don't have a lot of time. I need to know what you're going to do."

"What do you mean?"

"If you're staying, I need to set people in place to protect you. I need you to be safe." The muscles in Leo's forearm flinched under my touch.

"What are you talking about?"

"What I just said. Rewind." He was frustrated; I wasn't sure why.

"Leo, am I allowed to come with you? You know I have a lot of baggage. And I exposed the...*you*. It was my fault you were captured, and I could've started a war!"

Leo took my chin between his thumb and forefinger and lifted my head, forcing eye contact. "That wasn't your fault! Kal, you're so—stubborn! I don't blame you for any of this. I chose to come out in the open; it was time. I *believe* in the greater purpose, and if it was my destiny to be taken saving you, then that's a sacrifice I'm willing to make. And so is the King. He too would lay down his life for one of his people."

The door swung open. "Five minutes, sir. We really need to—"

"Just leave us!" I hadn't seen Leo snap at anyone but me before. He got up, his defined back towards me, rubbing his forehead.

"*What's wrong?*" I said after staring at the back of his head for a moment. "Why are you so angry?"

"I'm not angry, I'm—I don't know." Leo locked eyes with me again. "Just tell me if you're coming with me or staying and put me out of my misery."

That was bugging him? I pushed myself up, balancing on one foot. "Leo, do you really need to ask? I told you before I'd return to Narun. It just depends on whether I'm allowed to…and if you want me to."

He scoffed. "Kalika, nothing's changed."

Our past conversations whirled in my head. "*A lot* has changed; everything has changed. I have so many questions, but we haven't the time to get into it. We need to get you back to Narun. We need to *go.*"

The intensity evaporated from Leo's shoulders. "*We?*" His fingers looped around my wrist. "You're coming with me?"

"Of course, I'm coming with you! From now on, I'll do whatever you say."

He let go of my arm, a scowl forming on his face. "*Why?* Are you coming with me because I'm the King's son, or are you coming with me because you want to?"

"I'm coming with you because I never should've left Narun to begin with. Because I made a ginormous mistake that ultimately led me to the point where I couldn't be more broken but—" I took a sharp breath between my teeth. "*But* I get it now. The thing about hitting the bottom is that it makes you look up. It strips you bare but gives you the chance to climb up and rebuild yourself. So, I'm starting over—again—the right way, because I know now where my place is. I don't know what the future holds but I'm open to…to whatever it brings."

"Great. In that case, I'll reassign you as my personal maid on arrival back home. That's an order."

My heart fluttered at the familiar grin. I shook my head before the strange feeling took over.

"You *wish*," I muttered unimpressed.

"Well, my wish is your command. After all, I do out-rank you."

"Whatever." I hopped once on the spot, leaning onto a crutch. "Royalty or not, you're not getting any special treatment once this leg heals." I looked for my other crutch. Where had I dropped it?

"That's the spirit." Leo pulled me over too fast and I stumbled, needing him for balance. Slightly awkwardly, he held me at arm's length.

I took in his face. His eye was all shades of black and blue down to his cheekbone.

At least we matched.

In my head, I vowed to train hard when we got back. I would become stronger. If there was a way to train my gift, I would do it. I would do whatever I could to protect Narun, and Leo, to my death.

I lifted an arm onto his shoulder, hesitated, and pulled myself against him. Leo eased as my head tucked under his chin.

"I know what you're thinking." His breath warmed my ear. "But the best chance they have at getting to me is through you. So, *I'm* going to do whatever I can to keep them from getting to you. If you want what's good for Narun, don't do anything stupid. And for crying out loud" — Leo pulled at my hair gently — "start listening to me."

The door banged open. Leo swirled, instinctively pushing me behind him like a child. Jill, Tony and Joe, in that order, spilt inside. Jill's hands were shaking in front of her.

"Sebastian is here."

Chapter 43

'Damn my leg' was the first thought coming to me. *'Should've gone five minutes ago,'* was the second.

"Where?" Leo took a step forward, jaw taut.

"Downstairs. Jack called it in." Joe held a phone in his hand.

Leo collected my lost crutch, passed it to me and moved to pick up a black jacket. "Is he alone?"

Joe hesitated. A pale Jill took Tony's hand.

Not good.

"Come on, what are you not telling me?" Leo said, agitated and sensing the charge in the room as I had.

"He has three others with him, as far as we know," Joe explained. "They don't know our room, but they know we are here. And there's something else."

"H-he's got Lana," Jill blurted, her frame shaking along with her voice.

No, no, no, no, no, no.

Leo's knuckles bulged white from the force of his clenched fists; he appeared taller and stronger.

"It's true, sir," Joe said. "Tony confirmed it—he saw her. Sebastian's not playing by the rules."

If Sebastian had Lana it was because he couldn't get to me, or Tony or Jill. He was playing dirty. He would find every friend I ever made, down to the janitor I worked with, to get to us.

"Where are they now?" Leo asked.

"They're down at the lobby, talking to the receptionist. It won't be long until they find us, sir. We *have* to go," Joe insisted but remained still.

I tilted my head towards Tony and Jill enough for Leo to register and waited for him to give the order.

"Joe, call Jonas. I want him to go with Jill and Tony, get them out of here and take them to a safe house. He's to stay with them until further notice."

In an instant, Joe was on his phone and out of the room.

"We can't leave you here." Tony's arm circled Jill's shoulders. She was white as snow.

"Guys, it's time to say goodbye." I looked at my friends' faces, nostalgic and overwhelmed by how hard it felt to say goodbye.

Jill rushed over and pulled me in for a hug. "You'll get her back, right? Please get her back!" She squeezed me hard. "I'm going to miss you!"

One of the guards, presumably Jonas, entered. Leo and Tony said their goodbyes.

"We have to go *now*," Jonas said with a bass voice. He was the biggest of the three, built more like a bodybuilder than an athlete. He was in his early thirties I guessed, hair shaved an inch shorter than Joe's. He would keep them safe.

I pulled Jill into a final hug, promising to do everything we could to get Lana back unharmed. Leo rushing us, I clasped my arms around Tony, fingers digging into his back. I had everything to thank him for. Who knew where I'd be without him. It felt wrong to leave them in such a way, but Jonas's commands ribbed them out of my grasp, and then they were gone.

I buried the moment, and the emotions that came with it, for another day.

Leo handed me a knife and a padded zip-up jacket.

"I'd rather have my Sais back," I muttered as I pocketed the simple weapon.

Leo shot me a pointed look as he tossed one of the duffel bags on his back. Joe confirmed something with Jack, who was the third and youngest-looking guard, on the phone.

"Where's Sebastian now?" I demanded as Joe hung up.

"They're in the lobby, waiting," Joe said.

"They know we know they're here," Leo reasoned.

"What's their play?"

"I'm assuming they'll hurt Lana until we surrender." Leo's face was sombre.

I thought about it logically. Involving Lana was against the rules: both lands had agreed a long time ago that innocent people were left out of our battles. Yet Sebastian was working on a personal vendetta. He knew all my friends; I'd introduced him to them.

"What's the plan?"

"We're going to get Lana back," Leo stated plainly. I pictured him cocking a gun and shook my head at the image.

Lacking the lightness of foot, for obvious reasons, I followed Joe and Leo to the empty corridor. Leo picked me up on top of the stairs and I held onto the sticks. Two floors down Joe got an update: Sebastian and his men were moving to the adjacent parking hall. We picked up the pace.

We moved through the lobby, attracting attention like a magnet as we passed. Joe led the way with eyes everywhere. Leo's focus was split…because of me. I was a liability rather than an asset.

"How are we going to get her back?" I panted, painfully aware of it. Captivity had murdered my level of fitness.

"I don't know." *At least Leo is being honest.* "But we need to put an end to this."

I read between the lines. Sebastian had a long list of leverage. We'd have to stop him for good.

The parking hall was five storeys high, oblong with a circling drive in the middle. Air flowed throughout thanks to the open wall design. Lifts and stairs were at the side closest to the hotel; a walk-through tunnel joined the two on floor four, but we took the outside entrance.

The bottom floor was full of cars and there was no sign of Sebastian as anticipated. He would want more privacy. He would be on floor five.

Joe paused by the lift. "Jack is waiting on third."

The silent communication between the two men was meant to count me out. I eased my grasp on the crutches. As we entered the lift, I was surprised I was even allowed this far.

The lift stopped on the second floor and the doors chinked open. Joe popped out while Leo held the doors from closing.

"This is as far as you go. Wait for us by the people carrier." Leo pointed at the burgundy Renault Scenic, three cars from the lift, sandwiched between a Ford and a Jaguar. "Do *not* follow. That's an order. One of us will come for you. If we're not here in twenty minutes, run. Or hop, more like it."

Joe returned from the perimeter check and gave it an all clear. I hobbled towards my designated hideout.

"Kal, do you promise?" Leo shouted after me.

I hummed a sound in agreement.

"You're not going to say goodbye?"

"I'll see you in fifteen. I'm not that lost without you."

The chuckle was cut off by the lift doors closing.

Awkwardly, I lowered myself onto the smooth concrete. I pushed the crutches under the car and leaned against the front wheel, making sure I had a view of the exits. The little round light indicating which floor the lift was on stopped and stayed at three. I pictured Leo and Joe meeting Jack there, exchanging quick protocol and advancing to the stairs. Joe would be at the front, Jack at the back. Their first and foremost job was to protect Leo.

Noises of traffic carried up from below; I tuned in to the cars on the ground floor.

I feared for Lana, feeling guilty of thinking ill of her on previous occasions. I'd never made an effort with her and had instead judged her far too quickly. The worst thing was, she wouldn't have the faintest idea what this all was about. Sebastian might've fed her lies or not have said a word. Either way, he would be holding Lana as a shield. His men would aim to take out Joe and Jack, leaving Leo to solve the situation between himself and Sebastian.

I stopped my fingers from drumming the side of the car; I wanted to hear a pin drop if needed.

How would Leo get Lana back without surrendering himself again? Leo's downfall was his obsession to protect me, but in battle, his weakness was also his compassion: he wouldn't let an innocent person be hurt on account of him.

"Noooooo!"

I gasped audibly, feeling my pulse jump. I was up, holding onto the side of the car to restrain myself from running towards Leo's voice. My head whipped to the left. There was a piercing shriek as a body fell past the open sides of the parking hall.

266

Air emptied out of my lungs. *First beat*—who was it? *Second beat*—were they dead?

I scuttled to the direction where the body had fallen, taking support from car bonnets. My skin crawled like a thousand ants. I leant over the stone edge, refusing to think about the consequences of what I was about to witness.

My stomach sank.

"Lana!" The name escaped, echoing freely before my hand knew to clasp my mouth shut. Lana's delicate yet lifeless body lay in a puddle of velvet blood. For six seconds, I couldn't tear my eyes off the sight. On the seventh, reason slapped me into action.

My neck snapped up; three floors above I met Sebastian's smirk. He threw his body over the ledge, starting to drop down to my level.

I was an idiot to reveal my location.

I dove onto the ground, crawling behind the cars. I froze behind a small Kia as Sebastian landed with a thud to where I had stood less than a minute ago.

"Playing hide and seek?" his voice echoed. A car bonnet dented under his boots, quickly followed by another. He was nearing, and then he was a car past me. All he needed was the right angle and he would see me.

I uncovered the knife Leo had given me from my pocket and army-crawled between two cars, keeping an eye on Sebastian's boots from under the car. I pulled myself up to one knee and threw the knife.

A faint groan parted Sebastian's lips as the knife pierced the skin on his knee cap. Swiftly, he pulled it out and turned to me.

I took support from the bonnet to pick myself up.

"You think a little nick will stop me?" He lifted a corner of his mouth.

"No. That was payback for my leg."

With a scoff, Sebastian tossed the knife back to me. "Simply out of interest, I'll let you take your best shot."

I holstered the knife; he would only use it against me. Sebastian beckoned me with his hand.

Oh, I'll give him a fight.

267

I powered up from the car bumper and jumped towards Sebastian, my fist itching to rearrange his face. He dodged my punch, but I grabbed a hold of his neck and climbed on his back, one leg wrapped around his waist. Arm around his neck, I held on with the sheer force of my pent-up anger toward him, pulling against his larynx.

The air was knocked out of me as Sebastian slammed me against a pillar—once, twice, three times. The fourth time, he angled himself so the edge of the pillar hit my broken leg. My hold loosened at the sudden bolt of pain; Sebastian bent down and flipped me onto my back. Refusing my body's plea for a few seconds of rest, I rolled onto my side and jabbed at the wound on his knee. His knee gave out enough to put him off-balance, giving me time to scramble half-up and smash against him, falling on top of him.

But Sebastian didn't have the disadvantage of a cast.

He pinned my bad leg under his and rolled over, leaving me trapped underneath him. I cracked his nose with a right hook, but he blocked my left hand and locked his hands around my wrists. Blood dripped from his broken nose to my chest.

"*Hey!*"

The familiar voice came from behind me. I craned my neck enough to detect Leo's outline at the same spot where Sebastian had landed a while ago.

Sebastian muttered expletives under his breath and wiped the blood off his face. I used the distraction to jolt my hip up, rolling to freedom as Leo's boot made contact with Sebastian's chest.

I pushed myself upright as Leo and Sebastian, both born fighters, stared each other down and attacked. The balance of call and response was equal to the eye.

I had underestimated Leo—he was fast, and he was sharp.

It was only when I saw a glimmer of a triple-bladed dagger in Sebastian's hand that I snapped out of voyeurism.

I dug out the knife again and threw it towards Sebastian's neck. As hoped, Sebastian leaned back enough to duck while Leo ran up the concrete pillar, kicked into Sebastian's right shoulder, and landed with a roll on the floor. Simultaneously, he picked up the dropped dagger.

Sebastian was quick to recover. He curled a lip at me and re-tracked to get the knife I had thrown.

"Go," Leo ordered with a tone hard to disobey, standing as a shield in the space between me and Sebastian.

I limped towards the door for the stairs.

"I should've killed you when I had the chance!" Sebastian spat and for a brief second, I wondered if it was meant for me or Leo.

Blades clashed against each other as I neared the door. I shoved it open with my body weight—and flew flat on my back in a sloppy arch. Large hands, with a symbol tattooed on the inside of the left palm, took hold of my jacket and yanked me up in the air until my feet dangled. A man I didn't recognise pressed me against the wall.

The next three things seemed to merge into one: Leo losing his focus because of me, Sebastian nicking Leo on his shoulder, missing his neck by inches, and my feeble body being thrown down the stairs.

The cast cracked in several places. My cheek felt moist against the landing. Then things went dark.

Chapter 44

Snippets of sights protruded into my consciousness: stairwell, cars, drops of blood on my legs, sudden daylight.

Next came the sounds: police sirens, chatter, a car door banging shut, and an engine forced to its max.

Lastly, I became aware of the pain pulsating throughout my body as if I'd been caught in a spinner filled with rocks. Hairline fractures on my ribs and fingers, bruises, concussion—nothing that wouldn't heal. No internal bleeding, but the leg needed re-casting.

The vehicle carrying me eased into a steady speed and I wished nothing more than to sleep the pain away.

But there was something pressing I had to recall. My eyelids lifted, and I stared out the windscreen without taking anything in. Someone shuffled.

"You're cut," I said to Leo—the man behind the wheel—my voice sounding foreign.

"You're alive," he retorted wryly. "Are you okay?"

I met Leo's intent eyes lazily, nodded, and reached over to inspect the cut near his neck.

I winced more than he did. "You need stitches." His wound was clean-cut but deep.

"And you need the full works. There's a clinic a few miles from here. They don't ask questions." Leo let his anxious gaze rest on me a little too long.

We drove through the edge of town, passing a wealthy housing estate—family homes with large, well-kept gardens, a few people jogged by, a dog ran loose. It was still light, but the sun was considering going down to rest.

"Quite a fall you took," he continued in a clipped tone. "Are you sure you don't need the hospital right away? How do you feel?"

"Achy." I straightened up, sucking in the pain. "What happened?"

"You fell down the stairs."

"I know *that*. And I didn't fall. I was pushed."

"*Thrown* like a rag doll, more like it," Leo corrected, displeased.

I exhaled slowly, temporarily easing the pain in my ribs. "What happened after? Where's Sebastian?"

Leo drew a breath. "Joe and Jack showed up once they had taken care of Sebastian's men. With their help, taking out Sebastian and the other guy was easy."

"Where are they now? Is Sebastian dead?"

"He's under arrest, both of them are. My guards will take them back to Narun."

I checked the wing mirror. Nobody was following. "Shouldn't they be with you?" If there was ever a need for his guards, it was today.

"No," he said curtly. "We need to lay low for a while." He stretched his arms out. "It's easier to hide if it's just the two of us. It was my decision."

I bet that decision didn't go down well: the Prince travelling without protection during one of the most crucial times in Narun's history, unprotected and *known*.

"I'll keep you safe, don't worry," Leo added, hesitant of my silence.

"I'm not worried about *me*." Suddenly, I recalled where I had seen the symbol tattooed on my attacker's hand. "He was a Hunter, that guy, wasn't he? He was after you."

Leo shrugged.

I pressed gently under my ribcage to relieve some of the pressure. "That means Sebastian has already gotten the word out. They know who you are." *We were too late. I was too late. The damage is done.*

"Looks that way." Leo kept his eyes on the road.

"You do realise *everyone* is going to be after you."

"Yup."

"And that's all you're going to say?"

"Uh-hu."

"Leo!" I smacked the seat with a loose fist. My fractured fingers didn't thank me. "I don't wanna be responsible for getting you caught a second time!"

"I've no intention of getting caught."

I cradled my hand against my chest, breathing out the spasms of pain. "You need your guards," I said slowly. "We need to get you to Narun, ASAP, under protection."

Leo was quiet for a moment, but I doubted he would actually change his mind.

"It's too risky. The main harbours will be scouted. Planes and trains, too. We'll be safest by car, on our own. Besides, it's better if we let things cool before returning."

Yeah, that's going to happen—never.

"What exactly are you suggesting, then?"

Leo joined the motorway; the worst of the post-work traffic had passed.

"Getting better, hiding, being on the run, and then using a less obvious way of getting back home."

"Why don't we send for the Guard and ship you back? That would make more sense." I rasped as a stab of pain jolted me again.

"Draws too much attention. I don't want to put any more lives on the line."

I sucked in my bottom lip, assessing what was left of the cast. "You'd be safer without me. I'm a hindrance, a very slow one," I muttered, and Leo scoffed. "They don't want me, they want *you*, Leo. You need to get back home! I'm sure that's what the King, your *father*, would want."

"He knows my intentions and he's behind me." Leo shot me a firm look. "Besides, we're in on this together. I'm afraid you're just as much on the wanted poster as I am, and not just because you're a way to get to me."

I swallowed awkwardly, trying to rid the taste of blood from my mouth. The Hunter tossing me down the stairs had made me bite my tongue.

Guilt suddenly speared my chest.

"What happened with Lana?" I forced myself to face the harrowing mental image of her mangled body. Her life was on my conscience.

273

"Sebastian never intended on letting her go. As soon as we got up there, he stabbed Lana and threw her down." Leo looked as responsible for Lana's death as I felt. Her family and friends would never know the truth. They would never fully recover—and neither would Jill.

I shuddered, forcing myself to push the mourning until later.

"What's going to happen to Tony and Jill?"

"They should be at the safe house with Jonas. Hey," Leo brushed the side of my arm, "don't worry, no one will get to them."

I missed them already. It'd be a long time before I'd see them again.

"Where're we headed, anyway?"

"Clinic and then stop for food. I've got essentials. We can sleep in the back of the van tonight."

"Well prepared." I attempted to slide down, but the seatbelt locked and held me up.

"Comes with the life."

There was very little I knew of Leo's past. There had always been rumours and speculation regarding the King's son, much of which I assumed not to be the truth. I'd have to ask him one day.

I tried sliding sideways this time, needing to rest my head. I got as far as my head reaching Leo's arm when it felt like my ribs were going to snap. I gasped in pain and immediately, Leo pushed me back upright.

The sun decided it was time to give night its reign as the sky darkened.

There was a lot to process. My kidnapping seemed weeks ago when it was merely days. Today felt a week long. But Leo was alive and safe, for now. And my friends were safe. Sebastian would be of no more trouble. Sure, there were others to worry about but that was a thought for a new day. We would run, hide, heal. Time would give us shelter. Time would help me sharpen my skills. Time would make us an invincible pair—

"Wait, what am I saying?"

"I didn't realise you were saying anything." Leo took an exit last minute as if he'd been distracted by his own thoughts. I groaned as my arm thumped against the door.

"Us as partners is never going to work. What are we meant to be?"

Leo slid me a look, trying to catch my train of thought.

"You're the heir," I clarified. "You can't be Guard or go on missions! You don't need a partner! Which means...was the prophecy a lie?" It felt as if the ground shook underneath me.

Leo rested his head against two fingers, searching for an answer. "Nothing's changed but my title."

"*Everything* has changed. All this started with the prophecy, but obviously, it must be flawed." Had Kailen been wrong?

"It's not," Leo said with conviction, and then frowned. "When we were at the cabin, I altered some details to keep my identity a secret." He gripped the wheel with both hands. "It's complicated. There are things you—*we,* don't need to know yet. Things are changing. There's a day coming when it's time for kings and heirs to join in the ranks."

My mind cast to the only place where I'd ever felt at home. What had changed in the time I'd been gone? What was still to change?

Shivers ran up my spine. "Are we going into war because of all that's happened?"

"It's not out of the equation."

Leo's honesty startled me. The past years had changed me to almost unrecognisable. I wasn't ready for home being different, too.

"Then...where does that leave us?"

"I'm still asking you to be my partner. Fight with me," Leo added the last words hastily as if needing to clarify.

"The King's son doesn't need someone to fight with; you and the King are what we're fighting for. Unless... I serve as one of your bodyguards?"

Leo scowled at me so unimpressed I let the idea die a prompt death. Heavy on the gas pedal, he ate up the road like it was a triple-chocolate sundae.

"Don't over-think," he said after a while. "Forget all the other stuff. It's me asking if you'll fight with me. Like Kailen wanted."

It still hurt to hear his name out loud.

I gulped air, throat dry. "Okay." I stared at my palms. "I won't make the same mistakes again. As far as I'm concerned, we're a team. And I'm going to stick by you until you say otherwise. I made that decision even before you made yourself royalty."

"I was always royalty," Leo countered. "You just didn't know it."

I whacked the air between us, lacklustre.

"You sure you're okay with all this?"

"Of course. I came to my senses." I was only half sarcastic.

"See." A crooked smile spread on Leo's face. "I always get what I want."

Again, I slapped the air somewhere in his direction.

"Seriously, that's *pathetic*. I may reconsider joining forces with you."

I curved my mouth and blew a sigh. Something still troubled me. "I gotta ask one thing… Are *you* going to be happy with *just* this?"

"Kal, you don't have to marry me."

Blood rushed under the skin of my cheeks at his bluntness.

"I know, I know. Forget it, it's stupid." I angled my head toward the side window. *I'm an idiot.*

"*Kalika.* At this stage, I don't think it's a secret how I feel about you, but I know you're still in love with Kailen. I don't expect anything. We're pretty unconventional as it is."

I nodded slowly, not knowing if he was watching or not. "I just don't want you waiting for something to happen in the future."

"Don't worry about it."

I couldn't look at him, though I was dying to see his face.

Leo switched on the radio to break the awkwardness.

"Leo—"

"You can call me Elikai, you know. It's just the two of us now. For a loooong time." He winked in my direction.

"Elikai." I sampled the name on my tongue. "I want you to know though that you *matter* to me, and not just because of who you really are. I want things to be as they were."

He glanced back, clearly tickled by something I had said. "As they were? I drove you crazy."

"You *used* to drive me crazy. Lately, you've been all right. You're kind of fun—and useful to have around."

"You don't say." He laughed. "As soon as you're better, I'm going to whip you into shape. Let's see how much fun you think I am then."

"I'm counting on it. I want to be better, stronger." My eyelids were starting to droop but my conscience gnawed on me. "I'm…sorry I couldn't save you, before, when you were taken." Other than receiving a beating, I wasn't much use with Sebastian either.

"Don't be daft. You've nothing to apologise for."

"I do. I didn't save you when you needed saving. I'm not the hero."

"Kal," a frustrated sigh passed his lips, "it's not about who saves who. It's the end result that matters."

"I know, but—"

"No buts. We're all working for the same goal. The Man of the Match might be different every day but it's still a team effort."

I lowered my chin. Of course, the same principle had been ingrained into us from the day I became Guard.

"You tired?" Leo's voice took a concerned tone as I couldn't hold off the yawn any longer.

"Very. How many more miles?"

"A few." The car accelerated a notch. "You've had a rough couple of weeks. Once we get you checked out, I want you to sleep. For a week."

No argument there.

I was sure someone was physically pulling my eyelids down. I drifted…and came back to on account of Leo's nudge.

"Don't fall asleep. Concussion." A finger pointed at the back of my head.

"Elikai?" I whimpered as I struggled to find a comfortable position.

"Yes, Rosebud?"

"I think I'm going to stick with Leo." My head rested back. "It's more... you."

* * *

Acknowledgements

I never thought I'd get here. It's been a long and daunting process to get my debut novel published. Any self-published authors out there—I salute you. The journey from chapter one to seeing my book on Amazon has a been a roller-coaster ride; it was during writing and editing this book that I learned about writing in the first place!

There is one person who without none of this would have happened and that is my Lord Jesus. From the day I was born You have guided my life and I am so grateful that You enabled me to do this. Writing in a language that's not my own would have been impossible had You not gifted me with the ability to do so...! For everything, to You be the glory.

The amount of people who've helped me along the way is vast and without their help, I wouldn't have got here.

Thank you to my beta readers who read some of the first drafts— I'm almost sorry you had to read it but thank you for nudging me in the right direction. To my beta readers who read the more improved 2.0 version—thank you for your comments and encouragement that helped me further polish this. And to my latest beta readers who brought the novel to where it is now—thank you for your time, effort and kindness. A special thank you to Amber, Blake, Danielle, Eris, Janeal, Liz, Natasha and my very first reader, Debbie. Without beta readers, this book would have sucked. Honestly. Each and every one of you is awesome.

Thank you, Gail, for saying yes to a very long-winded request to proof-read some of the book! You are brilliant. P.S. Hope you still have some wine left in your cupboards.

Thank you to Tereza Ghatt at Tereza Ghatt Photography for the incredible cover photo. You were a joy to work with and the end result is amazing! Thank you also to the dazzling Marija Varzinska for being the cover model—you are truly beautiful, inside and out. And I hope you didn't freeze.

Nathan Smith, thank you for hopping on board and creating me my first ever website! Your encouragement and tips have been much valued.

A HUGE thank you to my family for believing in me and encouraging me even though you had no idea what the book was about or if I could form a readable sentence. I'm so blessed to have you and I love you all. Olette ihania! Kiitos.

Carlos, I'll get to the ironing pile soon (maybe). Thank you for your patience, support and understanding. Love you always.

Readers… *Thank you.* Thank you for giving *Shadow Soul* a chance. Thank you for giving an unknown author a chance. I hope you enjoyed the book!

If you have any comments/questions/corrections on those wretched prepositions, or a simple hello, please do contact me on authormjbavis@gmail.com and/or visit my website at www.mjbavis.com. Also, if you enjoyed the book, please would you be so kind to leave a review on Goodreads, Amazon or your blog. Again, thank you!

If *Shadow Soul* has taught me anything, it's that one should never give up. Whatever your circumstances, whatever your dream, however high you've stumbled—rise and rise again. There is always light at the end of even the darkest of tunnels.

Follow the Light.

About the Author

M.J. Bavis coined her first book as a teenager and it was about horses, mean girls and a misunderstood heroine—and a worrying amount of violence.

It took a move from her Finnish childhood home to the UK, a degree in Criminology and a whole lot of (she hopes) maturing to realise horses and mean girls weren't her thing. Still, she loves writing young adult novels with a bit of fantasy, mystery, big emotions and headstrong (and slightly damaged) characters. When she's not writing she's fangirling over the Arrow, browsing for her next book to read, or mentally preparing herself for what the weather will throw at her on the next school run.

She calls many places her home, but her permanent address is in West Yorkshire, England.

To find out more information on her upcoming books, head over to: www.mjbavis.com

Or connect at:

authormjbavis@gmail.com

Printed in Great Britain
by Amazon